Errand into
the Wilderness
of Mirrors

Errand into the Wilderness of Mirrors

Religion and the History of the CIA

Michael Graziano

The University of Chicago Press
Chicago and London

The University of Chicago Press, Chicago 60637
The University of Chicago Press, Ltd., London
Published 2021
Paperback edition 2023
Printed in the United States of America

32 31 30 29 28 27 26 25 24 23   1 2 3 4 5

ISBN-13: 978-0-226-76740-6 (cloth)
ISBN-13: 978-0-226-82943-2 (paper)
ISBN-13: 978-0-226-76754-3 (e-book)
DOI: https://doi.org/10.7208/
chicago/9780226767543.001.0001

Library of Congress Cataloging-in-Publication Data

Names: Graziano, Michael (Religion scholar), author.
Title: Errand into the wilderness of mirrors : religion and
the history of the CIA / Michael Graziano.
Other titles: Religion and the history of the CIA
Description: Chicago ; Illinois : The University of
Chicago Press, 2021. | Includes bibliographical references
and index.
Identifiers: LCCN 2020046181 | ISBN 9780226767406
(cloth) | ISBN 9780226767543 (e-book)
Subjects: LCSH: United States. Central Intelligence
Agency—History. | United States. Office of Strategic
Services—History. | United States. Central Intelligence
Agency—Religion. | United States. Office of Strategic
Services—Religion. | National security—United States—
Religious aspects. | Intelligence service—United States—
History—20th century. | Intelligence officers—United
States. | Cold War—Religious aspects.
Classification: LCC JK468.I6 G737 2021 |
DDC 327.1273—DC23
LC record available at https://lccn.loc.gov/2020046181

♾ This paper meets the requirements of ANSI/NISO
Z39.48-1992 (Permanence of Paper).

To my parents

Contents

Contents

Introduction

Charting the Wilderness

> Understanding the system of ideology that operates in one's own society is made
> difficult by two factors: (i) one's consciousness is itself a product of that system,
> and (ii) the system's very success renders its operations invisible, since one is
> so consistently immersed in and bombarded by its products that one comes to
> mistake them (and the apparatus through which they are produced and dissemi-
> nated) for nothing other than "nature."
> Bruce Lincoln, "Theses on Method"[1]

> These values of freedom are right and true for every person, in every society.
> *The National Security Strategy of the United States* (2002)[2]

In 1988, American spies dispatched psychics to observe Pope John Paul II.
Known as Project Sun Streak, the operation was part of the US Army's
and Defense Intelligence Agency's (DIA) "remote viewing" program that
tested whether telepaths could observe targets from an extraordinary distance.[3] Stationed in a room in Fort Meade, Maryland, the "viewers" were
given anonymized descriptions of the Pope ("Although he may not have
been born in this country, he respects the American flag") and instructed
to report whatever details they could discern. The DIA officer in charge of
one session noted that viewer 025 "worked brilliantly to answer specific
questions about Pope Paul's [*sic*] personality and clothing."[4] Viewer 025
also produced this image of their target (see fig. I.1).

Project Sun Streak is now remembered largely as an object of derision
and as a legacy of a Cold War national security state that had more cash
than good sense. This book suggests other interpretive possibilities. To
Jonathan Z. Smith's argument that "the disciplined study of any subject
is, among other things, an assault on self-evidence, on matters taken for
granted, nowhere more so than in the study of religion," we might append
intelligence work.[5] The strange and the exotic are familiar to both the history of intelligence and the history of religion but, in each case, to rely
solely on these elements is to miss the larger picture.

Approved For Release 2002/05/17 : CIA-RDP96-00789R001400180001-7

FIGURE I.1 Viewer 025's remote viewing depiction of Pope John Paul II (1988)

We can tell a different story about psychics spying on the Pope. That story begins thirty-eight years prior when, in 1950, President Truman signed National Security Council Report 68 (NSC-68). The top-secret document explained how the United States understood the conflict that would govern nearly the next half century of global history.[6] It also represented a kind of teleology, an understanding of which way the world was going and why. In the view of NSC-68,

So long as the Kremlin retains the initiative, so long as it can keep on the offensive unchallenged by clearly superior counter-force—spiritual as well as material—its vulnerabilities are largely inoperative and even concealed by its successes.[7]

If we take seriously that many in the national security and intelligence communities perceived the Cold War as a zero-sum game in which defeat would be measured by a Geiger counter, we must reckon with the possibility that claims of a "spiritual counter-force" were not figurative. This spiritual counter-force shows up in familiar ways, like increased religious toleration, but also in ways less so, like Project Sun Streak. The conditions of possibility that made Project Sun Streak worth pursuing are different in degree, rather than kind, from the operations about world religions NSC-68 encouraged. These efforts came to represent what this book, borrowing a term from World War II American spies, calls the "religious approach" to intelligence.[8]

The religious approach to intelligence reflected American confidence that "religion" was a universally applicable lens through which the world could be understood and manipulated. This attitude influenced the choices, assumptions, and decisions made by American intelligence in World War II and the Cold War.[9] To study the religious approach is to grapple with intersecting developments in American and "world" religions, the growth of US empire, and the academic study of religion after World War II.[10] It is to study the ways that intelligence reports linked religion and race when analyzing Japanese behavior, or later reports' near certainty that appeals to the Virgin Mary were a sufficient condition to motivate Vietnamese Catholics. The religious approach was a shorthand for what Central Intelligence Agency (CIA) director Allen Dulles meant when he said in 1956 that the Agency had long tried to "bring to bear the force of religion on Cold War matters."[11]

This book is a study of how the Office of Strategic Services (OSS), and its spiritual successor the CIA, studied and engaged religious traditions around the world in the service of US empire and national security. American intelligence officers drew on existing, often stereotypical, information about "foreign" religions even as they revised these ideas to be more useful to national security goals. Between World War II and the 1979 Iranian Revolution, OSS and the CIA honed this new strategy in the context of two thriving discourses in American culture: a renewed attention to religious pluralism as well as a newfound national interest in "world religions."[12]

Telling this story weaves together the history of American religion, US intelligence, and the global Cold War to make three arguments about religion and national security at midcentury.

First, popular American ideas about the nature and function of religion as a global public good influenced US intelligence to understand "world religions"—a concept and object of study as well as a set of distinct religious traditions—as an element of US national security. Echoing the inchoate academic study of religion, intelligence officers saw religion as something that everyone everywhere possessed all the time. Religion's ostensibly universal presence and structure made it a profitable avenue to understand foreign cultures and peoples, the logic went, since knowledge of one tradition could be used to interpret another. As an element of human culture, religion was (and is) self-evident, obvious, identifiable, and universal—or so it seemed to the subjects in this book. When placed in the hands of intelligence personnel, this meant religion could also be a cultural resource marshalled alongside other human and natural resources. The idea that Americans had a unique connection to religion or an exceptional sense of *being religious* is a common one in US history, and focusing on the intelligence apparatus sheds light on what happened when this long-standing American idea fused with the Cold War national security state.

Second, these assumptions about the nature of religion were folded into an existing and powerful tradition of American exceptionalism, encouraging intelligence officers to view the United States and the world's religions as natural allies. In this view, "religions"—wherever they were found and whoever belonged to them—were fundamentally anti-Communist, pro-democracy, capitalistic, and supportive of human liberty and freedom. That this idea was largely self-evident to intelligence officers reflected not only how religion was understood in the academy specifically and American culture more generally, but also how American exceptionalism was itself rooted in American religious history. The US national mythos had long included the idea that Americans were fluent speakers of "religion," since religious values and ideas were inseparable from the US government and American identity. While American exceptionalism fueled the drive to understand other cultures (in order to overpower or control them), it also presented interpretive challenges for US intelligence officers. As the Cold War progressed, these assumptions blinded analysts to the prospect that religion and religious groups could seriously challenge US interests. American intelligence officers were too often unable to see how their own teleological confidence—a confidence in the trajectory of religion in the modern world—shaped the US response to international religious actors.

Finally, US intelligence work abroad bled into debates about religion at home as Roman Catholicism became the model through which the intelligence community could understand and manipulate other world religions. Catholicism, readily accessible to American intelligence officers yet remaining distinctly "foreign," served as a prototype for other national security applications of religion.[13] Intelligence officers believed the lessons they learned from Catholic informants were applicable to other religions and operationalized them in other times and places. In so doing, they influenced how Americans thought and spoke of religion—from Catholicism to other religions of the world—in ways more suited to America's new national security challenges. This process encouraged intelligence officers to bridge the familiar with the exotic, and their work at home with their work abroad. As a result, OSS and the CIA operationalizing their knowledge through the "religious approach" was never a story that was solely foreign or domestic. Recognizing the intimate connections between the "foreign" and "domestic" in both American religion and national security helps explain how and why intelligence officers attempted to manipulate American Christianity at home just as they tried to manage world religions abroad. As the religious approach crystallized in the worldview of NSC-68 during the crucible of the Cold War, US intelligence officers would look to other, increasingly "foreign" religions in their pursuit of anti-Communist allies.

In what became an important part of the "cultural Cold War," the religious approach created a demand for intelligence officers with expertise in religion. This demand was entwined with the study of "world religions" taking root in the nation's universities as well as a renewed focus on religious pluralism in the broader culture.[14] By the 1950s, American popular attitudes toward the world's religions increasingly assumed that all religions (simply by virtue of being "religions") were functionally similar. This echoed the "world religions paradigm" (WRP) then becoming prominent in the academy.[15] The WRP understood global religious systems as roughly analogous to one another and interchangeable in terms of function and purpose (if not content) on account of sharing a common core or essence. This idea appealed to intelligence officers in part because it suggested that religious meaning was universally translatable across otherwise stark divides of language, culture, and ethnicity. When US Army general Willard Wyman encouraged the 1950s CIA to work with "world religions" because all religions are "basically the same," he was riffing on the world religions paradigm as found in popular books and college classrooms.[16] These intellectual changes were never far from geopolitics: it is no coincidence that

LIFE magazine published a world religions encyclopedia—complete with a bronze Buddha on the cover—as American forces inherited responsibility for French imperial security in Southeast Asia, or that the US Navy would soon produce a similar volume of its own.[17] The development of academic scholarship on religion and the strategic management of religious groups went hand in hand.[18]

The academic study of religion in the early Cold War shared assumptions with intelligence officers—and most Americans—in that world religions were thought to be pre-existing entities easily recognized in foreign countries. Unlike their academic counterparts, however, intelligence professionals did not spend much time theorizing religion's origins or definitions. If a reference book or expert described a group as religious, or if the people being analyzed engaged in recognizably "religious" behavior, that was usually sufficient. While intelligence officers may have approached some analysis with an anthropological imagination, they did not concern themselves with small groups or understudied factions. This was a feature, not a bug.[19] These analysts worked to advance American empire, and they viewed global political power as aligning neatly with relatively well-known and long-established religious identities: Christian Europe, Hindu India, Buddhist Southeast Asia, the Muslim Middle East, and the atheistic Soviet Union. Intelligence officers shaped how Americans learned about world religions and the ends to which that knowledge was put. The study of world religions helped America translate the world to Americans even as American intelligence officers used it to translate America to the world. This approach encouraged intelligence officers' confidence in their religious models, sometimes at the expense of understanding complicated on-the-ground realities. Consequently, the intelligence community became hamstrung by their own development of religious expertise.

Expertise has a history. By the mid-twentieth century, American intelligence was working with religious information originally produced and studied by colonial powers and the academics they employed.[20] As historians of religion have shown, the discourse of "world religions" was a byproduct of the Enlightenment quest to categorize and order human nature, which became an effective tool in the imperial quest to map the "strange periphery" at the edge of the metropole and its understanding of the world.[21] Early American intelligence officers, heavily influenced by their more experienced British colleagues, inherited this legacy and uncritically applied it to their new global domain to help govern the *Pax Americana*.[22] In so doing, American intelligence officers took their belief systems and certainties local to the United States and projected them outward around the globe. While these developments sometimes happened incidentally, this does not make these changes any less important, or their consequences any less profound.

Intelligence histories are curious things.[23] They often focus on the secret and the exotic, yet ultimately reflect the people doing the work itself.[24] This conundrum should be a familiar one to those who study religion. Is the object of study limited to the exotic or, to paraphrase Jonathan Z. Smith, should it instead focus on what we see around us every day?[25] In this work, it is both. Understanding intelligence work, or the study of religion, means looking carefully at the mundane choices made by people trying to make sense of other people. In this effort, histories of intelligence and histories of religion have a great deal in common. Both fields try to make sense of how others make meaning, and why they do what they do. As a result, studying intelligence work ultimately tells us more about intelligence officers than the people they worked with or the places they studied.

If it is a cliché in intelligence work that the best sources are usually hiding in plain sight, then it is a cliché that also applies to historical investigations of intelligence work. The CIA's CREST database is the most complete (and, not coincidentally, the only) government repository for CIA records. Until 2017, CREST was housed exclusively on four computers at National Archives II in College Park, Maryland, that recorded both the researcher and their keystrokes. Incomplete and heavily redacted, however, the CIA's record of itself is a history of deliberate obfuscation. Other archives are necessary.[26] The most useful records were provided by everyday people who found themselves wrapped up in larger plans, and whose recollections and correspondence were never classified in the first place. These stories have always been visible, if one knew where to look: a best-selling book, the outcome of an election, or a graduation ceremony.

To tell these stories, *Errand into the Wilderness of Mirrors* is organized chronologically, beginning with OSS's development of the religious approach during World War II. Chapter 1 investigates how OSS director William Donovan's Catholicism informed his leadership of OSS and shaped the intelligence agency's interest in working with the Vatican as part of its initial foray into the religious approach.[27] Chapter 2 tracks how OSS developed these early relationships by drawing on academic expertise about religion and then applying it operationally, as in Operation Pilgrim's Progress, a massive information-sharing network that constituted OSS's largest operation with religious groups during World War II. As OSS continued to refine their "religious approach," they began applying their generalizable theories of religion to non-Christian traditions. The third chapter investigates OSS operations involving North African and Southeast Asian Muslims, as well as Japanese religious traditions. The eventual Allied victory bolstered OSS confidence in their methods, even as that victory masked methodological shortcomings in studying world religions through a uniquely American lens.

Despite OSS falling victim to postwar budget cuts, important elements of its religious approach were carried forward into the Cold War. Chapter 4 explores how the Eisenhower administration coordinated a revised religious approach from the White House, prioritizing religion's presumed anti-Communist nature. The crown jewel of the Eisenhower administration's religious approach is chronicled in chapter 5, involving an audacious CIA campaign to bolster US support for South Vietnam by linking Vietnamese Catholics with American religion and US ideals of religious freedom. Intelligence officers manufactured public tolerance toward and cooperation with Catholics, even as they attempted to conceal the very processes of manufacturing. Chapter 6 investigates the career of legendary American intelligence officer Edward Lansdale to show how the religious approach was used as an element of counterinsurgency in the "small wars" of the expanding US empire. The final chapter tracks how American understandings of Islam in the early Cold War shaped the CIA's late 1970s assessment that Muslim actors were unlikely to pose a serious threat to the shah of Iran. The CIA's failure to anticipate the 1979 Iranian Revolution revealed the analytical shortcomings of an overly generalized religious approach. The book concludes by considering how the CIA, newly aware of its own blind spots, assessed new religious challenges like liberation theology in 1980s Latin America.

My pursuit of these arguments does not entail a comprehensive history of American intelligence. This is a study of how and why religion came to be a subject of interest for American intelligence professionals, and how they developed and deployed "religion" as a necessary component of national security. Religion was not the only, nor the most important, focus of intelligence officers, but the reasons why intelligence services became interested in religion—and how they pursued that interest—are a useful window onto other, larger changes in American religion and culture during the Cold War. To illuminate these changes, this book examines "religion" from multiple vantage points: as a personal affiliation and identity marker, as a category of human experience, as a weapon and a strategy, and as Cold Warriors' assumed—and flawed—ideology. Doing so also provides a reflection onto our own time, when religious identity and national security are again at the forefront of the assertion and expansion of US empire, and its sustainment through strategic pluralism at home.

Making Sense of a New Wilderness

More than half a century ago, Perry Miller's *Errand into the Wilderness* (1956) described the plight of the New England Puritans, strangers on a strange shore, seeking to revive anew the mission to which they were sure their group was called.[28] The Puritans felt a sense of disquiet and unease in a new wilderness as they began to understand themselves as a people apart from the England from which they came. In their own estimation, they had *succeeded* in their "errand" but, thanks to the English Civil War, no one back home was watching their city on a hill. It was a hollow victory. "There was nobody left at headquarters to whom reports could be sent," Miller wrote in his book that would come to reshape the study of religion in America for the remainder of the century.

The idea for Miller's book, according to the author's preface in *Errand*, came to him while he stood on the banks of the Congo River.[29] Much has been made of this moment, and its role in shaping American studies and US intellectual history.[30] It is all the more telling, then, that the Congo story was at least partly fabricated. "Yes, there is a kind of truth in Perry's romantic reference in *Errand*," wrote Elizabeth Miller about her husband's scene, "but Perry, who was a writer, was in part creating, after the fact, an effective anecdote as well as an explanation of why his own errand had been undertaken."[31] While the Congo story may not have been entirely true, Miller did have opportunities to see and think about the American mind in a global context. During World War II, Miller worked for OSS in Germany, where he specialized in psychological warfare, a domain that frequently applied the knowledge gained through the religious approach.[32] The accuracy of *Errand*'s account was not nearly as important as how it was delivered and what it achieved. William Donovan, Miller's boss and the director of OSS, would have been proud.

Hundreds of miles to the south of Miller's wartime operations, another OSS officer was hard at work in Rome. James Jesus Angleton would develop a reputation within OSS as an expert in counterintelligence — protecting against foreign espionage — in part through his vetting of the religious approach at the Vatican. Like Miller, Angleton was a university man at heart, but unlike Miller — who, according to his OSS file, "wants to return to his position in the Harvard faculty as soon as possible" — Angleton stayed in intelligence work after the war.[33] Angleton eventually became the

CIA's legendary counterintelligence chief. David Atlee Phillips, a career CIA officer, described Angleton as

> CIA's answer to the Delphic Oracle: seldom seen but with an awesome reputation nurtured over the years by word of mouth and intermediaries padding out of his office with pronouncements which we seldom professed to understand fully but accepted on faith anyway.[34]

Both OSS officers, Miller and Angleton were tasked with understanding and manipulating the human mind. It was not easy. Angleton, quoting a verse from T. S. Eliot, described the business of espionage as a "wilderness of mirrors."[35] While their postwar careers led them to different institutions—the CIA for Angleton, Harvard for Miller—their work was not entirely dissimilar. They were experts at crafting a useful story to influence how others think about America in the world. They were both, in their own ways, masters of American studies.

Success in the war brought about different uncertainties, and the CIA was left alone with the world: a wilderness different in scale rather than kind. Empowered with considerable independence and little oversight, the CIA became the "headquarters" to which reports would be sent. While Miller never worked for the CIA, the strategies the Agency employed—like the religious approach to intelligence—were not all that different from the ones Miller used to understand the Puritans in 1956. Miller and the CIA took ideas seriously. Many of the intelligence officers in this book would likely have agreed with Miller's confident pronouncement that "the mind of man is the most basic factor in human history."[36] If one could understand how humans thought, then one could understand how humans worked. Armed with this knowledge, one could influence people toward particular ends. The major question—and errand—of the religious approach to intelligence was to determine how the human mind could be used to shape the future of humanity, radiating from the United States outward into the world.

This confidence in America's ability to understand and influence the world is at the core of the religious approach to intelligence. It was also sometimes wrapped up with a disregard for the consequences of these efforts to understand. "You have to understand the culture of the clandestine service," former Director of Central Intelligence Robert Gates explained.

> You haven't been through what they've been through. They've put their families through hell at times . . . some may eventually end up in London or Paris.

But they start out in Third World hellholes without even a Western doctor when their kids get sick. They have a strong sense that almost no one understands them or what they do. So they feel defensive and misunderstood.[37]

And yet, they felt compelled to understand everyone and everything. To work for the CIA was to be part of an institution that saw knowledge of the world as one way to secure freedom in it. Carved in marble at the CIA's original headquarters is the Agency's unofficial motto, from the Gospel of John: "And Ye Shall Know the Truth and the Truth Shall Make You Free."[38] The authors of the Gospel of John saw Jesus as the divine *logos*, revealing the divine order of the universe for all to see. The CIA had an errand in this new, postwar wilderness, bringing truth and freedom to other peoples beyond the borders of nation or religion. The Agency's own accounting of the word made flesh sits across the lobby: 133 stars that make up the Memorial Wall, one for each CIA officer killed in the line of duty.[39] This is one measure of the human costs of these efforts, but it is not the only one. As this book shows, the reality of intelligence operations was far more complicated, with profoundly troubling consequences for people around the globe.[40]

This book begins with the CIA's predecessor, OSS, and its influential wartime leader, William Donovan. Under Donovan, the intelligence agency became a unique place to study religion, combining considerable financial resources, spotty oversight, and a desire to know everything about everywhere. William Casey, who got his start in Donovan's OSS and went on to lead the CIA under President Reagan, explained that "Donovan's grasp of this elusive, multiple yet crucial nature of intelligence led to the CIA . . . becoming not merely a spy outfit but one of the world's great centers of learning and scholarship and having more PhDs and advanced scientific degrees than you're likely to find anywhere else."[41] Those who served with Donovan viewed him as the demiurge of American spy craft, imbuing OSS with the certainty that the world could be understood and manipulated according to American aims. "We *can* know," OSS officer Stanley Lovell explained, "Iron curtains and Bamboo curtains are only impenetrable to those who will not open their eyes."[42] This story begins by charting the efforts of American intelligence officers, alone in a new wilderness, as they learned to see.

Chapter One

American Spies and American Catholics

"Mr. President, is Bill Donovan's work still a secret?"
"What?"
"Is Bill Donovan's work still a secret?"
"Oh my, yes. Heavens, he operates all over the world."
 From President Roosevelt's November 10, 1942, press conference[1]

"What civilization needs is men who can be trusted without being watched."
 William Donovan[2]

President Franklin Roosevelt formed the Office of Strategic Services (OSS) in 1942 to coordinate US intelligence and espionage activities.[3] Before the postwar bureaucratic reshuffling closed OSS in 1945, it produced voluminous research, gathered intelligence, and conducted paramilitary operations around the world. Organizationally separate from the US military, OSS's mission was to both collect and analyze information pertinent to the war effort, as well as execute "such special services" as directed by the Joint Chiefs of Staff.

OSS was an unusual organization. Given its wide-ranging portfolio and trusted with relatively little oversight, the organization was free to experiment in its strategies and personnel. OSS recruited an eclectic variety of academics, soldiers, and businesspeople. William Casey, the devoutly Catholic OSS officer who would later direct OSS's spiritual successor, the Central Intelligence Agency (CIA), once said that OSS

> was probably the most diverse aggregation ever assembled of scholars, scientists, bankers and foreign correspondents, tycoons, psychologists and football stars, circus managers and circus freaks, safe-crackers, lock pickers and pickpockets . . . You name them, [OSS director William] Donovan collected them.[4]

Not entirely coincidentally, OSS records occasionally verge on the absurd or whimsical. Interdepartmental memos were spiced with diagrams of exploding pencils and other James Bond-esque gadgetry.[5] The OSS material is charmingly direct, as in the case of a booklet appropriately titled "Arson: An Instruction Manual."[6] The rumor in wartime Washington, DC, was that the ideal OSS officer was "a Ph.D. who can win a bar fight."[7]

Historians and historical actors have long disagreed about OSS's value to the war effort.[8] OSS made material contributions to the future of American intelligence work through its focus on research and analysis, as well as its training of a generation of American intelligence officers. Yet many of its World War II operations met with limited success and were overshadowed by other intelligence exploits. Critically, OSS was not part of the "Ultra" or "Magic" projects, codebreaking coups that enabled the Allies to read German and Japanese communication—a feat accomplished by the British and US military intelligence, not OSS. Yet when OSS worked, it worked well. General Dwight D. Eisenhower, for his part, praised OSS's work during the Normandy landings.[9]

Much of the credit (or blame) for OSS goes to William "Wild Bill" Donovan, the first and only director of OSS. Donovan was given free rein over the organization, shaping both OSS and the future US intelligence community in his image. With his outsized personality and creative approach to bureaucratic oversight, Donovan embodied the organization he led. Though Donovan never worked for the CIA, he trained the first generation of intelligence officers who helped lead the Agency through the Cold War. When the United States underwent a dramatic evolution from intelligence novice to global presence, it was Donovan's protégés keeping watch at Langley. There, in the CIA's headquarters, only one statue oversees the work they conduct, and it is of Donovan. In marble and memos alike, Donovan's spirit lives on, immortalized in the very structure of American spy craft.

Donovan was a man toward whom it was difficult to feel neutral, and his colleagues seem to have either felt adoration or revulsion, with little room in the middle. As one of his colleagues later recalled, "Bill Donovan is the sort of guy who thought nothing of parachuting into France, blowing up a bridge, pissing in Luftwaffe gas tanks, then dancing on the roof of the St. Regis Hotel with a German spy."[10] Donovan lived an eventful life. In addition to leading OSS and influencing the establishment of the CIA, he won the Medal of Honor in World War I and argued cases before the US Supreme Court. When he died, President Dwight Eisenhower remarked, "we have lost the last hero."[11]

Neither brains nor brawn, however, made Donovan's approach to intelligence unique. In its earliest days, Donovan imbued American intelligence with the peculiarly American idea that religion was everywhere, free, and individual: a natural ally in war and diplomacy. By war's end, OSS would argue that mastery of foreign religious information and intelligence work went hand in hand. Each were explorations of the unknown, excursions into the geopolitical and intellectual wildernesses that Americans would have to confront after 1945. For Donovan and his team, this was a task uniquely suited for OSS. "It remains my view that the religious approach," OSS officer Ferdinand Mayer wrote to Donovan, "aspects of which none of the regularly constituted agencies such as State, War, or Navy could effectively or properly operate, is one of the super-secret activities that the Central Agency could best manipulate."[12] This "religious approach" would be part of the experimental methods, techniques, and ideas Donovan's OSS developed that became norms at the CIA. Combined with other US government efforts in the military and in the public square, this encouraged Americans to see religion as a component of national security.

Understanding the religious approach means understanding the people who pursued it. Donovan's sizeable influence on OSS, and consequently the CIA, began with his experiences as an American Catholic in the early twentieth-century United States. Donovan was a Catholic lawyer, politician, and soldier at a time of widespread anti-Catholicism, profoundly shaping his professional career and the work he directed in OSS. His life traced the American dream and its limits during the interwar period. These challenges made clear the strategic value of religious tolerance. Donovan's argument was simple: the demands of national security rendered old prejudices not so much immoral as strategically foolish. Donovan's story is a reminder that the early US Cold War national security bureaucracy was a product of late nineteenth- and early twentieth-century social challenges — as were the people who staffed it.[13]

Donovan developed OSS's relationship with Catholic individuals and the Vatican at a time when such relationships were explosive political liabilities.[14] The origins of what OSS would later term its "religious approach," then, began with haphazard interest in the Vatican and Catholicism — what might be termed OSS's "Catholic approach." A vast international organization like the Catholic Church appealed to an intelligence organization tasked to collect, analyze, and operationalize information around the world. OSS was not the only wartime organization interested in the Catholic Church, nor was it the first to see the Catholic Church as a source of valuable information.[15] But in the US context, the value of the Catholic Church in OSS operations demonstrated to many powerful Protestants in government the benefits of strategically tolerating Catholics during and after the war. Eventually, OSS's interest in—and success working with—Catholicism bled into other religions, influencing an intelligence strategy that treated the religions of the world as valuable national security assets. OSS was interested in psychological warfare and viewed religion as a key component in understanding and manipulating the human mind. This approach would have enduring consequences for not just American Catholicism, but the relationship between religion and American national security during the Cold War. OSS's successor organization, the CIA, would have its own approach toward the religions of the world—an approach that got its start in OSS offices studying the Catholic Church. For OSS, Donovan explained, the chief lesson of the war was that "hyphenated Americans were useful."[16] This was no passing remark. Donovan's career, capped by his leadership of OSS, reflected his own trials as a hyphenated American. If the CIA's interest in religion began with OSS, OSS's began with William Donovan.

A Catholic and Catholicism Between the Wars

Donovan's life paralleled two developments that profoundly reshaped American religious life, and influenced Donovan's decision to pursue the "religious approach" with OSS. First, as the United States ascended the world stage in the twentieth century, American religious practices grew more diverse. As generations of immigrants built American industry, they also built American churches, mosques, and synagogues upon conflicting— and sometimes contradictory—views, giving lie to the idea that "Islam," "Judaism," or "Christianity" was, or could be, a singular thing. American society reflected the increasing diversity of American religions, selectively incorporating global influences into domestic culture.[17] Second, Americans tolerated—and legally protected—a greater spectrum of belief and practice. While demographic shifts ensured greater religious diversity, minority religious groups confronted an American legal framework that had long extended full religious freedoms to only a select few groups. A series of legal battles ensued, reaching all the way to the Supreme Court.[18] While protections for others, particularly African Americans, would be slow in coming, this did not stop other minority and dissenting groups from developing new ideas about who would be protected as full US citizens and challenging the status quo.[19] More so than his Protestant colleagues, Donovan could see the benefit of OSS strategically working with "foreign" religions because he knew well how religion could influence national unity.

Born in 1883 and raised a Catholic, Donovan was a product of the last great systematized attempt to keep American Catholics out of political power within the United States. Donovan's family hailed from Ireland by way of the Irish shantytowns that dotted nineteenth-century Buffalo, New York. Donovan's grandfather labored along the railroads in upstate New York, and his father worked at Buffalo's Holy Cross Cemetery. Though his family dropped the "O" from their name—transitioning from the O'Donovans of County Cork to the Donovans of Buffalo—they did not drop their religious affiliation. A grandson of Irish immigrants, Donovan was educated in parochial schools and Niagara University, a Catholic institution in upstate New York.[20] Donovan went on to law school at Columbia, where he rubbed elbows with classmates like Franklin Delano Roosevelt and learned from professors like future Supreme Court Justice Harlan Fiske Stone.[21] Yet in the white and largely Protestant world of power, professional success did not entirely negate his Catholicism. Courting Ruth Rumsey, Donovan's future wife, meant objections from her Protestant family, who saw an Irish Catholic as socially inferior and a poor match for their daughter. "Most of the time," Donovan wrote to Ruth, "my heart was in my mouth. I wanted you so much and yet thought you would choose rather some one of your own class." Nevertheless, the two were married—in a Catholic Church, no less—in July 1914. Ruth's mother was troubled to learn that the couple had agreed that any children were to be baptized in the Catholic Church.[22]

Placing importance on Catholic cultural markers, such as infant baptism or a marriage Mass, did not necessarily mean that Donovan—or any other American Catholic—was a devout believer or a doctrinaire theologian. Individual belief is difficult to pinpoint historically, and ritual participation does not always correspond with belief. Religious practice is no less (or more) meaningful when belief is ambiguous, ambivalent, absent, or even openly questioned.[23] Donovan was someone whose Catholicism mattered largely because of the obstacles it presented: to ignore it would play into the hands of those who wished to penalize that identity.

The tension between what broader American culture thought of American Catholics compared to how Catholics themselves understood their experience shaped much of American Catholic life in the early twentieth century. Al Smith, perhaps the period's most famous Catholic, was the Democratic Party's 1928 presidential nominee. When a critic challenged Smith to respond to papal encyclicals condemning the separation of church and state, Smith famously responded, "what the hell is an encyclical?"[24] Encyclicals were papal statements on doctrine, and it is doubly telling that Smith knew neither their content nor how influential they were presumed to be in his life. This perspective was representative of cultural Catholicism in America: being an American Catholic never required lock-step agreement with—or even knowledge of—Vatican policy, but it did require responding to such stereotypes. There is no evidence that Donovan was moved by the doctrine of transubstantiation or thought deeply about the rightful authority of the bishop of Rome, yet he was still an American Catholic. Donovan and Smith are more representative of American Catho-lics (and members of other denominations in their own ways) in the early twentieth century because they identified and publicly participated as such regardless of personal belief. Marrying in a Catholic church was good, as was baptizing your infant children—encyclicals were something for priests to worry about.

For most of the world, though, getting married in July 1914 meant a short honeymoon. Within weeks, Austria-Hungary declared war on Serbia and the great powers of Europe mobilized for what would become known as the Great War. Like many others who went on to leadership positions in World War II, World War I was Donovan's baptism by fire.[25] Variously shelled, gassed, and shot, Donovan earned his "Wild Bill" nickname when, after chiding some of his troops to keep up with their thirty-five-year-old lieu-tenant colonel, one replied: "But hell, we aren't as wild as you are, Bill."[26] Donovan's leadership made him a memorable figure at the front. He once refused the French *Croix de Guerre* when the award was not also offered to a Jewish soldier who had fought in the same engagement (both men eventually received the award).[27] Donovan's stature as a military hero and notable American Catholic grew—helped in part by his own lobbying to be awarded the Medal of Honor, something he received in 1923.[28]

Donovan returned to the United States in 1919 and resumed legal prac-tice as he transitioned back to civilian life. But the wider world beckoned. Shaped by the war and his own experiences as an American Catholic, Donovan began his own "religious approach," entering a phase of his life when he began studying religion and reflecting on its place in American life. Yet, as was the case throughout his life, "Wild Bill" found it difficult to stay in one place for very long. He and Ruth spent two months cruising the ports of North Africa and the Middle East aboard the *Homeric* in 1923. Though the trip was relaxing, Donovan—apparently something of a music connoisseur—was disappointed in the entertainment options ("When they do jazz over this way," he wrote in his diary, "their conception is to make the music as inharmonious as it can be done").[29]

While the trip served as a much-needed vacation, it also revealed how Donovan's wartime experiences had strengthened his interests in history and religion. Donovan's notes were full of practical considerations about wars both recent and ancient. He mapped past troop movements onto the terrain he was seeing, for example, and was intrigued to learn about British attempts to form an all-Jewish unit in World War I to sway Jewish opinion toward the Allies.[30] The voyage took Bill and Ruth to ancient mosques, churches, and monasteries across the region, from the Alcázar of Seville to the Church of the Holy Sepulchre in Jerusalem. As the pair visited Tunis, Cairo, Damascus, and ventured into Palestine, Donovan paired it with studies of Judaism, Christianity, and Islam. He studied the life of the Prophet Muhammad, for example, and read James Frazer's *The Golden Bough* (1890), among the earliest and most influential studies of comparative religion. Donovan also made time to read Ossendowski's *Beasts, Men, and Gods* (1921), recounting the tale of a Polish spy lost in Siberia after coming out on the wrong side of the Bolshevik Revolution. Saved through the timely intervention of Buddhist monks, Ossendowski recounted romantic tales of the mysterious East and its peculiar beliefs. Still, a vacation was a vacation: "would like to copy out some of his description of the Living Buddha," Donovan jotted in his journal, "but I am too lazy to do it."[31]

Back in New York, Donovan pursued new political opportunities but was repeatedly challenged on his Catholic faith.[32] An appointment as assistant attorney general in the Coolidge administration raised his political profile, and landed him on the shortlist for vice president in Herbert Hoover's 1928 presidential campaign.[33] Yet GOP insiders eventually decided that a Catholic on the Republican ticket would not help their chances against the Democratic nominee and fellow notable Catholic Al Smith. After Hoover won the election, Donovan was then widely seen as the president-elect's choice for attorney general—the *New York Times* reported it as all but formally announced—but it was not to be.[34] The idea that a Catholic and a "wet"—that is, someone opposed to Prohibition—could serve as the nation's highest lawyer was unthinkable to many Americans.[35] Hostile editorials were aided by pushback from the Ku Klux Klan which, at the time, carried considerable weight in mainstream America. Donovan had to settle for the position of deputy attorney general instead. When Al Smith had lost the election, a popular anti-Catholic joke of the day was that Pope Pius XI received a one-word telegram: "Unpack."[36] The joke was also on Donovan.

Whereas in 1928 Donovan was too Catholic for the national GOP, voters in Catholic-friendly New York—the same state that elected Al Smith as governor—feared Donovan was not Catholic enough when Donovan ran for governor in 1932. Rumormongers noted that Donovan's wife, Ruth, was a Protestant and his children—though ostensibly Catholic—were not educated in parochial schools. There were even whispers that, with only two children, Donovan and his wife must be using contraception—claims that weakened his Catholic credentials regardless of their veracity. Donovan's hometown newspaper, Buffalo's *Catholic Union and Times*, printed an editorial clarifying that Donovan was a Catholic in good standing, and that the bishop of Buffalo had personally confirmed Donovan's children into the Church.[37] Donovan need not have been a devout Catholic to find his bishop being interviewed about the spiritual health of his children particularly distasteful. In the end, it did not matter: Donovan and the Republican ticket were demolished in a Democratic landslide.

As the political defeats and personal embarrassments mounted, Donovan began addressing religious difference directly and in public. In a 1931 address to a "Fellowship of Faith" meeting to celebrate the Jewish New Year, Donovan argued that in the United States, "We have established the political right to freedom of conscience and religion. But we cannot truthfully avow that we have achieved tolerance and wiped out bigotry." Quoting the Lebanese-American artist Kahlil Gibran, Donovan shared parables that linked Moses, Jesus, and Muhammad as the proper role models for 1930s America. Though the Great War was over, Donovan warned that the Great Depression meant another war was already here—a war to have people live in the peace and contentment they deserved.[38] In a 1935 *Brooklyn Central* essay, Donovan argued that the Depression was the result of a moral—as well as financial—collapse in the United States. In chastising the errors of the age, Donovan claimed there was "no substitute for the great truths that have come down to us from men who have led spiritual lives; from Moses and the Ten Commandments, from the Songs of Solomon, from the Four Gospels."[39] The fix for what ailed America required a change not just in people's pocketbooks, Donovan argued, but in their hearts.

While Donovan focused on American unity amid religious diversity, he also recalibrated his approach to public life as a Catholic civil servant. Throwing caution to the wind, he began to speak openly of the need for more Catholics, and people familiar with Catholicism, in American political life. Rather than serving only their immediate "parochial" communities, Donovan argued, Americans needed Catholic leaders at a "national" level.[40] In making this argument, Donovan confronted one of American anti-Catholicism's central pillars and a stereotype predating the founding of the Republic: Catholics sought undue political power.[41] The more fever-dream variations on this idea usually added that, once acquired, Catholics would use this political power to demolish First Amendment protections and establish a Catholic theocracy modeled on the Vatican. Protestant fears that Catholics conspired to overturn church-state separation only exacerbated such worries. Many Americans expected successful Catholic politicians to both condemn the alleged power of the Catholic Church in US politics while ignoring the power regularly wielded by Protestant individuals and institutions. The KKK was self-evidently normal; a Catholic president was not.[42]

Catholics of varied ethnicities and theological commitments experienced anti-Catholicism as a challenge to their identity as American citizens. Donovan, no less than other Catholics, encountered these prejudices throughout his career in the civil service. Yet Donovan, like Al Smith, found himself caught between different species of American anti-Catholicism. As powerful Catholic politicians seeking national office, both men's religion marked them as theologically abhorrent to conservative Protestants. Yet, in their presumed loyalty to the Pope, each man was also politically untrustworthy to liberal Protestants and secular Americans. One did not have to look far to find examples of anti-Catholic ideas in liberal venues on the eve of World War II. *The New Republic* published a series titled "The Catholic Church in Politics" (1938) with the goal of curbing some of the perceived overreach by the Catholic Church into American public life. "When Catholic action begins to threaten the fundamentals of democracy itself and to stand in the path of social progress," the magazine explained in the series introduction, "it calls for description and comment, just as activities of any other organization or social body are discussed."[43] Essays like this envisioned American liberal democracy as interchangeable with Protestant individualism. Catholicism, in this view, disrespected proper American boundaries between the public and the private: "real" Americans knew that individual beliefs were private commitments inappropriate for public display (except for when they were).[44]

By speaking out, Donovan no doubt confirmed the fears of the most vocal anti-Catholic critics: American Catholics, once given a taste of political power, would always want more. Yet Donovan was not a passive victim, acquiescing to the prejudices of his day. Instead he engaged with mainstream prejudice, challenging and provoking critics of both Catholicism and religious diversity more generally. When Donovan worked in the Department of Justice, he led one of the most successful raids of the Prohibition era, seizing a great deal of illegal alcohol and money.[45] Ironically, his detractors pegged him as an anti-Prohibition activist since his religious affiliation was associated with that position. From Donovan's point of view, this assumption on the part of his political opponents was a self-inflicted wound. (Donovan was a firm believer that the best person for any job *was* Donovan.) In assuming that all Catholics behaved a certain way and believed in the same ideas, then, his detractors lost out on a well-qualified candidate to lead the Department of Justice.

By promoting the suitability of American Catholics for public service, Donovan sought to bring Irish Catholics and other marginalized religious groups (like Jews and Muslims) to the center of American life. His public record, including his failures as much as his successes, supported less politically and socially privileged Catholics by rejecting the critique that all Catholics thought and acted the same. Parts of Donovan's lifestyle—not least of all that he was wealthy—also made him stand apart from other American Catholics in the interwar period. He benefited from great social and financial resources the average American Catholic would not have known, and some of his fellow Catholics resented him for it.[46] Receiving Catholic criticism alongside Protestant intolerance provided Donovan with a unique vantage point to understand religious identity and difference in America: he was marginalized *from* Irish Catholics *by* Irish Catholics even as he was marginalized from the white Protestant American mainstream *as* an Irish Catholic. He was not an outsider, but not quite an insider, either.

These experiences with anti-Catholicism positioned Donovan to think critically about religious identity in American politics and culture. He understood—personally and professionally—that religious identity was not deterministic, and he brought an appreciation for the value and diversity of religious minorities with him into the world of intelligence and national security. From his own experience, he knew that being Catholic did not necessarily make one opposed to Prohibition, a member of the Democratic Party, or supportive of fascism. He understood that infant baptism or respect for the priesthood did not affect an American Catholic's ability to uphold the rule of law or defend the United States. Crucially for the interwar period, Donovan understood the link between lay Catholics and the Vatican, often assumed unbreakable by those Americans with little knowledge of Catholicism, to be far more tenuous. Making sense of religion, Donovan knew, was a messy business. This knowledge—that came from being *in* power but not *of* it—would help Donovan develop the religious approach in OSS.

OSS, Catholicism, and the Religious Approach

Roosevelt appointed Donovan as director of the Office of Strategic Services in 1942. Responsible for both collecting intelligence and operating on it, the nature of OSS's work meant a reliance on deceit and subterfuge. This involved psychological warfare, which Donovan understood as a strategy of demoralization, getting in the enemy's head and breaking them down by sowing "confusion and doubt and delusion." Donovan knew critics might dismiss the psychological aspect as gimmicky parlor tricks when there was "real" fighting to be done. Yet Donovan insisted that psychological warfare was crucial to winning the war. "There is really no mystery about that term and there is nothing new in it," Donovan told his officers. "It is as old as warfare itself."[47] When one OSS officer worried to Donovan about the public perception of their work, the director became exasperated:

> Don't be so goddam naïve. . . . The American public may profess to think as you say they do, but the one thing they expect of their leaders is that we will be smart. Don't kid yourself. P. T. Barnum is still a basic hero because he fooled so many people. They will applaud someone who can outfox the Nazis and the Japs.[48]

Whereas other Americans worried about the propriety of spy craft, Donovan saw these efforts as a natural extension of war—and one that, if OSS did its job, might even shorten the conflict.[49]

OSS pursued its goals in ambitious and unorthodox ways. Dismissive of bureaucratic constraints in the paperwork-bound world of intelligence and national security, Donovan attracted likeminded thinkers with similar quirks. Tom Braden, an OSS officer who parachuted behind enemy lines in Europe, remembered that "All you had to do was go to Bill Donovan and say, 'Look, I want to hang off the back of an airplane and drop a bomb on a squad over here in the trenches.' And Bill would say, 'Fine. Let's give it a try.'"[50] Carleton Coon, who worked for OSS in North Africa, recalled that "We were never under orders. We were always asked, 'Would you like to . . . (e.g., get yourself killed?)' To which we always said 'yes.'"[51]

Even though OSS's purpose was clear to Donovan, he still had to carve out a role for the organization in relationship to the massive federal wartime bureaucracy. The military branches did not trust Donovan's upstart organization. General Douglas MacArthur banned OSS from the South Pacific because, as his intelligence chief later explained, MacArthur did not have time to "sit back and ransack libraries."[52] The domestic security services were little better. FBI director J. Edgar Hoover viewed OSS as a competitor for funding and saw Donovan as a rival for FDR's time and attention. Over Donovan's protests, Hoover's FBI remained responsible for intelligence work in Central and South America during the war. There was no love lost between the two men. "The Abwehr [German military intelligence] gets better treatment from the FBI than we do," Donovan grumbled.[53]

As Donovan sought support for the new OSS to distinguish it from its rivals, he reached out to prominent American Catholic leaders like New York archbishop Francis Spellman and Bishop Fulton Sheen. For Donovan, these men were not only important Catholic figures but also valuable pieces of an international information network. Wartime bureaucratic favors for Spellman kept Donovan in the archbishop's good graces.[54] Bishop Sheen, for his part, was particularly keen on referring people to Donovan for OSS employment in creatively vague terms ("His talents are most unusual," Sheen wrote enigmatically about one prospective candidate). It likely did not hurt that Donovan hired the celebrity-priest's brother, Private Al Sheen.[55] One of Donovan's officers would later recall how the director worked tirelessly to "help priests and others linked with the church who were risking death" during the war.[56] While OSS was not unique in pursuing Catholics—the FBI recruited potential agents from Jesuit schools, believing those institutions produced the ideal form of "Christian manhood" demanded by the Bureau—Donovan's Catholicism did add a personal touch to his efforts.[57]

Donovan's outreach reflected larger government interests, too. From the perspective of FDR and other government leaders, the need for national unity was paramount: religious divisions—and, to a significantly lesser extent, racial divisions—were understood by American leaders to weaken the US position against the Axis powers.[58] The president, for his part, had gone so far as to send a personal representative to the Vatican on the eve of war—a far cry from a formal ambassador, but a move that aroused a public outcry all the same.[59]

These conflicting efforts and tensions provided the backdrop for Donovan's meeting with the Apostolic Delegate in Washington, DC, in early 1942. In an ironic twist, it was Donovan—whose dream to be on a presidential ticket had run aground on anti-Catholic fears—who would be the American to meet secretly with the Pope's representative in his nation's capital. The two men discussed what the Vatican might be able to do—unofficially—for the United States during the war. After the meeting, Donovan sent a memo to FDR outlining what had been discussed:

> I had a long visit with the Delegate and from him obtained assurances that there would be made available for us information from all over the World that would be received from their various delegates. He recognizes that a Hitler

victory might well mean a modern Avignon for the Papacy. I think that he is very anxious, unofficially, to help in every way possible.[60]

While the delegate stressed to Donovan that the Vatican's public position would be that of "strict neutrality," Donovan reported to the president that "when the war finally ends their position must be beside us."[61]

Donovan personally tended to the US-Vatican relationship during the war, including a meeting with Pope Pius XII. Judging from Donovan's memos to FDR, a papal audience could cover a range of topics. They discussed specific intelligence issues such as "the question of the Japanese embassy placing their radio transmitter in the Vatican" as well as geopolitical developments more broadly, including "communism, Germany, Russia," and US politics. (The Pope "expressed great interest in your re-election," Donovan wrote to the president.[62]) Though Donovan could be irritated with much of Pius's perceived "fence-sitting," he liked Pius "immensely as a person."[63] Addressing these delicate political questions was made more difficult because all of the belligerents made overtures to the Vatican during the war, aiming to win the Vatican's support or at least deny it to their opponents.[64] This meant that any potential advantage—like Donovan's personal touch—became all the more appealing.

Over the course of the war, OSS met well-placed Vatican officials interested in quiet cooperation with the United States. A pattern developed in which Vatican officials would "leak" documents to Allied intelligence with their ecclesiastical superiors seemingly aware of their actions. OSS believed that Pope Pius knew about these information "leaks," leading American officers to conclude they also had the support of the Holy Father.[65] OSS was happy to exploit what it termed "the willingness of the Church to collaborate." Once, an African American soldier hiding in Rome became trapped when Axis forces conducted house-to-house searches in his part of the city. Unable to move freely without attracting attention in the largely white city, aid came from an unlikely source when the Vatican Ethiopian Legation arranged a hasty visit to the officer's location. The Legation left Vatican grounds with twenty in their party and returned with twenty-one. This was part of a larger trend: by 1944, OSS estimated that the majority of Catholic clergy in German-occupied Italy were working with resistance organizations.

Donovan and his senior staff saw a Church that was eager to cooperate with American aims, even if it could not say so publicly. A 1944 OSS assessment provided to President Roosevelt concluded that "the Vatican is a sure source of aid in [the] fight against the Germans . . . Diplomatically, the

Vatican insists on its neutrality. Actually, the Church in Italy is actively pro-Allied."[66] The Vatican stood to gain from this arrangement, too. The Holy See's location in Rome sometimes made access to outside information difficult, and the Vatican struggled with information security throughout the war. Occasionally the Pope's best access to news was through summaries provided by the British ambassador, which he himself gleaned from listening to the BBC on his personal radio.[67] For the Vatican, access to OSS meant access to external information networks and a link to the outside world.

While OSS pursued a relationship with the Vatican, OSS had to tread lightly around competing political realities, juggling anti-Catholic sentiment at home while mitigating anti-American sentiment held by Catholics abroad. Anti-Catholicism was a liability in wartime, since Vatican diplomats were fully aware of the anti-Catholic history of the United States. Along with Britain—another country with historically cool Vatican relations—this meant that two of the major Allied powers were to be kept at arm's length in the minds of some Vatican diplomats. One OSS informant at the Vatican reported that Vatican diplomats thought "the Anglo-Saxons" would never permit a peace to develop in the Vatican, "since the Catholic Church would obtain a too notable success." Underscoring the level of resentment, the source continued, "Vatican diplomats themselves say this openly."[68] Not for the last time, Donovan's OSS was in the curious position of convincing foreign Catholics that America was not really all that anti-Catholic, while simultaneously convincing suspicious American policymakers that while the Vatican did have a secret global information network, its intelligence could be trusted to benefit the United States.

OSS's assumption that it shared the Vatican's concerns sometimes combined with its general ignorance of the institution itself to produce well-meaning, if highly unworkable, suggestions. One of the more harebrained schemes involved a covert OSS operation which—to make a long and rather inventive story short—would strike both Mussolini and Hitler with sudden and irreversible blindness. This was the brainchild of Stanley Lovell, OSS's director of research and development. (If Donovan was America's James Bond before James Bond, Stanley Lovell was "Q" before "Q.") With both fascist leaders unable to see, Lovell suggested to Donovan that Pope Pius could then issue a "Papal Bull or whatever is appropriate" instructing Catholics that this sudden blindness illustrated the righteousness of the Allied cause. This was audacious even within the pantheon of colorful OSS schemes, which included bombs strapped to bats and weaponized goat dung.[69] Helpfully, Lovell also drafted a suggestion of what the Pope might say:

> My children, God in His infinite wisdom has stricken your leaders blind. His sixth Commandment is Thou Shalt Not Kill. This blindness of your leaders is a warning that you should lay down your arms and return to the ways of peace.

Since many German and Italian soldiers were Catholics, Lovell explained, they "will heed Pius" and end the war without firing a shot. While Lovell was sensitive to the criticism that "this may appear to be a suggestion of hypocrisy" on the part of the Pope, he thought the ends justified the means. "If he can use his high office to stop this killing," Lovell asked, "isn't he advancing the cause of Christianity more than any man on earth?" While Donovan's own thoughts on the plan went unrecorded (Lovell recalled Donovan's response as a judicious "hm"), the idea never left the planning stages and both Mussolini and Hitler died with their eyesight intact.[70]

Less dramatic but more important were the quiet conversations between OSS and Catholic leaders and the secret documents that changed hands. What began as an attempt to establish a listening post in Italy morphed into something more. Donovan's success in convincing the intelligence community of the Vatican's strategic benefits for US national security led to a demand for more people knowledgeable about Catholicism. In one 1945 memo, OSS officer Lt. Col. William P. Maddox requested additional men for Vatican duty, writing to his superior:

> You have doubtless noticed in recent weeks a considerable increase in the volume as well as quality of the intelligence reports being received through Vatican sources. These operations are acquiring increasing importance and should be given the most careful attention. I look upon the work as one of the most significant we can perform in this theater.

Maddox specifically wanted someone who was knowledgeable about the inner workings of the Church. What was needed, Maddox wrote, was someone who could speak to the "intricacies of church history and organization," the "currents of inside Vatican politics," and the "personalities of church representatives in Rome and abroad."[71] While relying on foreign informants was useful—indeed, it was a necessity—the secretive nature of some tasks made relying on non-Americans problematic. Breaking into sealed Vatican communiques, for example, was a task best left to proper OSS officers.[72] These actions were not outliers. By war's end, American spies were already reading as much of the Vatican's communication traffic as they could without detection.[73]

The Need for a New Approach

While Catholicism and the Vatican remained the largest and most important focus, OSS was developing a systematic "religious approach" to religious people, places, and ideas more generally. OSS's study of Catholicism was an important part of this process, since OSS leaned into an American understanding of religion that spoke to something innate and essential in everyone, everywhere. To study such a thing was the first step in manipulating it, and to manipulate it promised untold power over the minds and thoughts of people around the world. For there to be a religious approach, however, religion could not be approached haphazardly. It was a domain of expertise like anything else.

Donovan's push to see Catholicism as a wartime intelligence asset foreshadowed how the relationship between religion and American national security would change during and after the war. OSS developed new methods for understanding religion: one conceived and practiced within the national security state. Intelligence officers began considering a generalizable theory of religion, something that could be applied to a variety of people and places around the world. They began learning about the world's religions and asking themselves what these religions might do for the United States. To answer that question, OSS began organizing its own study of religion.

Chapter Two
Refining the Religious Approach

In a global, totalitarian war, intelligence must be global and totalitarian.
William Donovan[1]

If Hollywood made a movie about OSS, they could do worse than centering the plot on William Colby. Young, handsome, and Catholic, Colby's operational history could rival the stunning action scenes in any summer blockbuster. Colby was a twenty-four-year-old OSS officer when he parachuted into occupied France in 1944. Less than a year later, he led a ski-parachute team across the Norwegian wilderness to sabotage a series of bridges and railroads to delay the return of more than 100,000 German troops as the Third Reich collapsed. Colby embodied the popular image of the intelligence officer and special operator: dashing, daring, and bold.[2]

Yet the real-life Colby knew it was brains, not brawn, that defined OSS. When William Donovan pinned a Silver Star on Colby's chest at war's end for the latter's operational heroics, Colby recalled how

> Donovan referred first to his scholars and research experts in describing the OSS "team" and only secondly mentioned the "active units in operations and intelligence who engaged the enemy in direct encounter." In this he reflected his unique contribution to American intelligence, that scholarship was its primary discipline, that the acquisition of information was to serve it, and that its paramilitary adventures were an adjunct to its authority and expertise in secret machinery.[3]

It was OSS's commitment to brainpower that fueled its wartime efforts and set important precedents for the future of US intelligence, as Colby himself would come to appreciate when he went on to lead the CIA in the 1970s. Some of OSS's most important contributions were produced in the dingy stateside offices focused on mundane acts of analysis.

With scholarship as OSS's "primary discipline," the organization's "secret machinery" cultivated religious expertise, though that information was far more challenging to collect than population demographics or language skills. While OSS's early interest in the Vatican was a function of Donovan's leadership and personal relationships, the organization's broader focus on Catholicism extended well beyond Donovan and became institutionalized across OSS as an answer to conceptual problems in the religious approach. What, exactly, made religious organizations "religious"? Did working with religious organizations require entirely different approaches and strategies? What they needed—and what they found—was a model. When OSS's religious approach would eventually lead them to non-Christian traditions, Catholicism served as the most enduring model for how "religion" works.[4] For OSS, Catholicism was foreign enough to be worthy of study but familiar enough to be interpretable. Its simultaneous perceptibility and mystery made it the ideal "religious" prototype to apply in future missions in different locations with entirely different cultures and religious communities.[5]

At a time when the secular academic study of religion was gaining credibility at universities and colleges around the country, OSS assembled a team of anthropologists, historians, economists, sociologists, and scholars of religion to map the cultural terrain in which OSS would operate.[6] These efforts helped distinguish how the United States engaged with religion during a conflict in which many of the belligerents mobilized religion on behalf of their nation's war effort.[7] By war's end, Donovan and his key lieutenants thought this method was so successful that they proposed a centralized office to specialize in the "religious approach" to intelligence.[8] More than Donovan's personal interest in religion, OSS's development of the religious approach reflected a commitment to the production of expertise—including in the study of religion—that influenced a generation of American thinkers in the Cold War national security state.

Religion as Theorized by an Intelligence Agency

Much of OSS's intellectual heavy lifting happened at its in-house think tank, the Research & Analysis Branch (RAB). Charged with analyzing and understanding history, religion, and other aspects of human culture around the world, RAB was one of the most consistently productive parts of OSS.[9] It pursued global cultural knowledge of all kinds, employing prominent thinkers including political scientist and diplomat Ralph Bunche (who would go on to become the first African American to win the Nobel Peace Prize), future associate justice of the Supreme Court Arthur Goldberg, historian Perry Miller, filmmaker John Ford, and historian Arthur Schlesinger.[10] The chemist Stanley Lovell, head of OSS's scientific development, explained after the war that

> Those of us in applied sciences, working with tangible tools to meet the subtle demands of the resistance forces in Europe and Asia were, I think, inclined to belittle the work of this academic group. How wrong we were. It was intelligence at its best, and it had never been done before—until Bill Donovan created it.[11]

Donovan too gave credit where credit was due: "most of our intelligence came from good old-fashioned intellectual sweat," he reflected.[12]

RAB had a formidable task: Donovan wanted to know seemingly everything about everyone everywhere.[13] One representative Donovan memo to FDR outlined how OSS was studying the Aleutian Islands in advance of a possible Japanese offensive. Donovan promised the president that everything about the indigenous people of the Aleutian Islands would be made known: "religion, language, clothing, food, economics, etc."[14] One common theme with this work, and with the operations it supported and informed, was the degree to which OSS continued to work with religious groups and institutions. By war's end, the productive relationships with religious institutions and individuals spanned the globe and demonstrated that OSS was thinking creatively and strategically (if not always entirely plausibly) about how knowledge of, and relationships with, religious groups could work to the nation's advantage.

In an organization like OSS that prided itself on action, however, RAB had its fair share of critics. The branch's problem was twofold. First, the bulk of its personnel were academics roped into wartime service, a group who became known as the "Chairborne Division."[15] As it turned out, the pace of work at Ivy League institutions in the early 1940s was slower than an intelligence agency in the crunch of a global war. These academics were asked to think in new ways toward unfamiliar ends, and then communicate their findings in accessible, immediately applicable ways. These expectations ran counter to the "life of the mind" they had come to know in the ivory tower, and some of the academics-turned-analysts struggled to balance deliberation with efficiency. The OSS officer charged with wringing productivity from these academics wryly observed that "For reasons I do not profess to understand . . . it appears easier to get out a 250-page epitome of what Europe will be like in 1986, to be delivered tomorrow morning at 830," than "a 2-page summary of what you most want to know about the job you're doing."[16]

Even so, OSS leadership was convinced that RAB's strategic value lay in its stockpiling of cultural knowledge. William Casey, another young Catholic OSS officer and future CIA director, recalled how Donovan "realized, earlier and better than most, that 'stranded' information was not much good. It had to be analyzed, dissected, and fitted into the larger whole that modern warfare required."[17] To build this "larger whole," RAB assembled an impressive array of specialties under its roof. Expertise in Persian history, German economic policy, and Brazilian politics, for example, was hard to find outside the ivory tower, so turning to the universities for personnel made sense. William L. Langer, a renowned diplomatic historian and chair of Harvard's History Department, ran the Branch, and solicited colleagues in academia to recommend "a few good boys who will ruin their health for about $2,000 per annum."[18] The peer review was successful and RAB landed a number of intellectual heavyweights, including eight future presidents of the American Historical Association, five future presidents of the American Economic Association, one future director of the American Council of Learned Societies, numerous leading area studies specialists, and two Nobel laureates.[19]

While OSS studied any number of topics as part of the religious approach, sometimes the knowledge they sought—like the inner workings of the Vatican—was found in people rather than books. RAB could shed light on the policies of the Vatican Secretariat of State, but it could not tell you whether the Vatican's secretary of state, Cardinal Luigi Maglione, preferred dealing with the Soviet or Japanese ambassador, or whether he favored Jamaican rum or Scottish whisky. For this, OSS turned to expert informants. Crucially, OSS relied on these informants not just for day-to-day knowledge but for non-American perspectives on the nature of religion.

One key source who influenced the development of OSS ideas about religion was the Hungarian émigré Zsolt Aradi, who was formally approved to work for OSS's Secret Intelligence branch in 1944, where he specialized in Vatican affairs.[20] Aradi was a knowledgeable Vatican insider who OSS employed on many missions involving Central and Eastern European Catholics in the latter years of the war. Aradi's primary job was to acquire and vet information about the Vatican, as well as educate American intelligence officers about Vatican history, culture, and institutional peculiarities.

As OSS's interest in the Vatican developed into an interest in Catholicism more broadly, Aradi provided guidance on dealing with religious institutions and systematizing a "religious approach."

In his work for OSS, Aradi authored "Intelligence Through the Vatican," a memo outlining the distinctive challenges of working with religious organizations in general and the Vatican specifically. In it, Aradi pushed American intelligence officers to think in new ways about "religion." Working with religious groups, Aradi cautioned, had nothing to do with truth claims or whether intelligence officers "believed" it: "One may have any opinion on any religious belief, but one thing has to be considered; that on this terrain, that is on the religious terrain, a mistake can be fatal." Aradi was presciently concerned with what the academic study of religion would recognize as issues of "insiderhood" and "outsiderhood" as well as emic and etic categories of knowledge. It was not enough to know what people on the "inside" thought about the Vatican, for example, if one could not appreciate how being on the "inside" shaped that person's view of the world to begin with.[21] Even "outsiders" to a community could fall prey to "insider" thinking if they merely replicated the statements of their informants without contextualizing or thinking critically about the conditions producing such information.

Aradi also drew attention to American intelligence officers' erroneous assumption that the Vatican was a *religious* rather than *political* organization. "One has to keep in mind that Vatican policy was in the modern times not to make martyrs," Aradi wrote. Aradi was not criticizing the Vatican— he himself was a practicing Catholic—but rather chiding the Americans for the analytical baggage accompanying their peculiarly Protestant notion of religion. The supposed separation of church and state was a myth born and bred in the United States, not one universally shared across all nations or "churches." Above all, Aradi wrote, it was crucial that US intelligence distinguish the reality of the Catholic Church from the claims the Church made about itself:

> The "penetration" of the Vatican is completely different from any other intelligence operation because of the special and singular position of the Vatican. The Vatican is a State and at the same time it is not; the Catholic Church, the organization of the Holy See, is the greatest and oldest organization which has ever existed—and it is not; the Catholic disciplinate society of men and at the same time can be only a crowd of people who do not have the same belief but only the same traditional way of thinking.[22]

In other words, OSS needed to treat the Vatican no differently than any other institution by maintaining a strategic suspicion of the institution and its motives. This was why American officers working on this project need not be Catholic, Aradi instructed, since the "Vatican problem" simply required intelligence officers who understood a "great idea."[23]

Aradi cautioned OSS not to buy into the Vatican's rhetoric that the Church was a monolithic organization. On the contrary, there were real differences between the Vatican hierarchy and the priests in the field. "It would be a great error," Aradi argued,

> To misunderstand the devotion due to an idea of transcendency and accept any opinion expressed by the Vatican or by its representatives or to see in each Catholic priest an infallible Pope Ersatz. The Vatican is ruled by men who are very well educated and some of them try to guard a great impartiality but hundreds of thousands of the priests have not the slightest idea what they represent.

American intelligence officers, Aradi suggested, should not mistake the dominant view within the religious institution for the institution as a whole. To assume that the Vatican was not interested in military, financial, or political information simply because it was an institution also interested in transcendent truths would be a mistake. Aradi's instructions to OSS were an important marker in the development of American intelligence relationships with religious groups abroad. By recognizing the "immense difference between the work and sacrifice of the single Catholic or Catholic priest and the balanced policy of the Holy See," OSS should realize that while the Vatican was unique, it also—like any other institution—could be incentivized to act in certain ways. And, even as the Vatican issued official policies on doctrine, it was possible for individual members to challenge, dismiss, or ignore such proclamations.[24]

One of the ironies of OSS's religious approach is that learning more *about* religion also meant grappling with the ways in which religious people and institutions were no different from their secular counterparts. Scholarly expertise combined with a variety of Catholic experiences to make clear that the broader Catholic Church was, like any large organization, far from a monolith. It had any number of different people and perspectives within it. These internal differences offered numerous entry points for groups like OSS that were interested in developing relationships with Catholics beyond those it established with the Vatican.

Operationalizing the Religious Approach

When the Allies accidentally bombed parts of the Papal Palace of Castel Gandolfo in 1944, Axis propaganda framed the event as American troops not respecting "Catholic property," a sign that the once God-fearing nations of the West were now subservient to Soviet atheism.[25] Keen to avoid this perception, OSS responded by disseminating its own message "throughout Europe by all available means, including underground channels."[26] Part of this plan's "all available means" included a Catholic news and intelligence network Donovan had cultivated since the early days of the war. Known variously as the Catholic International Press or the Center of Information *Pro Deo* (CIP), it was a large Catholic journalism network with correspondents scattered across Europe. A largely lay organization, the CIP was managed by the colorful Belgian priest Felix Morlion, O.P. (1904–1987), who was committed to establishing "the place of God in public life." CIP sought to inform secular editors, reporters, and thought leaders about global issues that demonstrated the relevancy of Catholic ideals to current events and, hopefully, to entice non-Catholic audiences to consider its perspective. OSS's work with CIP became its most sustained and successful relationship with Catholicism beyond the Vatican during World War II, quickly making it a key component of OSS's religious approach.

Father Morlion ran CIP's Brussels office before the war, where his work was far from secret.[27] While CIP published for the masses, Morlion's primary target was leaders of public opinion. "News is a common denominator by which to gain the attention of every one," Morlion explained, "And what we must do is show the spiritual issues which underlie the news."[28] Morlion evangelized using the media, part of a larger battle to establish the "Apostolate of Public Opinion," as he understood it. This was years before the liberalizing reforms of the Second Vatican Council, and Morlion's interest in motion pictures and cinema made him a bit of an odd duck in an institution largely uncomfortable with the modern world. Morlion's subscription list had big names from the worlds of journalism and religion, including political commentator Walter Lippmann, journalist Arthur Krock, American Catholic radio personality Bishop Fulton Sheen, prominent American Jesuit John La Farge, and Director of the Office of War Information Elmer Davis.[29]

In July 1942, Father Morlion met with Donovan in New York, where the OSS director worked out an agreement with the Belgian priest.[30] In return for unfiltered access to CIP's network of correspondents, OSS would make a significant "donation" to Morlion's organization.[31] The following day, Morlion jotted a letter to the Belgian embassy in which he informed his home government that the Americans had "decided to create a special section to be better informed about the underground of the religious situation in Europe."[32] In true Morlion style—which is to say, an exaggerated one—he explained that he was utterly indispensable to OSS and the State Department. "Being the sole leader of the Catholic international information services which could be helpful to the American government," Morlion wrote, "my departure would mean the stopping of these different activities."[33]

Morlion's relationship with OSS became known as "Operation Pilgrim's Progress," which was less a spy network than an information-sharing agreement. As Catholic observers and journalists, CIP correspondents sent in reports to CIP as they had before. Unbeknownst to those working for Father Morlion, however, their dispatches and unpublished notes were routed through OSS headquarters, where Donovan and others sifted through them for useful intelligence. Donovan received each report directly, personally determining which to forward on to President Roosevelt or Secretary of State Cordell Hull.[34] "The outstanding quality of this material is its reliability," wrote one OSS officer charged with handling the documents. "[Morlion] has reached unimpeachably authoritative sources."[35] As the war progressed, OSS moved from simply skimming information from CIP's network to actively seeking information *through* CIP's sources, allowing US intelligence officers a ground-level window onto occupied Europe.

The program's nature—a network of journalists scattered throughout Europe—also meant certain drawbacks. The journalists were not trained spies, and they did not necessarily prioritize American concerns. Others in OSS disliked the program since its informants were wont to engage in "unadulterated propaganda," a critique that appears to have been made entirely straight-faced.[36] One OSS officer bemoaned the CIP's London correspondent's fixation on Poland, complaining that each report from London contained a "plentiful sprinkling of the rankest sort of Polish propaganda."[37] Ironically, this was precisely the reason why the CIP was valued in the first place—a source of "Catholic" views separate from formal institutional statements coming from the Vatican directly. Those opinions, of course, were less desirable when directed at the United States. OSS officers balked when they found themselves the targets, rather than the creators, of misinformation.[38]

The operational possibilities for Pilgrim's Progress expanded when the Allies took Rome in 1944 and moved Morlion directly to the Vatican, where the priest settled in among his Dominican colleagues.[39] OSS wanted Morlion to use his new perch on the continent to defuse critiques of American religion that might otherwise undermine support for the Allied cause in Europe. Morlion began working to address European Catholic critiques of the United States as too Protestant and materialistic. "The truth about the spiritual attitude of America," Morlion wrote in his guidance to CIP, "must counteract the strong prejudice about American 'materialism' and its dangers for the post war world." The plan called for using radio broadcasts to condemn the hypocrisy of pro-fascist European Christian leaders, lifting up the United States by comparison. In the operation's planning documents, the CIP argued that Catholics could be swayed by appeals to the theological necessity of religious liberty—which the CIP's programming portrayed as existing only in Allied countries. The CIP's broadcasts encouraged its listeners in occupied Europe to fulfill their Christian duty by resisting their occupiers in any possible way (though they were particularly keen on industrial sabotage).[40] Under OSS guidance, the CIP also launched a number of activities directed at American audiences, including a "daily supply of European news" for the National Conference of Christians and Jews, a group promoting religious tolerance within the United States.[41]

Operation Pilgrim's Progress was not confined to Europe. OSS directed Morlion to produce pro-American media in Latin America, where effective propaganda was thought to require "special knowledge of Catholic spirit and Catholic theology." Targeting popular Latin American papers, CIP placed articles designed to address the troubling questions "which bother Latin American Catholics." These pieces ranged from the scandalous ("Is Hitler ex-Communicated?"), to the likely not-flying-off-the-shelf ("Thomist Doctrine of Democracy as the Most Perfect Form of Government"), and articles answering questions that likely weren't being asked by many Latin Americans in the first place ("Have more than Fifty Percent of Americans Abandoned Christianity?").[42] Being cognizant of regional differences within globe-spanning religious traditions was an important development in the religious approach that allowed OSS to more effectively think about what religion looked like on the ground.

With funding and support from the US government, Morlion also expanded the CIP's information-gathering capabilities. OSS coughed up funds for two assistants to Morlion, financing CIP offices in Rome and Lisbon, a $500 monthly stipend for Morlion's personal upkeep, and the continued "basic payments to the C.I.P. network."[43] These funds went toward a variety of CIP activities beyond Morlion personally. OSS staff officer Frederic Dolbeare, charged with the unenviable task of regulating the Office's payments to CIP, estimated in 1944 that if OSS could stream-

REFINING THE RELIGIOUS APPROACH   37

line its various payments, Operation Pilgrim's Progress could run at about $25,000 per year, a figure "somewhat lower than our present one."[44]

OSS's substantial financial commitments to Operation Pilgrim's Progress signaled both the organization's commitment to the religious approach as well as OSS's recognition that CIP's value would be impossible to reproduce in-house. Accordingly, it had to be protected. As OSS learned more about how Catholicism and Catholic organizations functioned, they became more attuned to how these relationships could be strategically employed, and more sensitive to how they could be needlessly jeopardized. When the OSS-London station identified CIP in an internal memo as a "Roman Catholic Church Intelligence outfit" working for OSS, headquarters quickly clarified matters by replying that such an understanding was "misleading." The head office also noted, with a touch of understatement, that if this description should reach the ears of Church officials, "difficulties are bound to arise."[45]

OSS's insistence on an independent CIP resulted in a working relationship that was a mixture of friendship and tension in even the smallest details. The code names OSS gave to Father Morlion were often drawn from Protestant thinkers, including "John Bunyan" (author of *The Pilgrim's Progress*) and "John Calvin" (who wrote *Institutes of the Christian Religion*).[46] It is unclear if these code names were intended as a deliberate slight or simply the work of idle, educated minds attempting to be clever. Explicit anti-Catholicism within OSS is largely absent from the documentary record, though that record has been heavily redacted and only partially released. In any case, this led to much confusion throughout the war. In one exchange of memos, two confused OSS officers tried to figure out if their references to different Protestant thinkers referenced the same twentieth-century Catholic informant: "I am still not clear on our terminology," one wrote dubiously. "However, I know we are referring to the same thing."[47]

Yet whichever famous Protestant provided his code name, Morlion's CIP work kept him busy in Rome. In November 1944, Morlion sent a coded message to OSS advising that he had met with Pope Pius about expanding CIP operations into Brussels.[48] His private meeting must have gone well, considering a note Morlion received from Cardinal Montini, one of Pope Pius's right-hand men (and the future Pope Paul VI in his own right) expressing the Pope's appreciation for CIP:

> Following the audience which he deigned to grant you, His Holiness is pleased to witness anew the interest which he has taken in that which you have exposed on the different activities of the Centers of Information "Pro Deo" (CIP) and how he has been touched by the devotion with which you

personally and your collaborators carry on the important work for the penetration of religious ideas in public opinion.[49]

If Pius was aware of the double nature of Morlion's organization—that it was acting as an information network for American intelligence—the Pope seems to have tacitly approved, or at least allowed it to continue by not actively opposing its activities.

OSS's relationship with CIP was ultimately one of convenience for both sides. For its part, CIP emerges from the historical record as an independent-minded group concerned primarily with shoring up its operating budget and shielding Catholicism from the twin threats of Nazism and Communism. Yet American analysts often assumed that Catholic interests—and the Vatican's more specifically—squared neatly with US aims, a tendency that would become pronounced during the Cold War and reach its peak during the Reagan administration.[50] While the Vatican and many everyday Catholics did indeed fear Communism, many in OSS failed to understand that the interests of CIP and the Vatican *paralleled*, rather than *merged*, with American interests during the war—and that CIP and Vatican interests may have differed, too. When an OSS planning document, devising ways to employ CIP more effectively, suggested it be developed into a "Catholic Intelligence Agency" (with the acronym "CIA," no less), it betrayed an ignorance about the goals and motivations of groups like CIP.[51]

For Father Morlion, the war was never only about the defeat of the Axis. It was also something more: a chance to realize the "apostolate of public opinion" that Morlion had been pursuing for years.[52] The priest, for his part, continued sending reports to the CIA well into the 1950s.[53] Allen Dulles, an OSS leader and future CIA director, remained a fan of Morlion's after the war, when the priest's expertise in psychological warfare would be called upon in the Agency's battle against Communism.[54] Replying to a 1951 note from Gordon Gray, the director of the Psychological Strategy Board (PSB), then-CIA director Dulles was happy to vouch for the Belgian priest: "Father Morlion . . . worked with me in New York during the early days of the war. I have a most favorable impression of him."[55] After Communists were successfully repelled at the Italian ballot box in 1948, Morlion helped US intelligence sway Italian voters throughout the 1950s.[56]

OSS's own assessment of the project was mixed, emphasizing its unique capabilities while noting that it would require more attention to fully develop its potential. Some OSS reports argued that the most valuable part of the project was the network that had been established, allowing contact with people and groups close to but at times separate from the

Vatican. By war's end, some OSS officers argued that events had borne out the value of this information.[57] Those outside OSS who valued Operation Pilgrim's Progress, like the State Department, also cited the program's ability to acquire information in hard-to-reach locales like the Vatican, Italy, and Eastern Europe.[58] OSS was mindful of the looming postwar situation in which many anticipated (correctly, as it turned out) that Italy would be an early battleground between the United States and the Soviet Union. If Pilgrim's Progress was maintained, one report suggested, it should be leveraged to develop relationships directly with members of the Curia—which the OSS assessed as "both desirable and possible."[59] After the war, OSS assessed Operation Pilgrim's Progress as ultimately an investment "of considerable future value" in the American intelligence relationship with the Vatican and Catholic Church.[60] But Operation Pilgrim's Progress also offered broader lessons about the religious approach. The operation suggested that working with religious groups might mean also working outside of official, institutional channels. It suggested that religions were not entirely monolithic, and that paying attention to those internal differences might yield more accurate understandings of the situation on the ground. That these lessons were sometimes forgotten by future generations of US intelligence officers only underscores how contrary these ideas were to popular American understandings of "religion."

The VESSEL Affair

OSS's development of the religious approach existed in a tense and contradictory atmosphere of both domestic anti-Catholicism and a growing sense within OSS that the Vatican and the United States shared important goals. This tension—between target and ally, friend and foe—led to the VESSEL affair, one of the most embarrassing events in OSS's brief existence. OSS operatives bought Vatican documents from a highly placed Vatican source code-named VESSEL who offered the OSS access to valuable information, including tantalizing data about Japanese war plans. OSS officers in Rome verified the material, sending it to Washington, where Donovan and others prized VESSEL's wealth of geopolitical information.[61] The finished intelligence was treated with the highest secrecy and presented to President Roosevelt as an OSS intelligence coup.[62] Even while locked out of most of the Pacific theater, the reports suggested, OSS was skilled enough to shed light on it from half a world away. It was only after an investigation by James Angleton, the OSS counterintelligence chief (that is, the part of OSS guarding against foreign intelligence agencies) in Rome, that VESSEL was exposed as a fabrication—the work of an unemployed Italian pornographer, no less.[63] That these reports wound up on the president's desk, eagerly endorsed by Donovan, compounded OSS's embarrassment.

Conspiracy theories have long swirled around both the VESSEL operation and Angleton.[64] Portrayed as either a genius or a madman—and usually a little of both—James Angleton haunts American intelligence history. After OSS, Angleton would go on to lead all CIA counterintelligence activity during the Cold War, an immensely powerful position in the national security state. He would eventually be forced to resign in 1974 at the height of the furor over the intelligence community's domestic overreach. His nicknames evoke the brilliance and paranoia Angleton's colleagues associated with him: the shadowy-sounding "Gray Ghost," "Orchid" (Angleton was an avid gardener), the "Fisherman" (and a fly-fishing connoisseur), and "Mother" (Angleton knew your business better than you did). Angleton would not be the only CIA officer to be a magnet for conspiracy theories, but his proximity to US intelligence work with the Vatican during World War II—as well as his later role in illegal CIA overreach during the Cold War—makes Angleton a kind of ready-made stock character in any CIA conspiracy theory, a person whose presence suggested the most untoward aspects of intelligence work. This reputation began in World War II, when Angleton investigated VESSEL.

No doubt buttressed by Angleton's involvement, a long-running conspiracy theory portrays VESSEL as not a spectacular failure, but an intelligence coup so valuable that OSS fell on its own sword to protect it.[65] Most versions of this story place the leaker as Cardinal Montini, one of Pope Pius XII's right-hand men and, later, Pope Paul VI.[66] In this account, the conventional history of VESSEL is a long con of staggering genius, a brilliant counterintelligence maneuver of Angleton's to obscure and protect the extent of America's secret relationship with the Vatican. Taken to its logical conclusion, these theories suggest that Angleton's counterintelligence maneuver continues to pay dividends with each book published on OSS that omits the "full story" of VESSEL.[67]

VESSEL conspiracy theories illustrate that OSS's religious approach existed in a deeply politically charged atmosphere. The confused and contradictory stories around VESSEL, Angleton, and OSS operations in Italy were used in Soviet and Italian Communist propaganda, which occasionally republished the most lurid VESSEL material. The chance to portray American intelligence as hopelessly incompetent—purchasing forged documents from an unemployed Italian pornographer and calling it a good day's work—was outweighed by the chance to frame American and Vatican interests as one and the same: an imperial opiate opposed to the proletariat. In what may well be one of the most peculiar echoes of that operation, the *Moscow Literary Gazette* ran an article in 1983 — nearly four decades later — titled "Seventeen Moments of Spring," outlining how Angleton and OSS had recruited "bishops, cardinals, and a future pope" in his scheming. Sadly for the reader — if fitting for the subject — no names are named.[68]

VESSEL's failure also reveals a curious contradiction at the heart of OSS's engagement with the Vatican and Catholicism. Donovan's experiences as an American Catholic soldier and politician allowed him to see the value of working with the Vatican during World War II even as his motivations for doing so were entwined with the same anti-Catholic assumptions that made engaging the Vatican politically dangerous in the first place. Donovan's, and OSS's, assumptions about the intelligence value of the Vatican did not always square with reality. Ironically, the image of the Vatican as an oasis of secret knowledge — awash in information valuable to the Allies, if only they could access it — stemmed from the same anti-Catholic tendencies in American culture that derailed Donovan's earlier, promising political career. That Donovan himself bought into these perceptions testifies to the power and reach of anti-Catholic assumptions in then-contemporary American culture, a phenomenon to which the OSS was not immune.

A Religious Approach Beyond Catholicism

In the view of OSS leadership, however, there was more to be gained than lost by further developing the religious approach. As the war wound down, OSS leadership was concerned about the organization's relationship with the Church. With the postwar world taking shape, it was clear to many American intelligence officers that the United States and Vatican would need to work together. But how would OSS protect this working relationship in an atmosphere of anti-Catholicism? CIP information was already laundered before being routed to places like the State Department, lest the Department be open to attacks that it was under the sway of the Pope.[69] There was also growing concern within OSS that Father Morlion — or one of the many OSS officers who had worked on Operation Pilgrim's Progress — would speak publicly about the covert relationship between the American government and Catholic groups. Whether this "will in future cause any embarrassment," one report summarized, "it is impossible to say."[70]

Protecting the organization's efforts to standardize its religious approach became a priority for OSS. Lester C. Houck, the chairman of OSS's

Reporting Board, described the difficult position faced by OSS in its desire to protect sources within "high Church circles":

> To remove all indications of any connection with the Church would be to destroy the meat of this material. Needless to say, however, any slightest leak regarding the origin would greatly embarrass both the United States and the Vatican and would completely "blow" highly valuable sources.

The solution was a fitting one for an intelligence agency: hide the evidence. "Since the appearance on the manifest of such titles as 'Country: Vatican—Subject: Appeals to the Pope' would be rather revealing," Houck wrote, OSS thought it unwise to label them normally. Instead, three days after Japan's surrender, OSS approved a program to relabel intelligence relationships with high Churchmen and Catholic groups under the innocuous code name "Snapdragon."[71] The political and the religious were to be kept separate even in the archive.

This put OSS in the curious position of going to great lengths to hide what was a largely undramatic working relationship with a major religious group in the United States. The situation also presented challenges for the future. As American intelligence officers looked toward the rebuilding of postwar Italy and the elections that would accompany it, they were already aware that the Vatican's support could prove pivotal for American plans in the region. While there was something to be said for the Americans preserving the Vatican's perceived neutrality, worrying about anti-Catholic sentiment within their own government was an unnecessary hurdle. Of course, OSS was by design a secret organization. The organization's contribution to American pluralism was not in the form of public service announcements or media campaigns (those would have to wait for the CIA). Two future CIA directors were Catholic OSS officers who had served under Donovan, William Colby (1973–1976) and William Casey (1981–1987). OSS's influence can be seen in the CIA's use of various religious organizations, Catholic and otherwise, during the Cold War. In the meantime, Donovan's work did not go unnoticed by the Church. At a ceremony at Cardinal Francis Spellman's personal residence in 1946, he was awarded the Papal Order of Merit of St. Sylvester.[72] Donovan told the *New York Times* that "the award was symbolic of the work done in the war by OSS."[73]

For all of Protestant America's long-standing critiques of Catholic Americans, including that the Church was more political than religious and that its members could not be trusted to safeguard democracy, there is a certain irony that Catholicism became the blueprint for the religious approach by OSS and its successor organization, the CIA. Within a decade of OSS's dissolution, the CIA would rely upon Catholic help in Italy, Vietnam, and other geopolitical hotspots. When the time again came for help from Americans of faith, future American intelligence officers would not relegate Catholic contributions to the shadows. Indeed, they would go to great lengths to make sure that Catholics found the spotlight.

Before the war ended, however, the OSS would be called to engage with religions beyond Christianity. Building on its engagement with Roman Catholicism, the OSS scaled up its religious approach to intelligence as the organization found itself pressed to quickly learn about a variety of other religious ideas, institutions, and groups around the world. How OSS studied and used other world religions would leave a lasting impression on American intelligence, and would represent a crucial link between an interest in Catholicism and a "religious approach" to intelligence that sought to engage the religions of the world.

Chapter Three

The Great Jihad of Freedom

> Behold. We the American Holy Warriors have arrived. Our numbers are as
> the leaves on the forest trees and as the grains of sand in the sea. We have
> come here to fight the great Jihad of Freedom. We have come to set you free.
> From OSS propaganda to North African Muslims[1]

> We deserve to go to hell when we die . . . It is still an open question whether
> an operator in OSS or in CIA can ever again become a wholly honorable man.
> OSS officer William Eddy[2]

As OSS broadened the religious approach beyond Italy and the Vatican, the
organization looked to the borders of the European theater and into the
Pacific. Yet American intelligence officers struggled to match this expanded
operational ambition with their own interpretive prowess. Diverse languages, religions, and cultures from North Africa to the Indonesian archi-
pelago posed stark analytical challenges to the largely white OSS. For
Americans thinking about "Asian religion" during the war, this meant juggling foreign and then-little-known religious systems like Shinto—a tradition that OSS understood to be uniquely (and exclusively) Japanese—as
well as Buddhism and Islam. From Muslim tribes to Shinto shrines, OSS
officers tried to harness these and other "world religions" as a means of
manipulating local cultures and conditions in service to the Allied cause. As
the OSS engaged world religions, a resilient strain of American exceptionalism guided their approach, denigrating foreign peoples and ideas even
as it sought to understand them. This sense of superiority paired with an
enduring Orientalism—a worldview in which peoples of the "Orient" are
seen as simultaneously barbaric, primitive, and romantically exotic—that
permeated intelligence analysis of both Muslims and the Japanese.[3]

These ideas were not new. They could be found on American coffee
tables and in waiting rooms. In August 1944, *TIME* published an article in

its Science section called "Why are the Japs Japs?" that promised to explain how "the" Japanese mind worked. Like other Orientalist coverage, *TIME*'s article presumed that Japanese customs and society were fundamentally different from "normal" American culture. According to the Yale anthropologist Geoffrey Gorer, *TIME* explained, these differences originated in the "severe toilet training of Japanese infants" in which young children were "ferociously punished" by their parents, ultimately resulting in the violence and barbarity of the Japanese military.[4] These explanations for Orientalist stereotypes reveal how thoroughly ignorant Americans were of their opponents in the Pacific. That Gorer had never visited Japan was not an obstacle to the article's conclusions, since Japan and its people were largely blank spots on America's intellectual map: Japanese culture required explanation.[5]

For many in OSS, the appeal of the religious approach was that it offered explanation of even the most seemingly confusing human practices. For example, OSS saw Japanese beliefs as notoriously difficult to understand, since the Japanese "do not follow a logical way of reasoning similar to ours," and they wondered why the Japanese held strange ideas like favoring a "beautiful defeat" over an "ugly victory." To make matters worse, the Japanese language itself was "never precise in its expressions," they thought, which made interpretation all the more challenging.[6] Yet if religion was everywhere and everyone "had" it, as the world religions paradigm (WRP) suggested, even seemingly "exotic" cultures like Japan's could be made legible through the religious approach.

But these acts of interpretation existed in a predominantly Christian framework, informed by both a generic American Protestantism as well as OSS's work with the Catholic Church in Europe. Lacking other examples, OSS's complex relationship with the Vatican and its understanding of Roman Catholicism writ large provided the theoretical grounding for working with all "foreign" religious groups. OSS projected its vision of Catholicism as simultaneously exotic, valuable, and pro-American onto "world religions" in general. The transposability of all religions meant that OSS assumed whatever worked (or did not work) for Catholicism would work (or not) with other religious groups.

This new errand, and new wilderness, would uniquely challenge OSS's pursuit of the religious approach. The wealthy, largely white upward-bound Americans who made up OSS leadership did not vacation in Osaka or pick up a fluency in Malay at Yale. The shortage of American specialists compounded the lack of general cultural familiarity. In the months preceding OSS's formation in 1942, more than 70,000 US citizens of Japanese ancestry (along with tens of thousands of additional non-citizens) were forcibly relocated to concentration camps.[7] Vast resources of possible human intelligence were literally imprisoned by the same federal government searching for ways to understand Japanese culture. As a result, OSS was sometimes hamstrung by the very assumptions they sought to promote. Nevertheless, due in part to these efforts—and sometimes despite them—OSS deployed the religious approach to serve the American war effort.

Making Sense of "Religion" in the Pacific Theater

As Allied forces island-hopped across the Pacific, credible intelligence on Japan was at a premium. Geography and culture combined to make the Japanese islands difficult to breach covertly. Allied politics did not help, either. General Douglas MacArthur, supreme Allied commander for the South West Pacific, gave OSS director William Donovan headaches by keeping OSS out of the Pacific theater for much of the war.[8] MacArthur's orders, however, did not stop OSS from *studying* the Japanese. With the Research and Analysis Branch (RAB) on the job, the OSS set out to make "sense" of Japan.

Compared to the vast research available on Christianity, reliable information on Japanese traditions was harder to come by for OSS. Part of OSS's struggle to understand Japanese religion stems from the history of "religion" itself, which is not a native term for much of the world's population.[9] For a few hundred years before the war, European missionaries, rulers, armies, and scholars had imported Christocentric ideas about "religion" into Asia, where local people encountered these ideas in a context of cultural imperialism and settler colonialism.[10] In British India, for example, European powers "discovered" religion as a distinctly different area of social life that often bore little resemblance to the ideas of indigenous people who lived in these regions.[11]

The study of Japanese religion was itself bound up with Japan's unique relationship to European colonialism, which differed from other colonial encounters in Asia. Japan's long-standing isolationist policies were breached in 1853 by the arrival of a US fleet under Commodore Matthew Perry. The United States aimed to compel Japan, through violence if necessary, to accede to US trade and diplomatic demands. Part of the negotiations and eventual treaty involved how to handle "religion," an idea ostensibly distinct from both Christianity and missionizing activity. The Japanese government's translators responded by strategically translating these terms to challenge the new foreign presence, making "religion" a site of political struggle in Japan.[12] Japanese intellectuals and government officials—familiar with European colonial ambitions and the imperial playbook—retrofitted the term "religion" to make sense in Japanese culture alongside traditions that predated it, such as Shinto, Buddhism, and Confucianism.

Nearly a century later, academic experts in religion—especially anthropologists—were called in to guide OSS through these treacherous historical and cultural waters.[13] While OSS analysts assumed Japanese religious culture required expert interpretation, the assumption that religion was strategically important—that it could be isolated and studied, that as an idea it must be a powerful influence on the Japanese mind—went largely unquestioned. This left OSS in a curious position with respect to religion in Japan: no one could make sense of it, but no one doubted its power to influence the Japanese.

OSS's primary focuses for the religious approach in the Pacific were Buddhism and Shinto. Both appeared strange compared to the Christian traditions OSS had encountered in Europe and the Americas, and OSS knew so little about these systems that its primary focus was on collecting whatever information it could find. In OSS's "Plan for Psychological Warfare Against Japanese Government," for example, American intelligence compiled a bibliography of scriptures, commentaries, and academic works, carefully noting when Western scholars produced information or when it came from Japanese experts like D. T. Suzuki.[14] This intentional delineation demonstrated their focus on authorship and origins as salient information for strategic deployment. Japanese experts would not only have a unique perspective on their object of study, this reasoning went, but their work would be easier to weaponize for Japanese audiences. Drawing upon existing academic and popular typologies of Buddhism, for example, OSS propaganda highlighted the apparent contradiction between Japanese warmaking and Buddhism's ostensibly non-violent nature. OSS officers perpetuated these assumptions through their research and briefings as well, going so far as to pair specific Japanese actions against particular sermons attributed to the Buddha. OSS hoped to shame and demoralize Japanese Buddhists by arguing that they were complicit with the Japanese government's immoral leadership.[15]

Unlike in Europe, OSS had little access to quality human intelligence about Japan that might have refined its propaganda program. Instead, OSS gathered information from trusted sources who had earned their credibility in different contexts. One of OSS's best (and not coincidentally, one of the only) sources of human intelligence was Father Candeau, a French Catholic priest affiliated with Operation Pilgrim's Progress. Working for many years in Japan as a Catholic missionary, OSS valued Father Candeau's unique position to explain the Japanese mindset. Candeau's portrait of Japanese religion and culture was rich in Orientalist tropes, such as his conviction that Japanese religious beliefs were essentially irrational. The Japanese, explained Candeau, "consider their Emperor a God and do not find anything unreasonable in such a belief." What was peculiar about the Japanese, according to Candeau, was that these self-evidently absurd beliefs could not simply be attributed to a lack of education, since Japanese society had ready access to European thinkers and philosophers. It was, instead, something particular to the Japanese mindset, an innate Japanese characteristic that tolerated irrationality.[16]

Father Candeau suggested that if OSS wanted to understand why Japanese soldiers were so willing to throw their lives away—especially in seemingly irrational actions like the *kamikaze*—the Americans should look to religion.[17] When the Japanese went to war, the priest-informant explained, they leave home "without the desire to return," since they have a "spirit of sacrifice" that is "instinctive and natural." Buddhism and Shintoism, according to the priest, "are unclear and vague in what they teach about life after death." Candeau speculated that this made the Japanese challenging opponents, since they lacked a coherent afterlife that could encourage rational behavior during wartime. Speaking to Japanese diplomats at the Vatican confirmed Father Candeau's suspicions about the role of Japanese religion in the war. These diplomats, he reported, were "rather optimistic" about Japanese resistance and dismissive of Allied demands for an unconditional surrender—something that the "Japanese mindset" simply could not accept.[18] As a result, Father Candeau anxiously concluded, these mindless warriors would be difficult for the Allies to beat even with numerical and technological superiority.

Confident that Japan would be dedicated to war for essentially religious reasons, OSS focused its attention on using this information to US advantage. The idea that Japanese belief could be influenced in order to manipulate Japanese action was an attractive one for OSS officers, but they struggled to execute these plans given their reliance on a number of faulty assumptions. OSS's difficulty in making sense of Japanese religion was part of its larger struggle to recognize differences within and among religious traditions, and its reliance on Christianity as the basis for understanding all other worldviews further reinforced a narrow model for understanding the relationship between belief and action.[19] Many officers were also entrenched in a racialized, Orientalist thought process that approached Japanese culture as something that could be isolated, inventoried, and manipulated. For example, when a young OSS officer named Edward Lansdale—who would go on to play a major role in the CIA's relationship with world religions—proposed weaponizing Japanese proverbs, the reason given was simple, straightforward, and wrong: "The Japanese, like all Orientals, love proverbs."[20] While this assumption may have squared with the limited research at OSS's disposal, it had no bearing on operational success.

Faulty intelligence and failure to think in sophisticated ways about how particular cultural traditions may or may not apply to modern warfare led OSS to intervene in the Pacific theater in perplexing ways. For instance, while working for OSS in Burma, anthropologist Gregory Bateson dumped yellow dye into the Irrawaddy River because the Burmese believed yellow "portended the end of a foreign occupation." By dyeing the river, Bateson argued, the Burmese would revolt against the Japanese. (It did not work—the dye was designed for salt water and sank in the fresh water of the Irrawaddy.[21]) Bateson's error was not merely in preparing the dye incorrectly, but in presuming belief mechanically determined action. If the religious approach was to gain any traction in the Pacific, OSS would need a more familiar terrain of ideas on which to operate. As OSS worked to understand and control Southeast Asian cultures, American intelligence officers increasingly relied on Islam, a tradition that Americans found marginally more familiar yet still readily applicable in "Oriental" locations.

A Race for Islamic Literacy with Japan

Though Islam was not widely practiced in Japan, Muslims played an important role in how OSS pursued the religious approach in the Pacific theater. Japan had conquered many Muslim-majority areas in Southeast Asia, and OSS saw these Muslims as among the most likely populations to revolt against their Japanese occupiers. Islam also seemed more naturally "religious" than the Japanese traditions, and thus at odds with Japanese governance. Muslims better fit into what OSS saw as the philosophical underpinning of the religious approach to intelligence: the conviction that religion everywhere was naturally linked to human freedom and democracy (and thus, sympathetic to American ideals). OSS propaganda linked democracy and religion, arguing that only democratic governments could safeguard the individual autonomy that authentic religious belief (like Islam) required. OSS could then claim to Muslim audiences that "the Fascist attack on democracy was also an attack on the Islamic democratic institutions."[22] This echoed OSS assumptions fueling the religious approach in other theaters: that the United States and religion were natural allies, a sentiment that would resurface in other OSS (and later, CIA) operations.

The problem—at least for OSS—was that the Japanese seemed determined to avoid conflict with the Muslims they now ruled. Japanese friendliness toward Muslims, one OSS officer gloomily observed, made it unlikely they would commit any "religious faux pas."[23] The Japanese were strategic in how they related to certain conquered populations, framing their actions as part of an anti-imperialist effort to prevent British and American colonial expansion in Asia.[24] OSS well understood the Japanese strategy, since it was one they themselves were employing with other religious groups around the globe. Recognizing they were behind the curve, OSS analysts tried to develop a fluency in Islamic theology to improve their propaganda. In so doing, OSS found themselves in a race for religious literacy.

OSS busied itself subverting Japanese portrayals of themselves as pro-Muslim. Paying careful attention to the differences between Shinto and Islam, OSS produced comparative studies that would not be entirely out of place in a twenty-first-century world religions textbook. Hoping to stimulate feelings of Islamic superiority, OSS propaganda encouraged Muslims to defend Islam against heretical, foreign threats like Shinto. American intelligence contrasted Shinto claims about the superior nature of Japanese identity and government with Muslim claims about human equality. Shinto was an "ethnic religion," OSS noted, while Islam is a "revealed religion." According to OSS, this meant that Shinto remained intensely national and focused on local culture, while Islam embraced an inclusive worldview and saw humankind as one. The Japanese worshiped "super gods" and claimed other deities owed fealty to the Japanese gods. Once Muslims realize this, an OSS report concluded, they will inevitably "feel the superiority of their religion," compared to Shinto's "outdated superstitious, mythological character of an ethnic cult." In studies like these, OSS tried to subvert Japan's anti-imperialist credentials in order to shift popular Muslim support toward American interests and, simultaneously, disrupt Japanese stability and security in the region.

In a plan that was equal parts creative and audacious, OSS designed an operation to convince Muslims that Japanese war plans included "absorbing" the entire religion of Islam into Shinto. Project Windpipe, as it came to be known, was an elaborate disinformation campaign aimed at Japan's claim that it defended Asia from "Anglo-American aggression." Project Windpipe portrayed Japan's alleged defense of Asia as a cover for an outrageous plan to meld Shinto and Islam in the service of Japanese empire.[25] The OSS hoped to tarnish Japan's outreach to Muslims as self-serving while presenting the United States as stalwart defenders of religious freedom, a message that OSS presumed naturally appealed to all religious people. Muslims in Japanese-occupied territory, OSS officers assumed, would gravitate toward the United States once they understood that America, and not Japan, had their best interest—that is, their *religious* interest—at heart.

To help turn these two religions against one another, OSS fabricated evidence of a grand religious conspiracy. Project Windpipe called for manufacturing banners, coins, pamphlets, and other goods with carefully sourced Japanese materials in order to appear authentically "Japanese." For example, OSS planned to print the Islamic *Shahadah*, or declaration of faith ("There is no god but God, and Muhammad is His Prophet"), on flags and banners, but with a twist: each item would replace the Prophet Muhammad with the emperor of Japan. Banners were printed with the Arabic slogan "There is no God but God, and Tenshi-Sama is His Prophet," replacing the seventh-century prophet with the twentieth-century "Honorable Son of Heaven." This revised creed would be joined by two images on the Project Windpipe-made flags: a large red "rising sun" alongside a much smaller Islamic crescent moon. OSS's artistic direction made clear that "the Sun must be much larger than the moon," presumably to suggest that Japan held itself above Islam. No detail was too small: from the colors of the flag's tassels (red), to the quality of the fabric (Japanese silk), to the style of Arabic calligraphy. Mixing these "authentic" details together required extensive knowledge of specific cultures and their history, even as it assumed incredibly limited possibilities for how these ideas would be received and acted upon.

Project Windpipe drew upon widely accepted central tenets of Islam even as it underscored OSS's interpretive limitations. Through research, for instance, OSS knew one pillar of Islam was the hajj, a practice established by the Prophet Muhammad in which all Muslims who are physically and financially able make a pilgrimage to Mecca once in their lifetime. Awareness of this religious custom led the RAB to recommend the time between Ramadan and hajj for the most fruitful time to sow division between Shinto and Islam, and so they planned to debut these "authentic" Japanese materials in time for the hajj of 1944.[26] OSS hoped that imams sympathetic to the Allies would make it appear as if the Japanese were distributing these heretical items to the Muslims they occupied. The goal, of course, was to paint the Japanese as inept infidels bent on destroying Islam. One of the operation's planners mused, "This, we hope, will enrage the Muslims."[27]

The OSS expected this elaborate fabrication scheme, infused with a mix of "authentic" Japanese and Muslim traditions, to lead Muslims to recognize the United States as an obvious ally against Japan.

The hajj was another Muslim practice that captured OSS's imagination, since the pilgrimage appeared to be the kind of ironclad causal link between belief and action that US intelligence saw as an easy target for manipulation. The Americans' straightforward understanding of the hajj as a religious "requirement" also lent it gravitas as a propaganda ingredient in the minds of American operatives. Since Mecca remained under Allied control during the war, OSS was eager to capitalize on the inability of Muslims in Japanese-controlled areas to attend hajj.[28] OSS operations portrayed Japan as only superficially friendly to Islam, unable to respect God's will and negotiate safe passage for the pilgrimage. OSS propaganda exacerbated these tensions by inventing a Japanese scheme to make Muslims perform hajj to Tokyo instead of Mecca.[29] In contrast, OSS claimed, the Allies demonstrated friendship to Muslims by providing access to Mecca.[30]

As OSS devised plans to instigate Muslim uprisings against Japan in Southeast Asia, they also considered more direct incentives for resistance forces. OSS teams in the Dutch East Indies (modern Indonesia) discovered that local Muslims were uninterested in Japanese occupation currency. What Indonesians wanted, OSS teams reported back, was payment in the Maria Theresa thaler, a coin last minted in nineteenth-century Austria but one that had remained popular with Muslim traders along the trade routes of North Africa and the Middle East. The popularity of the thaler among Muslims in the Dutch East Indies was simple to understand, explained OSS chief scientist Stanley Lovell, once you applied the religious approach:

> Indonesians are Mohammedans and the law of Islam compels them, once in their lifetime, to make the "hajj" (or great pilgrimage) to Mecca and Medina during the holy period, or the "umra" (lesser pilgrimage) at any time. The only money that was sure to be acceptable in their holy cities was this Maria Theresa thaler, and since becoming eligible to the Muslim heaven with its black-eyed houris might depend on the pilgrimage, these coins were both desirable and precious.[31]

Given OSS's view of the hajj, American intelligence officers concluded that Muslims would do anything to get their hands on the thaler coins—even fight their Japanese occupiers.

Yet one problem with this plan was that the US government was fresh out of nineteenth-century Austrian currency. In a burst of numismatic creativity, Lovell and his team of OSS scientists brought the "extinct" coin back to life. Working with rare-coin dealers in the United States, Lovell's team obtained minting machinery and developed a procedure to artificially age the coins (the last of which had been minted in 1870). Lovell went so far as to insist on using real silver in the counterfeit coins, since he was sure the Indonesians would bite the coins to test their worth. The Dutch government in exile, less than keen on the prospect of rampant inflation in their occupied colony, only reluctantly agreed to the plan. As Lovell wrote after the war, the great lengths to which OSS went to produce the thalers was justified, since the thalers would serve as a motivator without equal. For these coins, he reported, the Muslim islanders would "promise to do anything: a mass revolt against the occupying Japanese soldiers, multiple assassinations and East Indian subtleties of attack too Asiatic and vulgar to be told in English."[32]

Beyond criticizing Japan's treatment of Muslims, OSS wanted to lift up American relations with Muslims by comparison. This was no easy task. OSS dealt largely in hypotheticals, stressing America as a bastion of religious freedom that would treat Islam the same as any other religion. OSS wove these arguments into their propaganda, as when they fabricated Japanese orders requiring mosques to be used as storage for ammunition ahead of an American attack. The fake orders explained that since an American bombardment would naturally spare the mosques out of respect for Islam, these houses of worship were the best place to store Japanese war material.[33] The propaganda served a dual purpose, painting the Japanese military as religiously intolerant while depicting the United States as a pluralist nation respectful of religious freedom. Yet again, long-standing ideas about American exceptionalism influenced OSS to see the United States as the natural ally of religious people everywhere. This strategy made good sense from a worldview like OSS's that presumed everyone, everywhere, had religion—and that all religions were basically the same.

This strategy appealed in part because OSS recognized the theological relationship between Christianity and Islam. OSS officers marked up reports detailing Islamic theology, and their marginalia offers a window into OSS assumptions about how religion generally, and Islam specifically, operated in the field. When one report noted that the Quran forbade warfare against Christians and Jews, an OSS officer circled it and wrote "Find this in Quran."[34] Studies of scripture and religious history led to OSS reports noting how Christians and Muslims were "natural" allies because the Allies were largely Christian and thus 'Ahl al-Kitāb, or "people of the book." OSS officers assumed the similarities Muslims and Christians shared—whether found in scripture, as Abraham's descendants, or in a shared geography of the ancient world—would naturally make Muslims and Christians ally with each other.

Playing up the familial resemblance between Christianity and Islam also highlighted Shinto's perceived peculiarity. American intelligence officers expected Shinto to operate according to Western assumptions about religion, and they were puzzled when it did not. When one report noted that "those who are not Japanese cannot become Shintoists," the reader underlined it and wrote "?!!"[35] Yet the idea that conversion is a standard feature of religions, or that religious identity is mutually exclusive, is far from a universal idea. This Shinto "fact" reinforced OSS's conviction that the Japanese viewed their own culture as superior. Research on Shinto suggested that OSS could "ridicule the Japanese conception of divinity itself" to break Muslim affinity for Japan. OSS attempted this by drawing attention to the Shinto idea of *kami*, an expansive category of spirits, forces, and powers, which they portrayed as material objects of worship. This strategy was clearly designed to trigger Islam's opposition to idolatry and polytheism. Unlike its Abrahamic counterpart Christianity, traditional Islamic theology had long opposed the idea of an incarnate God, or that it was even possible to represent the divine in physical form. Using Shinto ideas of *kami*, OSS presented followers of Shinto—and by extension, all Japanese—as idol worshippers. Since such a belief and cultural practice was anathema to Islam, OSS concluded, Muslims would "naturally" be repulsed and turn toward more suitable Abrahamic allies.

Yet even these "facts" were confused attempts to wrestle with the reality of diversity within religious traditions. By assuming that every religion was governed by certain rules, and that ideas within a tradition were held universally, OSS thinkers struggled to account for the reality that members of the same religion disagree, sometimes in profound ways. Many followers of Shinto might not see *kami* as objects of worship, for example, and would not even view Shinto as "religious" in the way OSS understood the term.[36] For its part, Islam's expansive history includes many different understandings of the nature of the divine. Mistaking the dominant view in a religion for the religion itself was a common mistake, something with which the academic study of religion has also struggled.[37] OSS needed information to be operationally sound, however, and neglecting internal diversity was one way to ensure that it was not.

OSS also tried to divide Islam and Shinto by appealing to ideas outside either tradition. Among the most powerful reasons Muslims should not trust Shinto practitioners, according to OSS, was that the Japanese were racist. Racism was thought uniquely objectionable to Muslim sensibilities and, according to OSS studies, one of the Prophet Muhammad's chief innovations was challenging racial castes. Employing a remarkable analogy, one OSS report explained that before the Prophet's time "the early Arabs had the same attitude toward the rest of the world as the U.S. 'southern gentlemen' have toward the negroes."[38] OSS understood Shinto to be racist against non-Japanese, portraying Shinto as an ethno-religious nationalism that celebrated the exclusion of other religions and nationalities. This was an ironic argument for OSS. The British, French, and Americans had colonized vast swaths of the Asia-Pacific for centuries, internally displaced indigenous people wherever they went, sustained a human slave trade, and yet proceeded to lecture Muslims about rejecting the Japanese incursion since, unlike Shinto, "the very core of Muslim doctrines is tolerance."[39] Moreover, OSS interpreted the centrality of tolerance within Islam as a similarity with — rather than a difference from — the United States.

Not only did the United States' own history of racism in Asia and at home weaken the strategy of focusing on Japanese racism, but the dismissive and vicious critiques of Japanese culture also undermined OSS propaganda. OSS relied on Muslim informants who portrayed Japanese people as efficient machines devoid of feeling or rational thought. While Islam has no ritual, this report argued,

> the Japanese are ritual crazy. Even outside of their religious life their best entertainment consists in things like the Tea Ceremony. Every movement is set before hand and God help you if anything unconventional is done by you.[40]

Praising Islam by suggesting it had no rituals echoed American Protestant claims that ritual was practiced by lower forms of religion, a critique often lobbed at American Catholics. Of course, this definition avoided classifying holidays, sermons, prayer, baptism, and other activities as "ritual." Similarly, in OSS's report, "ritual" has a negative connotation: it is a mindless activity performed by Japanese, not Muslims. Defining Muslim practices as free from ritual allowed OSS to elevate Muslim culture over Japan's. By fusing religious critique with racial critique, OSS echoed long-standing ways the category of religion had been used to mark and maintain religious and racial categories.

OSS operations in the Pacific theater demonstrate how American intelligence understood the religions of the world by filtering them through Eurocentric and colonial understandings of "religion." These ideas were then enlisted to help evaluate possible military outcomes with Japan. In a pattern repeated around the globe, OSS officers tinkered with a discourse of world religions for strategic advantage. This rudimentary manipulation, however factually challenged, revealed OSS's theorization of how religions influenced conflict around the world. Extensive research into foreign religious traditions made OSS confident in their understanding of these traditions, even as the assumptions supporting OSS's studies were rooted in problematic methodological assumptions about the universality of human experience and the causal relationship between belief and action. This colored OSS's own analyses of how people around the world would respond to OSS claims and, in turn, influenced the operations OSS undertook. OSS's tools to study these religious phenomena were incomplete and clunky, shaped as they were through a white, Eurocentric Christian theology and bureaucratic self-interest.

Using Islam as a wedge between the Japanese and the populations they occupied suggests OSS saw Islam as a usefully pro-Allied, "Western" religious tradition. They gave little consideration to the possibility that Muslims in the region would not want to be aligned with the Allied cause. Especially in the latter days of the Pacific War, the OSS saw Muslims as potential partners because American intelligence operatives had extensively worked with Muslims elsewhere. Examining how OSS made sense of Islam is key to understanding how OSS studied and interpreted religion, since American intelligence officers interacted with Muslims more than any other non-Christian religious group. The most sustained OSS engagement with Islam took place along the southern Mediterranean coast, where OSS hoped to incite Muslims against their fascist occupiers. In this corner of the world, a different but no less challenging wilderness awaited OSS.

Islam and OSS in the "Middle East"

OSS intelligence operations with Muslims in North Africa and Southwest Asia were only the latest chapter in American relations with the so-called "Muslim world" and "Middle East." Then as now, these terms do not identify actual geopolitical territories so much as imagined spaces that Americans helped create through popular media and academic writing.[41] This interpretive blind spot was not unique to OSS. "When Americans refer to the 'Muslim World,'" historical anthropologist Zareena Grewal explains, "they reproduce, amend, and complicate Colonial Europe's moral geography of the Orient."[42] OSS engaged this "moral geography," and their analysis reflected broader American cultural attitudes that a unified, cohesive Muslim world existed in the first place.[43] While OSS officers could no doubt identify major differences between the cultures of Christian-majority countries in World War II—for example, between Germany and Great Britain—a similar attention to detail was missing from the organization's approach to Muslim-majority countries. Instead, they drew upon existing stereotypes and assumptions about the "Middle East" and the "Muslim world" to form the basis of their research and operations. The most meaningful and accessible cultural associations to most Americans at the time, including OSS officers, were those rooting Islam in "Abrahamic" traditions found in the "Holy Land."

Americans had long used a relationship with the idea of an Abrahamic "Holy Land" to imagine a unique role for themselves in world history by inserting the United States into an expanded biblical narrative.[44] This practice extended back to early Puritan sermons reinforcing the notion that "Jerusalem was, New England is."[45] The Puritan image of the "city upon a hill" was but one manifestation of their insistence that they were the new Israelites in a new wilderness. In the nineteenth century, American missionaries who lived and worked in the region encouraged this connection to "Israel," as God's chosen people and as stewards of God's kingdom on earth. The first American institutions in North Africa and Southwest Asia, such as the Syrian Protestant College (later renamed the American University of Beirut) in 1866 and the American University in Cairo in 1919, reflected a paternal custodianship even if the relationship might seem more benevolent than British and French colonialism in the region. Although Americans did not formally govern residents, they nevertheless imagined Ottoman territory as a new American frontier. Here, American Christians believed they had another chance at converting the "natives" in lands that they understood as theirs by spiritual birthright. This allowed Americans, whether they missionized in the Middle East or visited only in their imagination through mission reports, travel narratives, or novels, to make sense of their nation's role in Christian history. This was a crucial ingredient in American efforts to craft a national mythology as the United States ascended the world stage in the twentieth century.

This history of primarily white Protestant missionizing motivated the OSS, and many of the OSS officers who worked in the region were the product of missionary families in the Middle East.[46] Children of missionaries were often bilingual and already familiar with the region's religious and social customs. Many were also connected through their extended family or church fellowship to the regional network of American educational institutions that had emerged from missionary programs. These connections left many officers with an affection for the region and a paternal sense of authority over its largely Muslim population.[47] Sharing a history did not mean that OSS was immune to Orientalizing stereotypes about Islam and Muslims found in mainstream American culture. Indeed, it often meant that OSS officers assumed they had immunities against flawed cultural logic or faulty assumptions because they were so personally familiar with the unique traditions and cultures of the region.

While all religion shared some essential qualities, the "religious approach" reasoned, each tradition displayed unique characteristics that had to be accommodated. OSS officers thought that Muslims (and Arabs, with whom OSS often conflated all Muslims) were substantially "different" from other religious and ethnic groups and thus required unique psychological targeting. OSS officers quickly found that many of their psychological warfare techniques, like targeted radio broadcasts and planted newspaper articles, were less effective than they had been in Europe. Rather than question the supposed universal efficacy of these mediums, OSS officers assumed their plans needed to better account for the innate characteristics (and deficiencies) of Islam and Muslims. One memo claimed that the "Arab mind" could only be swayed by the "leaders-sheiks" and religious leaders "to whom the masses of the Near East peoples still look automatically."[48] The Muslim mind responded best to order and force, one OSS observer explained, since "the military discipline has been the best moral education for Arabs up to now. Their religion allows all moral faults except inhospitality."[49] This Orientalizing approach echoed OSS's analytical missteps in its study of Japanese culture by assuming first that the essence of a culture could be distilled and, second, that this distillation governed how all people of that culture thought and acted.

These epistemological flaws were further complicated by OSS officers and informants observing Muslims in the region through the lens of Christianity. American intelligence officers often relied on information from explicitly Christian sources and frames of reference, such as the network of missionaries informing the OSS office in Cairo.[50] For example, OSS allowed Father Morlion's Pilgrim's Progress network to chime in with a Catholic perspective on Islam, advising OSS personnel to be "severe," since "Mussulmen like a man who can show himself a 'Great Chief.'"[51] The way these Christian informants understood Islam colored OSS's strategies for working with Muslims. This is particularly evident in RAB's 1942 guidelines for OSS officers in North Africa, which noted that the best time and place to target Muslim minds was after Friday prayers at the mosque, when the men "are in a more religious frame of mind" and "more receptive to rumors and propaganda unfavorable to non-Muslims."[52] Even so, approaching Islam from a Christian perspective unintentionally forced some Christian OSS officers to grapple with their own assumptions about what was normal. For instance, when talking to Muslims about religious matters, the RAB's guidelines implored intelligence officers to remember that "the Fatherhood of God" was not a universally acceptable term because it suggested to Muslims the deity's involvement in "sexual intercourse." Since Islam understood this to be "one of the most monstrous errors of Christianity," the RAB suggested avoiding the topic.[53]

As OSS tried to standardize its approach toward Islam, it occasionally reflected on the limits to its approach. In one write-up on Islam, one RAB analyst noted that

> one caution in assessing this material is necessary: Since it is derived from the judgments of foreign observers, it is not unlikely that some of the attitudes described are merely repetitions of stereotypes—and biased—foreign conceptions of what the native Moslems think.[54]

OSS officers recognized the possibility of biased stereotypes even as they often lacked the information necessary to identify it or the skills to correct it. This self-consciousness was calculated: the strategic value of Islam simply outweighed dismissive attitudes about it. Causing religious offense was not only rude, it was operationally counterproductive. Acknowledging the potential for bias imbued OSS with the confidence that they were likely to avoid it, even when that was not the case.

OSS personnel on the ground in North Africa illustrated many of these conflicting impulses. Early in the war, Donovan sent the Harvard anthropologist Carleton Coon to North Africa to survey the nomadic Muslim tribes then nominally under French rule. Working undercover for OSS, Coon's reputation provided adequate cover as he ran guns to French resistance fighters and networked with local Muslim leaders. Whereas Coon was there to study the local population—studies he pursued alongside his intelligence operations—his boss, William "Bill" Eddy, represented a different strand of American engagement with locals.[55] Donovan referred to Eddy as his "Lawrence of Arabia" which, uncharacteristically for Donovan, may not have been an exaggeration.[56] While Eddy's official job was US naval attaché in Tangier, he also served as head of OSS in North Africa.[57] Born in Lebanon to Presbyterian missionaries, Eddy was a World War I veteran fluent in Arabic and French. Eddy famously served as interpreter between FDR and the Saudi king Abdulaziz during their 1945 meeting aboard the

USS Quincy in the Suez Canal, and would go on to be a key figure in US-Saudi relations after the war.[58]

Coon and Eddy spent most of their time preparing for the Allied invasion of North Africa, known as Operation Torch. As part of the OSS vanguard, Coon and Eddy assessed the level of resistance Allied forces should expect during the invasion. To that end, they also did what they could to encourage the indigenous Muslim tribes to revolt against Axis occupiers.[59] "Coon is a world-famous anthropologist, scientist and author," his boss Eddy later reflected, "but I knew him as a fearless organizer of homicidal guerillas."[60] Theoretically, this was a task made easier thanks to Coon's fieldwork relationships with the Riffians and Berbers, and the anthropologist vowed to "crack" the local Muslim tribes.[61]

The situation reads like the plot of a bad movie: Coon, an Ivy Leaguer and social Darwinist with an interest in race science and no background in intelligence, was instructed to "busy myself with Arab affairs, to find out what the Arabs were thinking and how they could best be influenced."[62] The anthropologist-turned-spy was phrenologically measuring the heads of the very people he was trying to persuade to support the Allied cause. He even translated President Roosevelt's Flag Day speech into Arabic in order to distribute the translation among Moroccan Muslims and thereby win their loyalty to the US cause. Coon described how he and his colleague

> would reword the English in a more Arabic-sounding way, and Gusus [a colleague] would sing out an Arabic poetical version and then write it down. Every time Mr. Roosevelt mentioned God once, we named Him six times; and the result was a piece of poetry that might have come out of the Koran.[63]

Coon does not record the reaction of the Moroccan tribes to this message, though it seems doubtful that they mistook the words of Franklin Delano Roosevelt for Qur'anic poetry.

Coon was convinced that Islam was the key to igniting resistance against the Axis occupiers. The text of another of Coon's propaganda messages, addressed to Moroccan Muslims in anticipation of the Allied landings, makes clear how OSS wanted Muslims to view the mostly Christian soldiers who would soon be on their shores:

> This is a great day for you and for us, for all the sons of Adam who love freedom.
>
> Behold. We the American Holy Warriors have arrived. Our numbers are as the leaves on the forest trees and as the grains of sand in the sea.

We have come here to fight the great Jihad of Freedom.
We have come to set you free.[64]

On the eve of the Allied landings, Coon projected that 80,000 Muslims would rise up in Morocco to aid the US Army when it washed ashore.[65] Like much of Coon's work for OSS, that number was overly optimistic. Even so, intelligence historians typically credit OSS's role in Operation Torch as one of the organization's most important contributions in World War II. Part of that effort was tied to the confidence of American intelligence officers that the religious approach offered a beachhead where there was none before.[66]

Though both Coon and Eddy worked for OSS, they represented different approaches to US involvement in the region. Eddy was a deeply introspective critic of both himself and OSS. Eddy's journals and diaries depict a man ill at ease with intelligence work, and his writings shed light on the darker aspects of a job that often proved to be a dangerous business for both American officers and their local allies. After the war, Eddy remained haunted by the informants and intermediaries he empowered and rewarded—opium addicts, domestic abusers—in the service of defeating the Axis in North Africa:

> It is permitted to walk with the devil until you have crossed the bridge. The OSS was in a death struggle with the Gestapo and, like Churchill, allied itself with devils to survive. We deserve to go to hell when we die. We used Communists, telling them that we would help them overthrow Franco, which we did not do. We false-promised Riff Moorish officers to work for independence of Morocco from Spain . . . the OSS had no conscience. If Kurt Rieth, the Tangier Gestapo Chief, had bought thousands of Moors with false promises and loose change, he was merely smarter than we . . . it is still an open question whether an operator in OSS or in CIA can ever again become a wholly honorable man.[67]

Eddy suffered recurring nightmares in which an informant was caught and executed while under his protection. Eddy relived this night after night even as he realized he wouldn't have changed his actions: "Would I do the same thing again? Yes, in wartime, I would, but that melancholy conviction does not make it easier for me to live with myself."[68]

Eddy's concerns and criticisms only deepened his commitment to the religious approach. After the war, Eddy wanted alliances premised not on geopolitical whims but on deeply held religious values. An important figure in the formation of the CIA, Eddy advocated for a religious alliance between Christianity and Islam. With so much in common, Eddy argued, American Christians should tell the world's Muslims that "We'd like to be in the same camp, even though we are not in the same camp-meeting."[69] Whether it was fueled by guilt or theoretical commitments, this more empathetic approach to Islam went beyond Eddy and Coon. OSS officer Archibald Roosevelt Jr., a gifted linguist and grandson of President Teddy Roosevelt, took pains to understand his Arab and Muslim partners on their own terms. His time in OSS convinced him of the importance of Islam in world geopolitics. Like Eddy, Roosevelt argued to his colleagues that the United States should make itself "the great unselfish friend of the Moslems," and he continued to develop these ideas in his later career as a CIA officer and station chief across a number of Muslim-majority countries.[70]

Though fueled by bureaucratic self-interest, OSS began to realize it would be insufficient to study world religions solely through a Christian or American lens, since the resulting analysis would bear little resemblance to the reality on the ground. "Ready made products will not fit local conditions," one memo on Arab Muslims explained. "Blunders have already been made in assuming that propaganda appealing to the American mind will appeal to the minds of all others."[71] But this was easier said than done. American Orientalism and exceptionalism fueled the drive to understand other cultures even as it presented interpretive challenges for Americans building global intelligence capabilities. Foreshadowing CIA analysis in the Cold War, Muslims—as fellow "Sons of Adam"—would play a special role in how US intelligence understood the relationship between religion and national security.

The Value of the "Religious Approach" in a Postwar World

By the summer of 1945, the war in Europe was won and the OSS was turning its full attention to Japan. Planning for the postwar world was underway. When it became clear that the end of the war also meant an end to wartime spending levels, part of Donovan's argument for OSS's continued existence was the religious approach to intelligence. By mid-1945, OSS had drawn up plans for a dedicated OSS-Religion office to be headquartered in New York City. Using their wartime outreach to religious organizations as a "guidepost," OSS estimated that the Religion office could run on $75,000 per year in 1946. OSS officer Ferdinand Mayer thought that while the Religion staff might start out doing non-religion tasks, once they got into their jobs, "my guess is that very shortly this business would claim their full attention."[72]

OSS leaders' wartime experiences convinced them that the religious approach to intelligence would be a growth industry in the postwar world. In a memo to Donovan, Mayer confidently argued that in peacetime OSS would finally be able to expand its reach to the full range of world religions.

> What are we going to do about the religious approach? This includes not only Pilgrim's Progress and the Catholic world but the ideas Javelin [Lanning MacFarland, OSS chief in Istanbul] and I have had with regard to the orthodox church, the Mormon picture in Europe in general and Germany in particular and whatever development we can work out in the Moslem and Hindu worlds and indeed throughout the Far East.[73]

Yet OSS's days were numbered. Japan's surrender in August 1945 changed the strategic calculus, and President Truman axed OSS a few months later, setting off a bureaucratic scramble for control of US intelligence work. Even though the OSS-Religion office never came to fruition, the logic behind its proposal would prove persuasive in the Cold War. Whether the religion was Catholicism, Islam, or Shinto, American intelligence would continue to consider world religions in their work due to religion's presumed universality and the American ability to access it.

At war's end, however, the future organization of US intelligence was not immediately clear. Deprived of leading OSS in peacetime, Donovan threw himself into lobbying for a new, expanded US intelligence agency. Donovan wrote a 1946 article for *LIFE* magazine in which he critiqued the course of postwar intelligence and advocated for a renewed OSS, an idea that would eventually morph into the CIA. One of his chief complaints was that there were no visionary intelligence leaders (such as, presumably, himself) with the knowledge and skill to capitalize on American diversity:

> Within our borders, the same foreign-born experts who guided us so valuably during the war are prepared to help secure the peace. Regrettably, the present intelligence setup shies away from these people. In some instances government agencies require a pedigree of two or three generations before they will entrust an officer with intelligence responsibilities.[74]

Donovan believed that failing to make the most of America's diverse human resources was not simply intolerant—it was strategically foolish.

Support—or criticism—of implementing the religious approach abroad was never far removed from the American religious context at home. Donovan used his platform in *LIFE* to tell Americans that from the perspective of OSS, one of the war's most important lessons was that "Hyphen-ated Americans were useful." America's religious and racial diversity proved valuable to OSS and its operations. "An unusual circumstance that helped us was the melting-pot nature of the American population," Donovan wrote.

> No other nation has in its population so many diverse national strains as are found in ours. During the war some thought the unassimilated admix-ture would prove a weakness that our enemies would penetrate and exploit. Instead the vast pool of linguistic skills and special racial and regional knowl-edge became one of our prime assets. No matter what region was involved, we were always able to muster for intelligence work either American citizens or friendly aliens versed in its language, politics, history, and customs.[75]

Donovan's argument for these "hyphenated Americans" was part of the larger cultural and political movement toward "Tri-Faith America"—a union of Jews, Catholics, and Protestants—then building strength.[76] Donovan knew that OSS had benefited from cultural diversity, and he told the public that those markers of difference helped win the war.

The assumptions that fueled OSS's religious approach were also part of a larger relationship between American religion and US intelligence and national security during World War II, a relationship that would grow stronger as the postwar peace became a Cold War. That this began in World War II, the same event that remade the United States into a superpower, is not coincidental. The practice of empire and the study of world religions have long been linked, as the history of the British Empire makes clear. The very origin of the academic study of religion was a response to the "European discoveries of the absence of religion" as European empires expanded.[77] When the United States assumed responsibility for security beyond its borders after World War II, it also inherited imperial languages of control. American intelligence officers often took the conclusions of this earlier academic study of religion at face value, sometimes failing to think critically or suspiciously about the possibility of bias and stereotyping.

Whereas early scholars of religion "discovered" non-Christian traditions and attempted to organize them in a Christian framework, OSS officers had already imbibed and applied this worldview, and so their challenge was to account for why religious groups did not function like the theories suggested. OSS was blinded to these methodological weaknesses in part because of their own assumptions about the universal nature of religion, the manipulability of cultural norms, and the image of America as a natural ally of religious people around the globe. The first generation of Cold War American intelligence officers would soon learn that the religions of the world were a more confusing wilderness than they had imagined. While it would not be OSS that took up these challenges after 1945, many of Donovan's officers would soon return to "the business" with a new employer: the Central Intelligence Agency.

Chapter Four

On Caring What It Is

This conjunction of an immense military establishment and a large arms industry is new in the American experience. The total influence—economic, political, even spiritual—is felt in every city, every state house, every office of the Federal government.

President Dwight D. Eisenhower's "Farewell Address" (1961)[1]

By the 1950s, many in the American national security community had realized the strategic value of religion at home and abroad. US Army general Willard Wyman sent Director of Central Intelligence (DCI) Allen Dulles an article about "world religions" from a 1956 issue of *Collier's*: "Man Owes His Freedom to God," by Arnold J. Toynbee. Since all religions are "basically the same," Wyman mused to Dulles, he wondered "what the result would be if we could get people like our philosopher, Niebuhr at Columbia University, the Pope, the Dalai-lama and the head of the Mohammedan religion together."[2] Dulles was intrigued, noting that while the CIA does not influence the "structure" of religion, it had long attempted to "bring to bear the force of religion on Cold War matters." But Dulles was not sure that gathering religious leaders was the way to go about it: "Frankly, we are not sure they are ready to sit down together," he explained.[3] Other strategies would be needed, and the Eisenhower administration had a number of ideas. While the Office of Strategic Services (OSS) closed in late 1945, its people, approaches, and methods did not go away. Many personnel would eventually move to the newly created CIA or transition to other government roles. In the Eisenhower administration, the religious approach endured even as the institutional OSS did not.

The religious approach—or, as it was sometimes known in the Eisenhower administration, the "religious factor"—was a way to understand and study foreign peoples, ideas, and institutions in broad strokes. For many US leaders, including OSS castaways, the idea that the United States was uniquely religious, and that its national strength flowed from religion, was a familiar one. Whether in private or public life, a number of Eisenhower administration officials saw the religious approach as a useful tool in building a cohesive US ideology that could challenge Soviet Communism. It was at once an aspirational vision for American culture and a strategy for world power. As the hot war in Korea devoured postwar peace dividends and the world sank further into the Cold War, members of Eisenhower's administration revisited these ideas to chart a better way forward.

That the United States lacked a cohesive ideology on par with Soviet Communism was a common fear among senior administration figures, and more than one Eisenhower official saw religion as part of the solution. In this respect the Eisenhower administration built on the foundations established during the Truman presidency, in which American officials had launched important early initiatives in the "religious Cold War" that extended beyond America's shores.[4] From the beginning of Eisenhower's presidency, members of the Eisenhower administration recognized the value of the religious approach—including the president himself—and the need to do more with it, even as they disagreed on what that might entail.[5] In the Eisenhower administration there were different views on what, exactly, was "religious," and what constituted the best "approach." Even as administration officials differed on the details and implementation, most took a cue from their boss and argued that democracy required religion—even if that religion did not necessarily have to be Christianity (but all the better if it was). As a result, as America's intelligence and psychological warfare specialists approached the prospect of a sustained "cold" war with the Soviet Union, the religious approach they pursued reflected changing ideas about how religion was understood and theorized at the highest levels of government. This work would be deeply formative to US confidence during the Cold War, especially the certainty that religion could be studied, understood, and manipulated in the service of US policy at home and abroad.

Without the presence of OSS, where the religious approach was born and raised, it began to develop a life of its own. The religious approach was coordinated from the White House, to be sure, but it was developed across a range of federal institutions, think tanks, and private interest groups. It also developed at places like the National Presbyterian Church, where Eisenhower and other prominent administration officials worshipped. Their efforts did not remain within the walls of the church; they took them to the streets and to the halls of power found a few miles away. National Presbyterian's minister, Dr. Edward Elson, baptized Eisenhower in 1953.[6] He also helped create the Foundation for Religious Action in the Social and Civil Order (FRASCO), a conservative Christian organization highlighting

"Judeo-Christian" ideals. One of Elson's parishioners, Admiral Arthur W. Radford, was the chairman of the Joint Chiefs of Staff and the major proponent of "Militant Liberty," a program in which the Pentagon sought to win the Cold War by measuring human freedom. But the place to begin is with National Presbyterian's most famous parishioner, President Eisenhower. Eisenhower articulated a theory of religion that supported many of his administration's positions in intelligence, propaganda, psychological warfare, and national security. The teleological confidence that undergirded the religious approach, and that would shatter in the streets of Tehran in 1979, continued to develop at the White House, in the halls of Langley, and in the pews of National Presbyterian during the 1950s.

Eisenhower, Theorist of Religion

During a press conference in 1952, Eisenhower found himself explaining the differences between the Soviet and American systems of government. Pointing to the "self-evident" truths in the Declaration of Independence, Eisenhower offered his own interpretation. "In other words," the president explained, "our government has no sense unless it is founded in a deeply felt religious faith and I don't care what it is. With us of course it is the Judeo-Christian concept, but it must be a religion that all men are created equal."[7] In the decades since Eisenhower spoke, his remarks have provided fodder for scholars and critics to pair the president with a variety of worldviews. Did the president think that religion was generally good, but that Protestants, Catholics, and Jews were the best fit for democratic governments (as Will Herberg argued in 1955)?[8] Or did the president mean to say something quite different: that the particulars of religion don't really matter so long as it is "religious" (as Robert Bellah argued in 1967)?[9]

In one of the most persuasive arguments about Eisenhower's intent, Patrick Henry argues that Eisenhower wasn't saying anything unusual. According to Henry,

> the president was making, in extemporaneous and rather unpolished language, a point that many very sophisticated people would want to make: namely, that there are deep religious roots of democracy, and while for the United States these roots are demonstrably those of the biblical tradition, there might be other democracies with other religious bases.[10]

In other words, Eisenhower valued religion for its social utility. This did not foreclose on Eisenhower possessing meaningful personal religious beliefs. As William Inboden's work demonstrates, Eisenhower's interest in the social function of religion coexisted with the president's own religious convictions.[11] Religion was an important social glue and source of both individual and collective meaning for the president, but in both his personal and professional capacities, Eisenhower hesitated to prescribe exacting theological standards about what should constitute real "religion."

The president's primary professional interest in religion was as an aid to democracy at home and abroad. Eisenhower saw religion as useful for democracy—even if it wasn't Judeo-Christian (though it was for "us").[12] For US leaders concerned with convincing the rest of the world to reject Communism, this was not an abstract debate. Hindu-majority India, the keystone of the non-aligned movement, was by the early 1950s the largest democracy on the planet. These considerations echoed earlier uses of the religious approach. Just as OSS assumed that studying one religion would provide a cipher for understanding all others, so too did Eisenhower see religions as sharing fundamental qualities on account of being "religions": they were essentially anti-Communist, democratic, and supportive of individual liberty and freedom. Eisenhower's echoing of ideas popular in OSS—in this case, the world religions paradigm (WRP)—is not surprising. Not for nothing did Eisenhower eulogize OSS director William Donovan as "the last hero."[13]

Others in the administration argued that democracy rested on not just religious foundations, but a specifically "Judeo-Christian" tradition. The term "Judeo-Christian" has a complicated genealogy that, as historian K. Healan Gaston argues, complicates attempts to make it a "liberal" or "conservative" term. While some Americans used the term as a call for religious tolerance and inclusivity, others deployed "Judeo-Christian" as a kind of theological firewall preventing American democracy from making dangerous dalliances with secularism and religious minorities.[14] The question was this: was any kind of "religion" sufficient to protect democracy and resist Communism, or was there something necessary about "Judeo-Christian" values? However administration officials answered, most agreed that religion was an essential ingredient in any cohesive US national ideology. Not coincidentally, by the time of Eisenhower's inauguration, there were plenty of senior government leaders worried that America's national ideology was in dire need of repair—or replacement.

Haunting these conversations was what happened in Korea. US involvement in the Korean War (1950–1953) had presented unexpected challenges for the newly emergent superpower. President Truman's handling of the war had helped Eisenhower's prospects for the presidency, buoyed by the latter's resume as supreme Allied commander in Europe during World War II. But while Eisenhower eventually managed to reach an armistice and maintain an independent South Korea, it came at a heavy cost. Millions were killed in the fighting, including tens of thousands of US servicemembers. Difficulties with military equipment, defense funding, and civilian-military relations had spilled into public view, giving the military a black eye. To make matters worse, even after the Korean War "ended," American planners remained troubled by an additional problem: twenty-one American soldiers had defected to North Korea. While the reasons for these defections varied (including avoiding further torture), the issue caused a media firestorm when American leaders—including many in the military—framed the issue as a national failure to adequately prepare its fighting forces for the spiritual and political challenges of modern war. If American soldiers could be persuaded to reject God and become Communists, this line of thinking went, what did that say about the country that raised, educated, and trained those soldiers? Even as internal military studies argued that the Korean War POWs behaved no differently than POWs from World War II, military brass used the public relations crisis as an opportunity to emphasize the need for renewed nationwide moral and spiritual unity if the US military was to be victorious in a war fought both on the battlefield and in newspaper headlines.[15]

Many Eisenhower administration officials working in intelligence and psychological warfare were concerned that American pluralism, while valuable, would appear weak against Soviet one-party discipline. The USSR might be a totalitarian wasteland suppressing happiness and free expression, they thought, but the Soviets were certainly organized and cohesive as they did it. These officials feared that US public opinion was too diverse and too fractured to compete effectively with Soviet Communism.[16] If religion was understood as central to American ideology, however, the religious approach offered one way to address perceived shortcomings in US ideology. If religion and religious identity were not only a uniquely American strength, but an asset unique to free societies, it would follow that working *through* religious people, ideas, and institutions would simultaneously bolster US cohesiveness and challenge Soviet ideology. Eisenhower's "I don't care what it is" quote was a powerful endorsement of his theory of religion and of his conviction that an expansive view of religion writ large was necessary to strengthen US ideology. Eisenhower argued that democracy and religion should work together for realizable ends like the promotion of freedom and individual rights. The flexibility of Eisenhower's religious approach was also its greatest strength. If this was Eisenhower's theory of religion, the way in which his administration pursued the religious approach was a kind of applied religious studies at the highest levels of the US government.

The president's view was shared by other parts of the executive branch. In the first year of Eisenhower's presidency, C. D. Jackson and Edward P. Lilly exchanged a series of memos about the need for more attention to religion. Both men served on Eisenhower's Psychological Strategy Board (PSB), a relatively new coordinating agency for all US psychological warfare activities, and shared an interest in using psychological warfare to challenge Communism. A psychological warfare expert, Jackson had worked for OSS and in Henry Luce's media empire. "I guess I psychologically warfared them into giving me a job," he later put it.[17] Lilly, a veteran of the Office of War Information (OWI) and a former history professor at the Catholic University of America, was convinced that the way forward was to use religion.

The crux of the matter, for Lilly, was that democracy and Communism were fundamentally incompatible. American democracy was founded "on a belief in a Supreme Being and natural law," while Communism rejected any form of "spiritual and cultural values."[18] This was not simply a description of the stakes, but also a clue about how to hit Communism where it was weakest. In a memo titled "The Religious Factor," Lilly laid out his call to action. Lilly began by lamenting that while religion was "admitted by almost everybody" to be a critical driving force for human behavior, and President Eisenhower's public statements made clear that religion was vitally important in American life, the US government still had not "developed any major activity" along these lines. For administration figures like Lilly, the religious approach linked domestic and global religious concerns. In his view, to forfeit the United States' greatest strength and the Soviet Union's greatest weakness was morally and strategically foolish.[19] "The religious factor in the main is still undeveloped," Lilly worried to Jackson.[20]

To fix it, Lilly's plan was to gather US religious leaders and have them agree on a statement of religious principles. This would not be a "mere" statement of religious or theological values (as if that in and of itself would be easy to accomplish). It would instead "be a restatement of fundamental human values, for which America stands." Given the assumed self-evident connection between religion, democracy, and human freedom, Lilly reasoned that the religious leaders would be more than happy to cooperate. In this way, "these human values would be based on fundamental religious principles to which the leaders of the major religious sects would proclaim their agreement." With American religious groups on the same page, the program could be extended internationally to a meeting of global religious leaders. This would allow for an international statement of theological affinity, one making clear that "our opposition to communism is based on our acceptance of religious principles of human dignity and freedom."[21]

Lilly reached out to other national security figures in the Eisenhower administration to make his case. Writing to Elmer B. Staats, the executive officer of the Operations Coordinating Board (OCB)—a successor to the PSB charged with coordinating the increasingly wide range of covert national security activities—Lilly argued that religion was so powerful that the *particulars* of the religious group were irrelevant. "Even in Asia where monotheism is not supreme," Lilly explained, "there is great emphasis, and not purely formalistic, on the spiritual factors of life and their importance to a people and a nation."[22] In this way, Lilly took a side in a debate that would come up repeatedly in the Eisenhower administration: was involvement in religious matters a means to an end for US policy? Or did these efforts have a duty to move American culture toward a more traditionally Christian perspective with regard to morals and theology? For Lilly, as for the president he served, attention to religion in US policy was primarily functional.

Lilly wasn't the only Eisenhower official thinking along these lines. During the first two years of the administration, a number of administration officials brainstormed possible uses for religion in psychological operations. OCB official Byron Enyart wrote to Staats arguing that the "religious factor" should be considered at the highest levels of US national security policy.[23] With the president publicly emphasizing the importance of religion, Enyart argued that the time was right to capitalize on plans outlined by Lilly and others to more fully operationalize the religious approach. "If we are not able to accomplish something with a climate of opinion as generated by the present administration," Enyart wrote, "... then we are not deserving of the many great things that the Good Lord has given us." Enyart ended his memo with a personal touch: "I have been an elder and/or Superintendent of Sunday School for over 15 years, and I know that there is evidence every day of an increasing cooperation between various elements of religions existing in the US."[24]

The efforts of Lilly, Enyart, and others in the administration continued in the spirit of OSS's unfinished work. Just as OSS leadership had predicted, the religious approach was proving to be a growth industry in the Cold War. Lilly wanted to take what had previously been a haphazard application of applied knowledge about religion and systematize it, starting with a statement of religious principles. Before the decade was out, the Eisenhower administration would pursue this and much else besides.

FRASCO and the Public Square

The Eisenhower administration's religious approach included supporting public-private initiatives, including one led by none other than President Eisenhower's minister at National Presbyterian, Dr. Edward Elson. The Foundation for Religious Action in the Social and Civil Order (FRASCO) was born from Elson's desire to wage a "spiritual counter-offensive" to challenge Communism's war on "religion and liberty."[25] Elson recruited Charles Wesley Lowry, a former theology professor and minister specializing in the "philosophy and psychology of Communism," as a co-chairman, and received some staffing support from the White House.[26] The group had two goals: stress the need for religious truth in the "preservation and development of genuine democracy," and—perhaps more ambitiously—"unite all believers in God" against Communism.[27]

FRASCO operated in the public eye, holding a series of conferences that featured famous Catholic, Protestant, and Jewish speakers. The 1954 FRASCO national conference, for example, featured major speeches from public intellectual Will Herberg, President of Notre Dame Theodore Hesburgh, and FRASCO co-organizer Lowry. Together they reiterated that the Cold War was a fundamentally religious conflict. "Quite literally," Herberg opined, "it is a struggle for the soul of modern man."[28] Father Hesburgh reminded his audience that, though the times were dark, there were reasons for optimism (namely, FRASCO).[29] Lowry, for his part, attributed American "impotence" in psychological warfare to American confusion about their own government. Americans, Lowry explained, mistake their democracy for any other worldly form of government when it is, instead, a "resurrected democracy, child of a Jewish father and a Christian mother."[30] FRASCO linked this mystical understanding of democracy to US national security. Active-duty military officers and Defense Department officials sent their congratulations at the start of the conference (which were reprinted for participants to see). Elton Trueblood, head of the United States Information Agency's (USIA) Religious Policy office, mingled in the crowds and provided invocations.[31]

Attendees of these ostensibly non-governmental meetings would have learned that the free world has "done little in the battle for men's minds," and so the United States in particular was in dire need of an organization like FRASCO to step up and fight against tyrannical atheist powers in order to "revive in our people an awareness of the spiritual foundations of our democracy." FRASCO materials advised appealing to heaven to end "Communist slavery," and that FRASCO membership (perhaps strengthened with a tax-deductible donation) would help, too. Membership applications required interested recruits to declare their willingness to join in spiritual combat for "true Democracy." The appeal of membership, and the success of FRASCO's public engagement more generally, was no doubt aided by FRASCO's heavyweight supporters. The Foundation's national advisory council was a who's who of prominent American leaders in industry (Henry Luce), politics (former President Herbert Hoover), religion (including Catholics like Father Theodore Hesburgh, Jews like Rabbi Norman Gerstenfeld, and Protestants like Norman Vincent Peale and Billy Graham), as well as national security (including Elton Trueblood and Gordon Gray, Eisenhower's head of the Psychological Strategy Board and eventual national security advisor).[32]

But the biggest draw was Eisenhower's keynote address. Everyone was familiar with the foreign challenge of Communism, Eisenhower noted, since the Communists argued that "capitalism—Democracy—carries within itself the seeds of its own destruction." But the greater challenge faced Americans at home. With American spiritual will weakening, Eisenhower urged the attendees to redouble their efforts to build a spiritual "fervor that establishes self-discipline." Expressing himself "delighted" at the conference, Eisenhower encouraged FRASCO to keep working until "this kind of thing" would be found in every "city, town, and hamlet" around the country.[33]

FRASCO shows that the "religious approach" had important public-facing applications for the Eisenhower administration. While the Foundation differed from OSS and the CIA because it operated in the open, FRASCO agreed that (a certain kind of) religion needed to be taught and institutionalized if the United States was to oppose Communism successfully. Gaston argues that FRASCO represented the strain of Judeo-Christianity that considered itself both "fiercely anticommunist and anti-secularist," making clear that democracy had to be understood—and defended—on religious terms.[34] One major achievement of FRASCO's gatherings, as Inboden notes, was that FRASCO came closer than any other organization to producing a pan-religious statement of principles against Communism of the kind Lilly and other Eisenhower administration figures desired.

Behind the scenes, FRASCO was equally ambitious. Vice President Richard Nixon wrote to Walter Bedell Smith, a former CIA director and then undersecretary of state, to solicit support for FRASCO's global plans.[35] Nixon attached a FRASCO proposal for a "Spiritual Counteroffensive in Southeast Asia" that began: "Time to save men's freedom in Southeast Asia is getting shorter."[36] FRASCO recommended engaging indigenous religious leaders—including Buddhist leaders throughout the region and specifically Catholic leaders in Vietnam—to "intensify local anti-Communism," but that it was likely best to avoid making this an official US government undertaking. Serendipitously, FRASCO was willing to lead this project in exchange for $50,000 in seed money and the support of the US intelligence and psychological warfare apparatus at the OCB. The idea was to design conferences, materials, and publications that would engage these religious leaders through projects like comparing the teachings of Buddhism and Communism (conveniently modeled on a book of Lowry's titled *Conflicting Faiths: Christianity vs. Communism*).[37] Spiritual counteroffensives were required in Southeast Asia no less than they were in the United States because, as Elson and Lowry explained in their proposal, "the crux of the world civil war now raging is ideologican [*sic*] and that the neglected key to ideological victory is theistic religion—belief in Good and in man as created in the Divine Image."[38]

FRASCO's interest in getting "agents" across the North Vietnamese "bamboo curtain," and its passion for convening American clergy, business leaders, and politicians to bolster US religious strength, were two sides of the same coin. There was little practical difference between funding workshops for Buddhist priests in Bangkok or for American clergy in Boston. FRASCO's interest in the religious approach, at home and abroad, reflected the same deep-rooted ideas about the world religions paradigm—the idea that all religions shared a common core and their meanings were universally translatable—that led OSS to formulate the religious approach in the first place. While FRASCO was ultimately (and quite intentionally) a private organization, it hosted many influential figures in intelligence, psychological warfare, and national security grappling with the religious approach in the Eisenhower administration. Many of these same officials would soon be central to the most dramatic "religious approach" operation of the entire administration, working with American Catholicism during the early Vietnam War.[39] How they understood "foreign" religions, then, was never far from the ironclad link between God and the United States, the difference between a mundane government and a "resurrected democracy."

World Religions and the "Religious Approach"

When the Eisenhower administration looked abroad to see how the religious approach might be applied in other countries, it saw no shortage of opportunities. Working groups were established to research potential partners among specific world religions, especially Islam and Buddhism. One geographic hotspot was Southeast Asia, where the spectacular defeat of French forces at Dien Bien Phu in 1954 threatened to pull Eisenhower into a war in Vietnam. Buddhism was recognized as an important element in Vietnam and neighboring countries, and was seen as key to mitigating a potential conflict. The administration's methodical approach toward Buddhism had important consequences for the religious approach more generally.

Given Buddhism's global presence, the Eisenhower administration recognized that US engagement with Buddhism was grossly inadequate. A few months after the last French forces left Vietnam in 1956, the National Security Council (NSC) called for developing relationships between Buddhist organizations in Southeast Asia and other "free world religious leaders and movements."[40] Taking their cue from the NSC, the OCB convened a "Committee on Buddhism" with representatives from the CIA, USIA, and State Department to determine how best to engage with the "Buddhist church."[41] Chaired by Kenneth Landon, a former professor of comparative religions at the University of Chicago, the committee hoped not only to reach out to Buddhists but, in turn, to have Buddhists reach out to Americans.[42] The committee proposed a trip of US clergy (which should consist of "a Protestant, a Catholic, and a Jew") to Buddhist countries to build goodwill, perhaps coordinated with commemorations for the 2500th anniversary of the Buddha's death and organized through either the World Council of Churches (WCC) or the National Conference of Christians and Jews (NCCJ).[43] Reciprocal trips by Buddhists to the United States were to be encouraged, too, so that Americans could learn more about Buddhism and improve "inter-Church relationships" between Christians and Buddhists. The USIA proposed posting special experts with expertise in "comparative religion" who could both convey American religious information to their host countries, as well as report back to Washington about religion abroad. Geopolitical concerns meant they were primarily interested in Theravada-majority Buddhist countries of Southeast Asia, and so the experts would first be posted in cities like Bangkok and Rangoon before extending the program to Mahayana Buddhist countries, Muslim nations, and others.[44]

Like OSS before it, the Eisenhower administration recognized that this kind of foreign religious entanglement would not be palatable to all American observers. Landon was keen to make US government interest in Buddhism seem "invisible." The OCB echoed President Eisenhower's preference to downplay divisive differences in favor of the broad social utility of religion: "Care must be exercised to avoid the doctrinal or dog-matic aspects of religion which divide religious people and which create misunderstanding."[45] Others on Landon's committee recognized the value of further outreach to Buddhists even if it had to be done cautiously to avoid tricky church-state funding questions in Congress, and to provide US experts with enough time to learn about Buddhism in the first place. But since Chinese Communists "will do their best to subvert Buddhist priests," the Committee felt that the United States must try to get its message across even if it meant navigating choppy political waters.[46]

Beyond Buddhism, the documentary record also reflects inten-tional efforts by the Eisenhower administration to cultivate relationships with Muslims on explicitly religious grounds. While some of these early attempts to engage Muslims were clunky—like propaganda images that depicted Soviet premier Joseph Stalin as a "red pig" to pork-averse Mus-lims—they were clunky in a way that echoed the religious approach.[47] Wil-liam Eddy, who had been one of the most important OSS thinkers on the Middle East and Islam, remained active in the region in the early 1950s. Bouncing between the newly created CIA and the Arabian-American Oil Company (ARAMCO) in Saudi Arabia, Eddy continued advocating for his pet project: a "common moral front" between Christians and Muslims. In a letter to the journalist Dorothy Thompson in 1951, Eddy explained that his goal was not only to improve Muslim perceptions of Christians, but also to improve Christian perceptions of Muslims. Eddy thought it was crucial that American Christians come to understand the "moral strength and historical significance" of Muslims, a component that was "desperately" missing from US psychological warfare. Eddy's wartime intelligence work had provided him with lofty contacts in the Muslim world, and he didn't hesitate to lobby them on his proposed common moral front. Eddy reported working with the grand mufti of Jerusalem, Amin Al Husseini—who recognized that "all historic religion will be destroyed" if the USSR won the Cold War—as well as King Abdulaziz of Saudi Arabia. Noting that the king was the protector of the two holy mosques in Mecca and Medina, Eddy continued a trend that saw American intelligence officers understanding the Saudi king as the most important living Muslim.[48]

Eisenhower's State Department recognized that some anti-American sentiment among Muslims was due to perceived American indifference or contempt toward Islam and its long history—a position that echoed both Eisenhower's desire for Americans to learn about foreign religions and Eddy's insistence that respect toward Muslims would have to precede cooperation *from* Muslims.[49] Yet the desire to understand Islam was sometimes hampered by the popularly dismissive attitudes toward it, which were evident when the State Department hired Franklin Publications to devise, publish, and distribute pro-American materials in the Muslim world. While acknowledging the difficulty of penetrating the "rigid and traditional" system of Islam, the Department had no choice in order to weaken the "fanatical and irrational elements in Arab attitudes." The Department also pushed administration officials to learn more about Islam, since this would result in better psychological and intelligence operations. Once again efforts to increase strategic religious knowledge occurred through collaboration with scholars and institutions of higher education. The State Department-funded "Colloquium on Islamic Culture," for example, was organized by Princeton University and the American University in Beirut, and informally involved William Eddy and ARAMCO.[50] Designed to better familiarize American government experts with the Muslim world, the program symbolized the public-private fusion that would exemplify so much Cold War religious expertise.

These efforts reflected the Eisenhower administration's study of world religions, especially Islam, as a component of the religious approach. The NSC highlighted the importance of religion when it concluded that Abrahamic traditions' "repugnance of atheism" make religion a security asset in the Middle East.[51] Within a few years, the administration had compiled lists of international Muslim organizations, educational institutions, and tracked down all known public and private American ties to Muslim organizations.[52] Overall, the assessment found relatively few government or private efforts working with Muslims "as Muslims," which was to be expected in the OCB's view, since this paralleled the "secularization of society" happening in both the West and Muslim countries. Still, more could be done. Echoing work done by OSS in World War II, the OCB compiled a bibliography featuring early academic experts in the study of comparative religions, including Wilfred Cantwell Smith.[53]

Islam was also studied in the intelligence and psychological warfare community. The PSB undertook a major study of Islam during the first year of Eisenhower's presidency. The study's goal was to detail the best practices for psychological warfare in Muslim nations, so that intelligence officers and psychological warfare specialists could make sure the "'American Way of Life' theme is appropriately tailored" to each Muslim country.[54] The PSB report concluded that Islam made an excellent ideological ally in the Cold War but the religion's role as "an effective barrier to the communist influence cannot be taken for granted."

In supporting this conclusion, the PSB report signaled two major themes that would resurface in later Cold War US intelligence assessments of Muslims and Muslim-majority states. First, from the perspective of PSB, Islam and the modern world were fundamentally in conflict with one another. Islam offered a "total way of life, encompassing both religious and secular activities," but lacked a central authority to manage healthy, organized developments in the modern world. As a result, Muslims were listless and without direction. The second theme built on the first: that Muslims were prideful, often irrational, and struggled to adapt. For Muslim leaders to most effectively challenge Communism, these US intelligence analysts thought, they would have to reform their own religion and bring it up to date. But doing so makes Muslims feel "suspicious and insecure" because they then realize that Islam is not as advanced as Christendom. "Faced with the crumbling of their finite world," the report explains, some leaders may remain neutral in the struggle against Communism.[55]

Much like OSS during World War II, the psychological and intelligence apparatus of the Eisenhower administration occasionally tripped over its own dismissive efforts to understand "foreign" religions, societies, and ethnic groups. Indeed, the PSB also included dismissive analysis about Israeli Jews ("medieval"; "uncompromising and difficult to deal with"), Kurds (they "react like a group of a children"), and Iranians ("incapable of self-discipline"). These analytical shortcomings, rooted in American teleological confidence about the modern world, would resurface in CIA efforts throughout the Cold War.[56]

Eisenhower also reached out to his minister at National Presbyterian, Dr. Elson, for advice when Islam intersected geopolitics. One exchange of letters between the president and his minister came during the Lebanon Crisis of 1958, in which Eisenhower deployed US forces to Lebanon after a variety of regional, ethnic, and religious conflicts threatened to topple its pro-Western government. Like much else about the Eisenhower administration's religious approach toward Islam, this exchange displayed both a desire to respect different religious groups even as it was complicated—and sometimes contradicted—by American racism and paternalism. Elson urged Eisenhower to remain focused on the religious approach, particularly when it came to Arabs and Muslims (terms Elson appeared to use interchangeably). "Atheistic communism is as hostile to Islam as to Christianity," Elson explained, and so

> I believe we must find the device for identifying ourselves with the proper
> aspirations of the people of the Middle East, interpret our spiritual moti-
> vations to them in their terms, and patiently and firmly guide them from

within. It is not too late to be to them again what once we were—their ideal and pattern for all life.

By taking advantage of Muslims' pride in their religion and affirming Islam's historical significance, Elson explained that "the Arabs will understand us if we communicate in spiritual terms" and so the president should "exploit the pride of Islam."[57] Eisenhower was of like mind: "The religious approach offers, I agree, a direct path to Arab interest." Whether it was in discussions with King Saud or other Arab leaders, the issue was never far from the president's mind: "I assure you that I never fail in any communication with Arab leaders, oral or written, to stress the importance of the spiritual factor in our relationships."[58]

The religious approach during the Eisenhower administration most commonly engaged with non-Christian religions like Buddhism and Islam, but Eisenhower himself often considered a third: domestic American religious life. The president grew frustrated with advisors who understood the power of America primarily in military terms. Foreshadowing the president's future farewell address in 1961—in which Eisenhower would warn that the dangers of a "military-industrial complex" could be felt spiritually—the president insisted that "the real strength of America must be described in values that are intangible."[59] Spiritual strength at home would strengthen relations with "less developed countries, including the Mid East." Eisenhower saw the foreign struggle as ultimately a domestic one—that foreign challenges would be fought first, and most importantly, at home. While the president could give speeches, Eisenhower explained, Americans from every walk of life ("especially the clergy") ought to be involved in this work if "belief in God should create between them and us the common purpose of opposing atheistic communism."[60]

Establishing that "common purpose" meant that the Eisenhower administration did not simply want to get Muslims or Buddhists to like American ideas, but to also make Americans become more familiar with Muslims and Buddhists. Multiple plans highlighted the importance of cross-religious exchange. The idea that Americans would naturally like these religious peoples (and vice versa) makes clear that the Eisenhower administration saw some commonality between these religious worlds. Over and over again, that commonality was identified as individual liberty, which many in the administration thought to be essential to all religions everywhere. A great deal of attention would be paid to individual liberty by Eisenhower's fellow parishioner at National Presbyterian, Chairman of the Joint Chiefs of Staff Admiral Arthur W. Radford.

Militant Liberty

Militant Liberty was an ambitious Pentagon program that symbolized much of the hopes and fears wrapped up in the Eisenhower administration's religious approach. The self-consciously scientific program sought the "meaning of freedom" in a series of equations that would allow Americans (through consultation with helpful charts and grids) to quantitatively assess the experience of freedom around the world and provide them with the means to improve it by focusing on "individual liberty." If performed correctly, these calculations promised nothing less than to unify American ideology, revitalize Western ideals, and provide a systematic method to combat Communism around the world. Yet by the end of the decade, Militant Liberty would be seen largely as a boondoggle. Though Militant Liberty was never implemented in the way its backers hoped, examining its development illuminates how important members of the Eisenhower administration thought about the religious approach. Militant Liberty is what happened when American planners, acknowledging the centrality of religion in their own culture, failed to understand the way in which religious ideas structured their own policy choices, leading them to mistake their personal preferences as both universal and neutral.

The origins of Militant Liberty date back to the aftermath of World War II. John C. Broger served in the US Navy in the Pacific theater during the war and, when his term of service was up, decided to stay in the Philippines. Feeling called to minister to the people of Asia, Broger co-founded a radio ministry known as the Far East Broadcasting Company (FEBC). A conservative evangelical educated at Southern California Bible College, Broger brought this Christian worldview to his work. The FEBC operated out of the Philippines and sent Christian messaging across Southeast Asia on the back of radio waves beginning in 1948.[61] The radio ministry made quite the splash: Billy Graham would later say the FEBC's story was like "reading a chapter added to the Book of Acts."[62]

During a visit to Hawaii in 1950, Broger met Admiral Arthur W. Radford, who was then serving as commander of the Pacific fleet. Broger's meeting with Radford at Pearl Harbor was fortuitous. Radford was worried about the state of the American soul, and was interested in what could be done to spiritually strengthen Americans so they would be ready to challenge Communism at home and abroad. The two men hit it off, and Broger shared with Radford an outline for a comprehensive plan to combat Communism he was devising known as "Militant Liberty." When President Eisenhower nominated Radford as chairman of the Joint Chiefs of Staff (CJCS), Radford was able to advocate for the program as the highest-ranking military officer in the United States and a key advisor to the president. It also meant that Radford could be a powerful advocate for government agencies to adopt new ideas—even if, as eventually happened with Militant Liberty, most agencies were not interested in them in the first place.[63] As CJCS, Radford hired Broger as a consultant to his office. It was in this capacity that Broger formalized his ideas on Militant Liberty and Radford pitched them to the rest of the federal government.[64]

The basic reasoning behind Militant Liberty went something like this: in "underdeveloped areas" around the world, traditional religions were losing their appeal, people were restless, and economies were stagnant. This diagnosis was not unique. Militant Liberty's planners drew on foundational national security positions in the Eisenhower administration, such as NSC 162/2, which argued much the same thing.[65] What made Militant Liberty different was the conclusions it drew. In the minds of Militant Liberty's planners, these areas suffered from a "cultural void" that would inevitably be filled by the strongest ideological system available that could provide a "new conception of the meaning of life." Based on Militant Liberty's perspective, the very same areas that the United States was trying to persuade in the Cold War were also the same areas most likely to flip toward Communism because of the latter's ideological strength. This was in part why military leaders like Radford found Militant Liberty so compelling: since the program presupposed a need to strengthen US ideology, it fit neatly with their assumptions about the relative strength of Soviet ideology.

Here there was both crisis and opportunity. Crisis, because American inaction would allow "militant Soviet Communism" to seep into these cultural cracks, and the United States would "lose" whole swaths of the developing world just as it had lost China. But there was also opportunity. "The old cultural ideas are to be replaced," the Militant Liberty program overview explained, and "they are most likely to be supplanted by a new faith, militantly propagated by articulate natives." But what was that faith to be? If the United States could beat the USSR to the punch, the Americans could install "militant liberty" instead of "militant communism." This multifaceted plan centered on the concept of "the true value of individual man" or, in the report's shorthand, "militant liberty." Rather than meekly wait for Soviet Communism to take hold, Militant Liberty proposed taking the initiative with programs to train indigenous leaders to "awaken" their cultures to a new "understanding of existence" about things like the "meaning of freedom."[66] Ultimately, Militant Liberty's success abroad would presumably boomerang back to the United States, bringing with it an opportunity to "revitalize the culture-ideals of Western man." The appeal of the plan was clear, especially to military leaders like Radford who feared that the United States was being too accommodating to Soviet expansion.[67] Rolling back Soviet cultural gains and revitalizing Western ideals contributed to a new "world order in accordance with the ideals and objectives of the United States."[68]

Militant Liberty proposed a sweeping organizational framework to match its lofty goals. As originally proposed, Militant Liberty would tap into most every major diplomatic, defense, and intelligence agency in the Eisenhower administration. The proposed workflow would start with the OCB identifying a target country and directing the CIA to prepare an estimate that would range from the ambitious ("a summary and explanation of the many complex historic culture-ideals of the people") to the more traditional, including insight on the country's economics, politics, and strength of the local Communist Party. With this estimate in hand, the OCB would formulate a "long-range unified economic-political-military and ideological program" for the NSC's approval. Operational responsibility for implementing this plan would be coordinated across a range of agencies, including the CIA, the USIA, and the Foreign Operations Administration (USIA's short-lived sibling), as well as the State Department and the Department of Defense.

All of this work was predicated on careful, ostensibly quantitative assessments of the area in which Militant Liberty programming would be deployed. These assessments were based on six categories (discipline, religion, civics, education, social order, and economic order), which were themselves graded on a scale from +100 (pure, individual liberty where the populace has a "Sensitive Individual Conscience") to −100 on the opposite end (where there was a "State-imposed 'Conscience'").[69] Militant Liberty's authors illustrated this idea with a helpful chart (see fig. 4.1).

As a proof of concept, the Militant Liberty proposal provided qualitative summaries of these six categories of life across eight countries: the United States, the UK, France, Germany, Italy, Japan, India, and the Soviet Union. At the end of each qualitative description, there was a "blank" where the reader could make their own quantitative assessment for the "percentage of liberty" they felt existed in, say, Italy's economic system. If enough informed American experts filled out these worksheets, an average liberty score for each country could be determined that would inform psychological warfare and intelligence work (see fig. 4.2). This heavily quantitative approach was supposed to provide a method for identifying ideological strengths in local areas as well as isolating ideological weaknesses that needed buttressing or

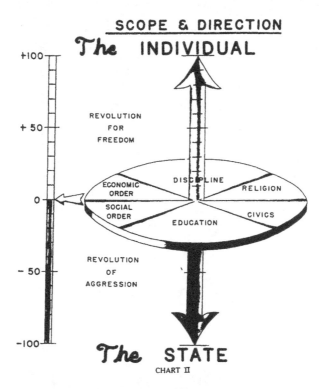

The INDIVIDUAL

+100

+50

REVOLUTION
FOR
FREEDOM

ECONOMIC
ORDER

DISCIPLINE

RELIGION

0

SOCIAL
ORDER

CIVICS

EDUCATION

REVOLUTION
OF
AGGRESSION

-50

-100

The STATE

CHART II

FIGURE 4.1 "Scope and Direction" ("Militant Liberty," p. 37)

reeducation. Each of these categories also fit neatly into the overall individualistic framework. Religion, for example, was defined as "all the beliefs, religious tendencies, moral code, etc., of the individual." True religion tended toward the individual and tolerance for other forms of religion, and was scored higher as a result. Low-scoring religion was religion that "tends toward the state," where the individual religious identity was washed out by a state that claimed for itself the mantle of religion.[70]

Militant Liberty also shows how religions less familiar to some American observers were assessed, particularly those religions that differed from the familiar terrain of Abrahamic monotheism. Militant Liberty's evaluation of India was conflicted, for example, because while India offered freedom of worship, its majority religion of Hinduism was a bit of a puzzle. More than a religion, it was a "religio-socio-economic system" that dominated daily life and provided personal direction, even as its caste system meant that "individual initiative is crushed at birth." From Militant Liberty's perspective, Communist gains in India were made possible by this failure of the caste system to provide properly religious, individualistic meaning in a way

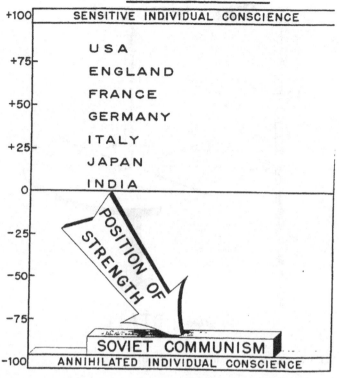

EVALUATION

SENSITIVE INDIVIDUAL CONSCIENCE

+100

+75

USA

ENGLAND

FRANCE

+50

GERMANY

ITALY

+25

JAPAN

INDIA

0

−25

POSITION OF STRENGTH

−50

−75

−100

SOVIET COMMUNISM

ANNIHILATED INDIVIDUAL CONSCIENCE

CHART III

FIGURE 4.2 "Evaluation" ("Militant Liberty," p. 38)

familiar to American Christian observers. Other Militant Liberty assessments left something to be desired, as when it evaluated the UK thusly: "no social problems exist because of religious differences."[71] Most interesting of all, perhaps, was Militant Liberty's assessment of the US religious scene in the 1950s: "No state church—complete freedom of religion—large percentage of citizens voluntarily attend church without feeling obliged to do so. Small percentage of atheists, agnostics, and some hypocrisy in churches. Also slight general indifference."[72]

Of course, devising numerical models and average liberty scores would have been fruitless if it failed to lend itself to operations in the service of US ideology around the world. Militant Liberty's planners thought previous American outreach attempts that relied on books or films were helpful, but they lacked the personal touch that would spark a "missionary zeal" for liberty in the target audience. Central to Militant Liberty was a training program for foreign nationals that would educate them about the "common denominator root meanings" of both Communism and freedom, apply the six categories of Militant Liberty, and be a "missionary" of individual freedom back in their home countries. In this way, Militant Liberty was intended to be an ideological force multiplier for American power that did not necessarily rely on American weapons or even, ultimately, Americans. By training friendly foreign nationals, Militant Liberty planners hoped this ideology would reproduce itself on its own soil. When these foreign nationals returned home, they would be part of a leadership cadre for a "Freedom Group" that would strengthen freedom and weaken Communism in their home countries.[73]

Militant Liberty was based on the bold—some might say audacious—premise that "freedom" and the "true worth of individual man" were uniquely appreciated in the West, but that these ideas were not "widely accepted" nor even sometimes "comprehended" outside of it.[74] According to Militant Liberty, this was due to Communism's "complete annihilation of the individual conscience" (helpfully footnoted with a definition of "conscience" from *Webster's Collegiate Dictionary*).[75] While freedom in the West went under many guises (the report notes things like "law, free enterprise, capitalism," and "the dignity of man"), the one "essential element" was "the sensitive individual conscience" without which a free, democratic society could not function. Yet individual choice was both a strength and a weakness, since it offered people individual agency without necessarily contributing toward a coordinated direction for society (something at which Communist societies, in this view, excelled).[76] For Militant Liberty, lacking a "positive philosophy of freedom" was the ultimate weakness of the Free World.

To model proper individualism, the plan drew up "The Basic Freedoms" and paired them with "The Basic Responsibilities." While some of these freedoms were quite specific (such as the "freedom to own means of production"), most remained general. Each list had ten items and was used to make clear the responsibilities of an individual in a free society. For example, the first Basic Freedom was "Freedom of worship and religion of individuals and organized groups," but this had to be paired with the first Basic Responsibility, which was "Responsibility for tolerance between the religious beliefs of individuals or organized groups."[77] In a free society, then, one was not free to believe things that required action against the beliefs of others: a vision of religion as less a system of mutually exclusive theological positions than as an aid to social cooperation. Even as Militant Liberty attempted to offer a universal message about freedom, the program's authors found themselves unable to think outside a worldview structured by ideas about individualism and religion as a cordoned-off area of existence that, while not necessarily Christian, certainly overlapped in foundational ways with the development of Christian thinking in Europe and the United States.

From the start, Militant Liberty's implementation faced an uphill battle. The program's chief proponent was Admiral Radford, who gave speeches, met with other leaders, and arranged introductions to get Militant Liberty in front of as many eyes as possible. The admiral was interested in Militant Liberty for a number of reasons, including especially as a panacea for the Korean POW "scandal." Radford had become fascinated by Communist brainwashing techniques and devising ways to guard against it. In a letter to CIA director Allen Dulles, Radford advocated for Militant Liberty by highlighting its ability to prevent brainwashing of US forces.[78] If the Militant Liberty program was implemented, the admiral argued, American troops would be adequately prepared to remain true to God and reject Communist philosophy.[79]

Despite Militant Liberty's heavyweight proponents, the program almost immediately ran into two problems. The first was that people outside the government found out about it. William Hale wrote a piece for the reliably anti-Communist *The Reporter* in 1956 that featured interviews with Pentagon brass about the proposed program. The article was a biting critique of the Militant Liberty initiative, aimed at the reader who might be wondering "just what the office of Admiral Radford is doing evaluating and assessing freedom." The article depicts Hale meeting staff around the Pentagon, including one colonel who memorably explains Militant Liberty as

> . . . just another of those front-office boondoggles. The Admiral says we need an ideology, so they hire a guy and appoint a committee that unanimously agrees we're all for clean living and American motherhood and the rest of it. So the fellow writes up a lot of stuff that was said much better in the Boy Scout Handbook, wraps it all up into a capsule, and now they think they've got something like ideological Little Liver Pills. This place isn't what it used to be.[80]

The second problem stemmed from the first: most federal agencies, as well as the military branches, opposed the program for being too sweeping and ideologically partisan.

The CIA's issues with Militant Liberty offer one example of these objections. One vocal critic inside the CIA was Frank Wisner's office, the Directorate of Plans (DDP). An OSS veteran, Wisner headed the covert, operational wing of the CIA for most of the Eisenhower administration. In a damning memo sent to CIA chief Allen Dulles, DDP staff dissected Militant Liberty piece by piece. They concluded that Militant Liberty was ultimately "untenable" and would never would have gotten off the ground without Radford's personal intervention. Furthermore, the CIA was also unsure of Militant Liberty's ideological underpinnings, noting that "Militant Liberty confuses a condition of the good life—Freedom—with its consummation." In other words, it was good and well to talk about freedom of worship, but a far more complicated issue to decide who or what to worship, and why.[81]

Furthermore, the very idea of the "sensitive, individual conscience"— trumpeted by Radford and Militant Liberty's authors as the universal key to freedom around the globe—was, for DDP, anything but universal. "It is a protestant evangelical emphasis," the memo explained, "which has had considerable influence in our part of the New World, but is meaningless if not repugnant in, for instance, the web society of Japan, or in those vast areas influenced by Buddhism and Mohammedanism." Even if Broger and Radford meant well, it argued, these ideas simply weren't translatable in the way the two men hoped they would be. These ideas "form part of our heritage . . . but should not be isolated for application by themselves as indoctrination."[82] In other words, it did no good to pretend that certain ideas were universal if they were not, since these ideas would be operationally useless on the ground. While the CIA's own track record in the Cold War demonstrated that it was not immune to mistaking the local as universal, DDP's arguments made clear that there were leaders in the Agency aware of the problem.

Faced with this grim assessment from his operations chief, Dulles wrote a personal letter to Radford and explained that the CIA had studied Militant Liberty, found some ideas in it valuable, but would not be able to incorporate it.[83] More than anything else, Dulles's letter reads like the CIA director was trying to end a conversation he was long past interested in having.[84] The director seemed frustrated in particular by Militant Liberty's conviction that what is good and true could be reduced to a numerical formula: "I don't think we can take any simple formula to measure the relative standings of nations in terms of our own concept of conditions for the good life." Dulles reminded the chairman that this outlook could do more harm than good in places like Japan and with foreign religious systems that would "deeply resent" the "implication that our particular formulations of 'liberty' constituted universal values." Given its reception at the CIA and other federal audiences, Militant Liberty was never fully implemented. The program's backers did not entirely give up the fight, however. Broger's influence would grow when, in 1956, he was appointed deputy director of Armed Forces Information and Education, an office he would go on to lead from 1961 until 1984.[85]

When the government-wide application of Militant Liberty failed to pan out, the focus for the program's advocates shifted to popular culture.[86] Radford's office arranged for sympathetic Hollywood figures to weave Militant Liberty themes into their films. Participants included the director John Ford—who produced films for OSS in World War II and whose four Academy Awards for best director remains the record—as well as the actors John Wayne and Ward Bond. The three men worked together on *The Wings of Eagles* (1957), a film that trumpeted the values of military service and the American way—thanks in part to the messaging that the Office of the Chairman of the Joint Chiefs of Staff was able to work into the film.[87] This interest in popular culture also makes sense in terms of the larger "religious approach." If the religious approach understood foreign societies as vulnerable to influence through manipulating their religious ideas or beliefs, it follows that Americans would also need to be on their guard against a "religious approach" used against them. While federal agencies rejected Militant Liberty as too sharply religious, Broger and others sought to apply Militant Liberty to American audiences for this very reason. Its success would rest on the ways it became innocuous.[88]

Though easy to dismiss as an overly theoretical panacea to the political challenges of uniting democracies and challenging Communism, Militant Liberty convinced smart, experienced people that this was the way forward in the Cold War. The program also shared important similarities with other activities conducted under the religious approach during World War II and the Cold War. Most strikingly, Militant Liberty was similar to the world religions paradigm (WRP) in important ways. While Militant Liberty dealt with issues beyond religion—seeking to fundamentally change foreign cultures in the service of American power—it shared with the WRP important assumptions about both the malleability of human culture and an optimism that the United States could successfully change it. Just as OSS assumed in World War II, belief was central to the worldview held by those for whom Militant Liberty made sense. If Americans could change what foreigners *believed*—in this case, about the essential value of the individual—they could influence these populations' *behaviors* and inoculate them against Communism.

Militant Liberty theorized about individualism—as part of the economic order, social relations, and government power—without explicit reference to Christianity. Yet as the CIA's Frank Wisner realized, that was a difficult thing for Americans to do. For Broger, Radford, and other supporters of Militant Liberty, their intellectual framework was indebted to powerful Christian ideas historically expressed in Western Europe and the United States. This lack of explicit recognition demonstrates how religious (and namely, Protestant) ideas form the roots of secular ideologies. American leaders struggled to recognize this influence, to realize just how important religion was, even as they saw it everywhere and relevant for every society. In their efforts to create a useful and universal religious theory, they misunderstood the particularly religious, even sectarian, origins of their putatively secular ideas.[89]

New Beginnings

On June 5, 1960, President Eisenhower delivered the commencement address at the University of Notre Dame's graduation ceremonies. The last full year of Eisenhower's presidency, 1960 would inaugurate a decade bringing major changes to American culture, politics, and religion. Though no one knew it at the time, 1960 would also be the last year for almost a decade and a half that the number of Americans killed in Vietnam numbered in single digits. That story involved the other honorary guests on the dais with the president, a group that represented the worlds of American politics, religion, and business. It is the story of the religious approach, the story of the first twenty years of the relationship between American religion and US intelligence.

On that sunny day in June, President Eisenhower received his honorary doctorate from Father Theodore Hesburgh, President of Notre Dame. No stranger to the intelligence community, Hesburgh was a broker for American Catholic influence and a friend of the man sitting a few chairs away, Dr. Thomas A. Dooley. Known as the "hero of Haiphong" and "Dr. America," Dooley gained international fame when he published *Deliver Us from Evil* (1956). His book told the stirring story of his aid mission to Vietnamese Catholics persecuted at the hands of Ho Chi Minh's Communists in Southeast Asia. The book's success made Dooley an American Catholic superstar and much in demand at places like Notre Dame. Yet some on stage likely knew what most in the audience did not: Dooley's publications and success were engineered by the CIA. One audience member who knew was Paul Hellmuth, a lawyer who served as Dooley's CIA intermediary—and Father Hesburgh's messenger of choice to deliver Dr. Dooley's personal invitation to receive an honorary doctorate.[90] Seven years later, Hellmuth's name would be splashed across national newspapers when he was revealed as the conduit through which CIA money flowed to ostensibly private groups like the National Student Association.[91]

The guests of honor were not limited to Americans. Seated to Father Hesburgh's left was a visitor from Italy, the archbishop of Milan Cardinal Giovanni Montini. An old Vatican hand, Montini had first encountered the CIA's predecessor, the Office of Strategic Services (OSS), as he steered the papacy of Pius XII through the dark days of World War II. After the war, Montini was an active participant in the 1948 Italian elections in which the CIA-funded Christian Democrats triumphed over the Communists.[92] Almost three years to the day after his appearance at Notre Dame, Montini would become Pope Paul VI.

A little farther down the dais was J. Peter Grace, a corporate tycoon and devout Catholic. Grace was president of the Eastern Chapter of the US Knights of Malta, whose members included William Casey and John McCone, both Catholics and future CIA directors. A few years prior, Grace and CIA chief Allen Dulles had approached Eisenhower's vice president, Richard Nixon, with an audacious idea: use CIA funds to pay for a Catholic (and anti-Communist) revival series in South America.[93] Grace's idea reached its fullest manifestation two years after his appearance at Notre Dame, when 1.5 million Brazilians took to the streets of Rio de Janeiro to welcome the CIA-sponsored Family Rosary Crusade.[94]

Though it may seem mundane and unremarkable on the surface, then, Notre Dame's 1960 graduation hinted at deeper changes working themselves out in American culture. These changes were not yet entirely visible, and for many gathered that day at Notre Dame the year promised to be a good one. In the words of the new—and Catholic—president elected a few months later, "the torch has been passed." Many of the honorees in attendance had been involved in South Vietnam in the 1950s, but the word "Vietnam" still referred to a place, rather than an event, in the American imagination. The CIA was near the height of its power, confident in its operational abilities and in its understanding of the world. The Catholic Church, too, was several years out from its own reckoning, when the Second Vatican Council (1962–1965) dramatically reimagined the place of the Church in the modern world. The commencement ceremony now appears as a moment frozen in time, reflecting the certainties of a confident America in the early Cold War.

In the Eisenhower years, the religious approach was not always covert. It was evident at graduation ceremonies, or in the Sunday pews of National Presbyterian. While certain programs may have trended toward offensively targeting foreign populations or defensively bolstering domestic American unity, in each case the Eisenhower administration's plans were understood to pay off in both directions: to be stronger at home meant to be stronger abroad, and vice versa. One program that exemplified these tensions — neither fully overt nor covert, neither fully public nor private — was the CIA's own religious approach in Southeast Asia. Though the Agency lacked a catchy brand name like Militant Liberty, the CIA's massive propaganda efforts around Tom Dooley, South Vietnam, and American Catholicism are one of the Eisenhower administration's most successful applications of the religious approach to intelligence.

Chapter Five

Baptizing Vietnam

America was made great by men who went out and hustled.
Tom Dooley, in an interview with Mike Wallace[1]

It is not often that a candidate for sainthood is derailed on account of CIA connections. Yet that was the case in 1975, when supporters of Dr. Thomas Anthony Dooley's canonization discovered a more colorful past than they had imagined.[2] Tom Dooley is now largely forgotten, but his life was profoundly shaped by the relationship between American religion and national security during the Cold War. The enduring strangeness of Tom Dooley lies in his simultaneous familiarity with and distance from Americans of the twenty-first century. Familiarity, because the messages in his books and speeches—that people everywhere yearn for religious freedom, that America is a friend to religious minorities—remain commonplace today. They are the stuff of politicians' stump speeches and Sunday morning talk shows. Yet Dooley was talking about Vietnam.

Dooley was present at the creation of "Vietnam"—an event, rather than a place, in American memory.[3] Dooley spoke earnestly of a place called Vietnam that was not unlike the United States. Dooley advocated for Vietnam's people—who were mostly Catholic, he explained—who only wanted to be free of Communist tyranny so they could enjoy religious freedom. A devout Catholic himself, Dooley argued that South Vietnam should be America's trusted ally in the region, a bastion of religious pluralism and democratic spirit in Southeast Asia. If Americans looked closely, Dooley seemed to say, they could see themselves in the reflections of the Vietnamese.

Yet the words were not entirely his own. Tom Dooley was a key figure in the CIA's religious approach in Vietnam. The Agency helped launch Dooley's career as an American Catholic celebrity so that Dooley, in turn, could explain "Vietnam" to American audiences. Using their newly developed expertise in religion, the CIA made religious appeals to both Vietnamese and American audiences (in part by leaning on a renewed sense of American religious pluralism) to build support for US involvement in Vietnam. The Agency's effort was the product of a formative moment in the relationship between religion, intelligence, and national security in the early Cold War.

Formed in 1947 from the wreckage of OSS and other wartime agencies, the CIA's job was to collect information from around the world (as well as from other US intelligence services), analyze it, and provide intelligence to American leaders. Victory in a global war was heady stuff, and many in the CIA—including a number of OSS veterans—attributed American success in World War II to OSS's potpourri of unorthodox ideas. Through the influence of these OSS holdovers and the machinations of the postwar defense bureaucracy, the Agency also became involved in activities well beyond its stated mission, including psychological warfare and paramilitary activity.[4] The result was that by the mid-1950s, the CIA was a young institution that surveyed the world through an ambitious horizon of possibility, empowered by a Cold War consensus that sought to remake the world in America's image.

The Agency's attempt to manage Dooley—as well as their broader intervention in South Vietnam—represented an evolution in the religious approach to intelligence. The Dooley saga signaled important changes in how American intelligence officers understood religion, the possibilities for its manipulation, and the benefits of doing so. In so doing, the CIA echoed broader changes in American religious culture during the early Cold War. Examining how these changes played out in national security, academia, and popular culture helps explain why the CIA succeeded in selling Tom Dooley, and why Americans eagerly bought into Vietnam.

Dooley's story helps explain how the rise of American religious pluralism after World War II was connected to the relationship between religion and national security in the Cold War. "Dooleymania," as it came to be called, was an attempt by the national security state to capitalize on the benefits of strategic pluralism during the Cold War, part of an ideological shift that became known as "Tri-Faith America." For the same reasons that OSS concealed the Vatican's assistance during World War II—it was overtly Catholic and foreign; American Protestants might assume it threatened the Republic—Tom Dooley's activities had to be publicized. While Dooley was of interest to American intelligence because of his Catholicism, his story reflected a growing practice among intelligence officers to use Catholicism as an interpretive link to the full variety of world religions. Dooley's story—about a patriotic Catholic who loved his God, his country, and his Pope—came to support American foreign policy objectives across a range of non-Catholic countries in Southeast Asia.

Yet Dooley's story became a darkly self-fulfilling prophecy. Dooley spared no effort in convincing Americans that it was their religious and national obligation to aid Vietnam, whatever the cost. In countless speeches, articles, and public letters, Dooley reiterated this message of necessity. No one sold America on involvement in Vietnam the way Tom Dooley did. With tragic consequences for both Vietnam and the United States, Dooley succeeded.

But in the mid-1950s, those realizations were still a long way off. Vietnam was a new errand and a new wilderness. Dooley's legacy provides a map for understanding how America's descent into Vietnam was guided by the religious approach. The promise of America after World War II was linked with the promise of American religion. As the last American helicopter lifted off from Saigon in 1975, both promises had been called to account for their contradictions and hubris. Before My Lai, before napalm and Tet and "peace with honor," there was Tom Dooley.

The Stories of Tom Dooley

Dooley hailed from a well-off Catholic family in St. Louis.[5] His college years at Notre Dame were interrupted by World War II and a stint in the US Navy. After the war, Dooley attended another Catholic institution—St. Louis University—for medical school. Degree in hand, Dooley returned to the navy and shipped off.

Dooley arrived in Southeast Asia as it became clear that the French Empire was imploding. The First Indochina War had raged since 1946, with France trying to reassert its authority against Vietnamese pro-independence forces, including Ho Chi Minh's Communist Viet Minh. A potent combination of French hubris and Vietnamese ingenuity resulted in the climactic defeat of French forces at the Battle of Dien Bien Phu in 1954. News of the disaster sent shock waves through France and changed the diplomatic calculus. The result was the 1954 Geneva Accords, which separated Vietnam at the 17th parallel and provided for a demilitarized zone. For an agreement that would have a profound impact on the next two decades of American history, the United States was not heavily involved in its outcome. Walter Bedell Smith, recently the director of central intelligence but then working for the Department of State, observed but did not participate in the negotiations.

The Geneva Accords guaranteed a period of free passage between the newly demarcated North and South Vietnams to allow for displaced people to return home. Dooley was part of the US Navy contingent sent to support the refugee exodus. This became known as Operation Passage to Freedom, a combined US-French operation to move hundreds of thousands of North Vietnamese refugees across the newly demilitarized zone to South Vietnam. As a navy doctor, Dooley provided medical care for the refugees.[6] Having made it safely to Haiphong harbor in the North, the tired masses boarded US Navy ships on their way to Saigon and the presumed safety—and freedom—in the South. These events form the basis for the stories in Dooley's best-selling book *Deliver Us from Evil* (1956).[7]

Through positive portrayals of both Vietnamese and Catholics, *Deliver Us from Evil* justified American intervention in Vietnam and presented Vietnamese Catholics as sympathetic subjects. The book was hugely popular. Its publication catapulted Dooley to stardom, and the navy doctor became the idol of many Americans around the country. Demand for Dooley was phenomenal. A 1961 Gallup Poll ranked Dooley as the third "Most Esteemed" man in the world, trailing only Eisenhower and Pope John XXIII.[8]

Part of the book's success was in its lurid descriptions of violence and drama. The book shocked readers with its accounts of Communist barbarism toward refugees. The Vietnamese refugees fleeing for the South were mostly Catholic, Dooley explained, and they fled because they were persecuted in the North by Ho Chi Minh's Vietnamese Communists. Dooley reported this as firsthand knowledge, recalling the countless injured, tortured, and crippled Catholics that passed by him on the docks in Haiphong.

In what quickly became one of the most reprinted portions of the book—excerpted in newspapers and magazines around the United States—Dooley tells how a group of Vietnamese Catholic schoolchildren were tortured by North Vietnamese Communists for listening to the gospel:

> In a voice loud enough for the other children still in the classroom to hear, the Viet Minh accused these children of treason. A "patriot" had informed the police that this teacher was holding classes secretly, at night, and that the subject of these classes was *religion*. They had even been seen reading the catechism . . . Now two Viet Minh guards went to each child and one of them firmly grasped the head between his hands. The other then rammed a wooden chopstick into each ear. He jammed it in with all his force. The stick split the ear canal wide and tore the ear drum. The shrieking of the children was heard all over the village.[9]

In dramatic scenes like these, Dooley recounted to millions of Americans the terror and violence inflicted on North Vietnamese Catholics as they desperately attempted to worship God in the Communist North. The schoolchildren tortured with chopsticks were hardly alone. The pages drip with tales of martyrs, while Dooley remained stoic about the likelihood of their survival: "How do you treat an old priest who has had nails driven into his skull to make a travesty of the crown of thorns?" he asks rhetorically.[10] In Dooley's telling, what the Vietnamese wanted most—what they were willing to fight and die for, if only they had help—was religious freedom.

The only problem with *Deliver Us from Evil* was that it was not, strictly speaking, true. Dooley's books and articles were manufactured by the Central Intelligence Agency and US Navy to influence how the average American viewed the conflict in Vietnam.[11] True, Dooley was in Vietnam and—by most accounts—did good work for refugees passing through the camps in Haiphong. Yet the published stories were the product of the Eisenhower administration's focus on the religious approach as a way to advance US interests in Southeast Asia.[12] Tom Dooley's biographer, James T. Fisher, did not put too fine a point on the issue when he remarked, "*Deliver Us From Evil* was a work of propaganda, pure and relatively simple."[13]

Relatively simple, indeed. The story of Tom Dooley is part of the larger story of concerted and covert attempts by the US government to shape popular American perceptions of Vietnam. The domestic impact of Tom Dooley was limited by the effective use of his image abroad, which in turn relied upon changes in the American religious order at home. The CIA's Dooley operations were the clearest sign yet that the religious approach linked the American religious context with the wider world. Recognizing this tension reshapes the story of early American involvement in Vietnam into one of covert government influence on American perceptions of religion during the Cold War.[14]

That story begins when Dooley deployed to Southeast Asia in the early 1950s. At the time, "Viet-nam" was a little-known place in the American imagination. Many Americans perceived Vietnam—to the extent they perceived it at all—as something of a backwater eclipsed by its northern neighbor, "Red" China. In *Deliver Us from Evil*, Dooley introduced Vietnam as an exotic locale before the word became a household name. "The China Sea washes Viet Nam's east coast and on the western border is the Kingdom of Laos with its elephants and tigers," Dooley wrote.[15] Leaning heavily on Orientalist clichés, Dooley's Vietnam was an ancient and mystical, if backward, jungle country. The deterioration of the French Empire received scant mention, even though its collapse brought the Americans to Vietnam in the first place. Dooley simply chastises the French for not putting into Vietnam what they took out.[16] The Americans, he said, would be different. Pervasive American ignorance about Southeast Asia facilitated Dooley's reassuringly simple take on matters. American knowledge of the human geography of Southeast Asia remained poor, and most readers would have been unaware of South Vietnam's Buddhist majority. Ancient kingdoms filled with tigers and elephants might seem exotic—and Dooley made sure it did—but he was also clear that Vietnam would not be entirely unfamiliar. Even if most Americans could not relate to lush mountain jungles, they *could* relate to the people who populated them: Christians. Catholic Christians, to be specific.

Dooley's decision to overemphasize the number of Catholics in a largely Buddhist country reflected a larger pattern in American Cold War propaganda. The CIA preferred not to cut propaganda from whole cloth: it was far easier to take existing facts and add a twist.[17] By exaggerating both the number of Catholics and their desire for American aid, the Agency leveraged increasingly positive ideas about Catholics in American culture to yield support for South Vietnam. In so doing, Dooley and the Agency buttressed efforts to make Catholics part of the American mainstream.[18]

Deliver Us from Evil had its roots in reports Dooley filed with the US Navy during Operation Passage to Freedom in 1954.[19] Dooley penned dramatic accounts of the evacuation process at Haiphong and the consequences it had for Vietnamese Catholics. The situation needed little exaggeration. Hundreds of thousands of refugees were processed, sprayed with DDT, shuffled aboard warships, and shipped south. Besides Dooley, one of the few Americans on the docks in North Vietnam was another US Navy sailor, Daniel Redmond. A Catholic himself, Redmond aided in the harrowing process of loading the terrified Vietnamese onto the ships: "One day I loaded three thousand people onto one LST [amphibious landing craft]," Redmond later recalled. "These goddamn French legionnaires were shoving people on like they were cattle. I felt like a war criminal, but at least I got them out of there." Even in 1954, Redmond recognized that the plight of the Vietnamese had more to do with the egregiously unjust administration of the French Empire than it did with the Viet Minh: "They were victims more of the French than the Communists."[20]

Yet Dooley's reports to navy brass reduced the colonial tensions of the disintegrating French Empire to a story of the US Navy saving God-fearing Vietnamese peasants from the clutches of Vietnamese Communists. Dooley's dispatches were relayed across the fleet in an effort to raise morale.[21]

One of those readers was US Navy commander William Lederer, then working as an information officer for the Commander of the US Pacific Fleet, Admiral Felix Stump. Lederer was an aspiring writer with a keen eye for a good story and interesting characters, a skill honed when he (along with Eugene Burdick) wrote the best-selling novel *The Ugly American* (1958) a few years later.[22]

Lederer found Dooley's dispatches at an opportune time. The navy was frustrated with the lack of media coverage for Operation Passage to Freedom, which had been overshadowed by seemingly more dramatic events like the Algerian War of Independence. Navy leaders were convinced that the operation should, and could, garner better press. Lederer was figuring out how to make that happen when he came across the young lieutenant. Dooley's reports had all the necessary ingredients of an epic tale: good versus evil, religion versus atheism, and (for good measure) the redemptive sacrifice of the US Navy.

Lederer was not the only official taking a sudden interest in Dooley. Another of the young doctor's admirers was Edward Lansdale, a legendary figure in CIA history.[23] A former advertising man from San Francisco, Lansdale cut his teeth on OSS psychological warfare programs during World War II. By the mid-1950s he was renowned for his ability to install pro-American regimes in Asia, and this reputation led CIA director Allen Dulles to send Lansdale on a special mission to Vietnam. One of Lansdale's colleagues remembered Dulles's straightforward orders: "It literally said, 'Save South Vietnam. God Bless you.'"[24]

This kind of grand mission was not out of the ordinary for the 1950s CIA. The Agency that intervened in Vietnam was at the apex of its self-confidence. Contemporary news coverage of the CIA was low on details but high on praise. In these puff pieces, the Agency came across as confident, focused, and ready to tangle with the Communists.[25] This was no façade: many within the Agency itself were confident in their world-shaping mission. From Guatemala to the Philippines to Iran, the Agency worked to install US-friendly governments through means both overt and covert. Vietnam was supposed to be more of the same.

Arriving in Vietnam during Operation Passage to Freedom and the massive refugee relocation, Lansdale and his team had two pressing concerns. First, they needed to maximize Catholic refugee relocation southward to build a Catholic base of support for the newly installed President Diem, a Catholic politician who ruled over the largely Buddhist nation of South Vietnam.[26] The problem was not so much logistics—the French and US navies could carry the refugees—as motivation, since the North Vietnamese Catholics had to decide to move south in the first place. To this end, Lansdale applied his expertise in psychological warfare. CIA personnel produced provocative propaganda leaflets designed to target Catholic sensibilities (or at least, what Lansdale and the Agency team presumed those sensibilities to be). Lansdale recalled that Washington "wanted to make sure that as many persons as possible, particularly the strongly anti-Communist Catholics, relocated in the south." Much of the propaganda played on the Communists' reputation for hostility toward Catholicism, like the leaflet that depicted "communists closing a cathedral and forcing the congregation to pray under a picture of Ho Chi Minh; the caption read, 'Make your choice.'"[27] Other US propaganda leaflets favored a more direct approach, like a map of Hanoi overlaid with an atomic blast or a map of Vietnam divided into a prosperous South and chaotic North, complete with churches in flames (see fig. 5.1).[28] No Protestant-designed appeal to Catholics would be complete without an appeal to the Virgin Mary, and in this the Agency did not disappoint: one leaflet read simply "The Virgin Mary is moving south."[29] The propaganda, combined with the lure of better jobs in the South under their co-religionist Ngo Dinh Diem, led many North Vietnamese Catholics to register for evacuation. One CIA officer noted that refugee registration tripled after Lansdale's leaflets were deployed.[30] While the CIA credited Lansdale for the refugee exodus, most North Vietnamese refugees had varied reasons for moving south.[31]

The CIA's focus on Catholics reflected the Eisenhower administration's religious approach in Southeast Asia. President Eisenhower had wanted to raise up a "Joan of Arc" to religiously unite South Vietnam. In a 1954 meeting of Eisenhower's National Security Council (NSC), the president's team debated how that might be accomplished. When Eisenhower asked whether it would be possible to "find a good Buddhist leader to whip up some real fervor," his team demurred. The problem, one explained, was that "unhappily, Buddha was a pacifist rather than a fighter." The room's laughter overshadowed how essentialist ideas about world religions continued to impact foreign policy. Similar to OSS operations in Asia during World War II, Eisenhower's NSC drew on the idea that world religions were essentially "one thing" that did not change through time. Though the NSC saw it as humorous that the Buddha was a lover rather than a fighter, *seeing* that humor relied on the idea that world religions had immutable characteristics. In this case, Buddhists were simply non-violent and could not be counted on to fight for their country—an assumption that would unravel in spectacular fashion within a decade. When Secretary of State John Foster Dulles suggested that there was also a sizeable Catholic popula-

FIGURE 5.1 "Come South," an example of USIA propaganda

tion that might be used instead, the president was interested and suggested that "the Catholics be enlisted."[32]

The Agency's second concern was to manufacture American popular support for this newly Catholicized South Vietnam. This was a trickier problem to solve. How could the Agency convince Americans, fresh from the morass of the Korean War, to support an Asian Buddhist country that few of them had ever heard of? Lansdale and Lederer, reflecting on just this problem, were quick to realize the value of Tom Dooley. Dooley and his reports—full of suffering Catholics and relentless Communist atheist aggression—were invaluable to American interests on both sides of the Pacific.

The Agency moved quickly. In May 1955, CIA director Dulles telegrammed Admiral Felix Stump, commander of the US Pacific Fleet, and requested Lederer's immediate services for a "special assignment."[33] Dooley had been trying to write a book about his experiences, and Lederer—a gifted writer and editor in his own right—was called in to assist Dooley with its preparation and publication.

If the sudden appearance of a navy-appointed editor—and an officer who outranked him, no less—struck Dooley as strange, there is no record of it in his papers. Assisted by Lederer, manuscript revisions quickly consumed Dooley's other duties. Dooley apologized to his mother for having "been remiss in my letters, but blame the BOOK . . . Commander Bill Lederer was certainly right when he said that giving birth to a baby is a cinch compared to fathering a book." (One wonders about his mother Agnes Dooley's reaction to that particular comparison.) Lederer encouraged Dooley to be "creative" with his own memory: "It is now being rewritten with emphasis on TAD [Thomas A. Dooley]," Dooley wrote his mother. "When I speak of the rescue work off the beach, instead of describing them as I was told they exist, I use poetic justice, or license or something. . . ."[34] The first draft of Dooley's book underwent a dramatic change once Lederer got his hands on it.[35]

Once Lederer and Dooley had words on the page, the CIA facilitated Dooley's celebrity and the commercial success of *Deliver Us from Evil* through a network of military and corporate interests. Most critically, Lederer helped Dooley arrange publication with Farrar, Straus & Giroux (FSG).[36] The choice of FSG was deliberate. CIA money kept the publishing house afloat in the early postwar years and, in exchange, FSG provided cover for Agency personnel operating in Italy. Roger Straus, one of the publishing house's namesakes, had served in naval intelligence during World War II and was open to working with the government: "I thought it was my patriotic duty to say yes," he later reflected. The Agency went so far as to install a separate black phone in Straus's office for communicating with the CIA.[37] FSG also had impeccable Tri-Faith credentials, with Dooley joining the ranks of Thomas Merton, Flannery O'Connor, and other prominent Catholics writing for the publisher.[38]

Lederer also provided Dooley with an introduction to *Reader's Digest* and its owner, DeWitt Wallace. The *Digest* agreed to publish an excerpt of *Deliver Us from Evil* as the April 1956 "Book of the Month." It was not the first time that *Reader's Digest* had provided favorable coverage to the Agency. (One 1953 *Digest* headline got right to the point: "The Central Intelligence Agency is good now and getting better under uniquely qualified Allen Dulles."[39]) In any case, Dooley's piece was a good fit for the magazine, a reliably conservative publication allergic to the slightest whiff of Communism. Ever the showman, Wallace sent copies of Dooley's *Reader's Digest* excerpt to Pope Pius XII in Rome. When Wallace received a cordial response back from the Vatican that offered "blessings" to the editor of the *Digest*, Wallace forwarded the note to Dooley and added, "Insofar as custom permits, we allocate a substantial part of that blessing to you and your associates in this hazardous project of Christian charity."[40]

After being featured in the *Digest*—with the largest domestic magazine audience in the United States—Dooley's sales exploded.[41] FSG rushed the printing and mass-mailed letters advising bookstores to stock up on *Deliver* while supplies lasted.[42] In late 1955, Wallace personally wrote Lederer to thank him for helping secure the rights to Dooley's work. The navy was pleased, too: Admiral Arleigh Burke, the chief of naval operations and one of the most senior officers in the navy, personally contributed the book's foreword. By then it was clear to everyone that the *Digest*—as well as the CIA, navy, and publishing house of Farrar, Straus & Giroux—had a winner on their hands.[43] With Lederer, Lansdale, and Wallace, the religious approach linked the worlds of defense, intelligence, and corporate America to produce an American Catholic superstar and new ideas about Vietnam.

An Agency-Approved Message to America

Deliver went to press in 1956. Both the published book and the highly popular *Reader's Digest* excerpt were central to a propaganda campaign that sought to influence American perceptions of Vietnam by changing how Americans thought about Catholics. The goal was not simply to make Americans sympathize with Catholics at home and abroad, but also to make Catholicism part of what it meant to be an American.

Dooley's writings modeled a new species of American Catholic, one more suited to the Cold War. As Dooley's handlers knew, the Cold War was not something that happened only in places like Vietnam. Indeed, as much Cold War propaganda made clear, the Cold War was everywhere. The moral backbone of America needed to be as strong as possible, and this meant drawing from the spiritual reserves of America's religious traditions.

This new American Catholic—or, perhaps more accurately, the US government's attempts to create the perception of a new kind of Catholic—were part and parcel of this larger campaign.

Curiously, *Deliver Us from Evil* accomplished this by portraying Vietnamese Catholics in ways reminiscent of earlier American anti-Catholic imagery. For example, Dooley portrayed Vietnamese Catholics as possessing a simple, powerful faith in the power of religious objects. Yet in Dooley's portrayal, this simplicity was evidence of Vietnamese Catholics' relatability rather than—as earlier, Protestant depictions of Catholics suggested—evidence of idol worship, or of their malleability for nefarious papal ends. The Vatican's influence was reimagined, too. Rather than the seat of a threatening foreign prince, the Vatican's influence in Vietnam was painted as a source of spiritual succor for beleaguered Vietnamese Catholics fighting for freedom of religion.

In this way, "exotic" or unfamiliar religious traditions and practices that may have previously given Americans pause were refashioned to contribute to a sense of pride in America's religiously pluralist democracy. To say that *Deliver Us from Evil* participated in these trends is not to say that Dooley or his handlers were always conscious of doing so. Rather, "Dooleymania" benefited from these trends in American religion and society even as it reinforced them. Dooley's work—and the CIA's and navy's efforts to make it happen—engaged and encouraged these changes in three key ways.

First, Dooley's work portrayed the Vietnamese refugees as explicitly Catholic. This is less significant for what it says about the Vietnamese than for what it suggests about how Catholicism was understood by the American public, whose support was necessary to pursue specific foreign policy goals. This built on government-sponsored World War II friendliness toward Catholics, a dramatic departure in US history.[44] It also made strategic sense to highlight Vietnamese Catholicism, since that would have been more familiar to American audiences than the reality of a non-white Buddhist South Vietnam.

In Dooley's writings, Catholic practices long criticized by Protestants were reimagined as potent Christian weapons against Communism. *Deliver*'s narrative features prominent and positive portrayals of infant baptism, the power of material culture, priestly authority, and even adoration of the Virgin Mary. When Dooley describes the Vietnamese refugees in his camp, he makes a point to say that they "invariably carried a religious object—a crucifix, statue or sacred picture"—three items that, even in the mid-1950s, were stock elements in anti-Catholic literature.[45] At one point Dooley tells the story of how US Navy ships, guided by Catholic priests, rescued a flotilla of refugee boats. In a scene that would not be out of place in an anti-Catholic dime novel, Dooley recounts how the refugees flew "the Papal banner, a yellow and gold flag displaying the Pope's tiara and the keys of St. Peter."[46] That in the mid-1950s, a best-selling book chronicled how the US Navy used foreign Catholic priests to rescue vessels flying the flag of the Holy See is a remarkable testament to the rapidly changing place of Catholics in American life.

Deliver details how the US military provided safe passage not just for Vietnamese Catholics, but also for their religious objects. Dooley recounts a fascinating story about the Our Lady of Fatima statue in Haiphong, a gift given to the people of Vietnam by the Pope. When Dooley wanted to evacuate the statue along with the parishioners, the Vietnamese priest responsible for it disagreed, because the statue would inspire Catholics left behind in the North. But Dooley, in his own words, "literally kidnaps" the statue when the priest is not looking, wraps it in a blanket, and transports it out of Haiphong on an army jeep to a nearby airfield. There, loaded onto a specially chartered US military transport plane, the statue of the Virgin was flown south. "And that's how Our Blessed Lady of Fatima, with a boost from American Aid, made the Passage to Freedom," Dooley explained.[47] In *Deliver*, the object, revered as it was, becomes not an object to fear but one so valuable that it was worth stealing to protect.

Identifying the Vietnamese as explicitly Catholic also helped blunt their exoticness to American audiences. Vietnamese Catholics were exotic, yes, but even in their strangeness they could be made understandable in reassuring ways. "The Tonkin mountain music is melodious, almost eerie, something like the ancient Hebrew liturgical chants," Dooley explained to his fellow Americans.[48] The parallel, like much of *Deliver*, is not subtle: the Vietnamese become the Jews to America's Christians—exotic but recognizable members on the same Tri-Faith team. The fluidity of Vietnamese identity reflected Dooley's ignorance of Vietnamese culture even as he sought to simplify the conflict for American audiences. Dooley closes one of his chapters with the words of Madame Ngai, a society matron who ran an orphanage for Vietnamese children displaced by the war. "We Tonkinese are a militant people," Ngai told Dooley, "much like those Texans you have told us about. We know that we will someday wrench our land back from the Viet Minh. Of this there is no doubt."[49] Through an Orientalist lens, the Vietnamese became empty signifiers, people who could be represented simultaneously as Hebrew, Jewish, Catholic, Christian, Texan, *and* American. That these markedly different representations made sense to Dooley's American audience speaks to how useful these identities could be in the right hands. Dooley successfully parleyed the "strangeness" of the Vietnamese into authentically American homespun.[50]

Second, the book forcefully argued that the core of Catholicism was love for religious freedom. Dooley missed no opportunity to remind his readers of the Communist threat to religious freedom, a hard lesson already learned by Vietnamese Catholics. "We Americans have got to take communism down from the clouds," Dooley told an interviewer, "and rub our noses in it. It's alive! It's devouring mankind in big gulps! We don't have time left for talk. Our only answer is God!"[51] Dooley was clear that Vietnamese Catholics simply wanted what every American already enjoyed: freedom of religion. Since America, too, was about religious freedom at its core, they were natural allies. Dooley reported that the Vietnamese Catholics, having imbibed the Viet Minh's anti-American propaganda, were shocked to find the American sailors kind and friendly. The US Navy, Dooley told his readers, "washed away the poisons of Communist hatred" through gifts of "loaves of bread, enormous quantities of candy, cigarettes, soft drinks and other articles"—even through acts of love. "I saw one notoriously loud, cursing boatswain's mate on the forecastle," Dooley related, "bouncing a brown bare-bottom baby on his knee while stuffing a Baby Ruth into its toothless mouth."[52]

Framing the Vietnamese conflict in terms of religious freedom was a strategic choice by the CIA and navy. Presenting Communist North Vietnam (godless, idolatrous) as an inversion of Catholic South Vietnam (God-fearing, pious) allowed Dooley to present Catholicism as an antidote to Communism. *Deliver* is a less-than-subtle primer on Communism's threat to American life, and the book's success meant the lessons were widely reprinted. Referencing a story in *Deliver*, a 1956 *Catholic View* article explained Communist opposition to the Lord's Prayer. The problems were the phrases "Give us this day our daily bread" and "deliver us from evil," Dooley explained. "In a communist country," readers learned, "your bread comes from the bounty of the government. You don't ask God for it. And in the second place, it is communist blasphemy to suggest that there might be such a thing as evil present in a communist atmosphere."[53] The practical appeal of this argument, at least from the navy's and CIA's perspective, was obvious: bureaucratic self-interest. It was important that American audiences understand the nature of the threat they faced and (not coincidentally) why this threat necessitated CIA and military budgets. But the narrative's focus on religious freedom also allowed Dooley and his handlers to sell their preferred species of Americanness. And Dooley was nothing if not a salesman.

With Dooley's story, American intelligence officers used the religious approach to portray religious people and ideas as hermetically sealed (and thus internal, ancient, and unchanging) and separate from economic and political factors. Deploying the trope of religious freedom proved useful to these institutions in the early days of American involvement in Vietnam, since it allowed them to flatten complex political and economic dynamics in debates over foreign policy. A long-running and messy conflict—part civil war, part revolutionary struggle—was hard to explain. In Dooley's telling, the stakes were immediately clear: the Vietnamese were dying for religious freedom, an idea that the United States was sworn to protect.

The Agency had even done some historical research to make sense of Catholicism's relationship to religious freedom. While there were plenty of surprising topics researched by the Agency in the 1950s, a lengthy report on the nineteenth-century papal encyclical *Testem benevolentiae nostrae* (1899) ranks among the more unexpected. The Agency reinterpreted the controversy around the "Americanism heresy"[54] as evidence of Catholics' undivided loyalty to the American state.[55] The memo demonstrated historically what the Agency argued contemporaneously: that American Catholics were unabashedly "American," celebrated religious freedom, and felt no political allegiance toward Rome. It made clear that Dooley was no outlier since he, and the Catholic Church to which he belonged, had always served the Republic.

Focusing on religious freedom also cleverly subverted traditional anti-Catholic critiques. The focal point of American anti-Catholicism had long been Catholics' curious relationship to the American state.[56] Debates about transubstantiation, the body of Christ, and other theological niceties—while important in some respects—mask the way in which anti-Catholicism drew its force from concerns about the subversive nature of the Catholic in liberal democratic states. The Pope's perennial threat to invade America and institute a Catholic theocracy had been the stuff of Protestant fever dreams since even before the American Revolution.[57] At a time of still relatively widespread anti-Catholicism, the genius of the book was to focus on the Americanness of Catholics and, crucially, their loyalty to the American state through their commitment to religious freedom. Catholics, like all Americans, had a duty to act as individuals in the fight against godless Communism and in defense of the American way of life. "America was made great by men who went out and hustled," Dooley explained in an interview to CBS's Mike Wallace. "They didn't turn to their government and say, 'Give me this, give me that.' In this era, all we do is turn to the government to solve our problems. It's not the government's business. It's my business. It's your business."[58] Dooley's work marked the explicitly Catholic as fully American, because American Catholicism was subsumed under the authority of the American state.

With this can-do attitude, Dooley situated himself (and his co-religionists) as self-evidently American and a servant of the American economic order. Fear of Catholic involvement in organized labor was a key component of anti-Catholicism before World War II, and these fears lingered in diluted form after 1945.[59] Dooley advocated enthusiastically for capitalism throughout the book. Once, when Dooley lacked funds to purchase medical supplies, he wrote letters requesting donations from major American corporations. Pfizer, Mead Johnson, and Pan-American Airways were among the private companies that donated medicine and materials. In the book, the generosity of American private enterprise stands in stark contrast to the fun-house critiques of the American economic system lobbed by Communists in North Vietnam: "This was the 'decadent capitalist system of America' responding," Dooley thinks.[60]

Finally, *Deliver Us from Evil* presented Catholicism as an interpretive gateway at an important moment in the history of American engagement with world religions. In Vietnam, Americans confronted the reality of Catholicism: a globe-spanning tradition with a rich history of internationalism, populated by diverse peoples with varying, and even esoteric, practices. Yet the parts were depicted as working together to form a harmonious whole. Thinking about Catholicism in foreign locales provided an analogue for thinking with, and through, other world religions. Scholars often root the emergence of the world religions paradigm at the historical intersection of Protestantism and European colonialism.[61] That intersection is an important part of this story, but it is not the entire tale.

Within the context of Vietnam, it was Catholicism—familiar as a people, strange as a foreign power—that demonstrated to Americans the utility of considering other world religions as strategic tools for American power. The global tapestry of Catholicism allowed it to serve Americans as a translator for things not understood and a testament to things not seen. The threat of Communism and the tortured bodies of Vietnamese Catholics were made real to American Protestants through a distinctly Catholic gaze. The intelligence community's role in making this view accessible had consequences for how Americans thought of the world and the religions in it. The American empire, confronted with new domains after World War II, began articulating a new language to govern the *Pax Americana*. A discourse of world religions, forged and sharpened in the heat of the United States' own religious differences, helped America translate the world to Americans even as Americans used it to translate America to the world. But from the perspective of the national security community, Catholicism's global presence offered unique strategic advantages. Yet because specific forms of Catholicism were the gateway to this larger discourse of world religions, it was imperative to privilege these forms of Catholicism over others. Dooley's success illustrates how many individuals—working more or less independently and housed across a variety of public and private institutions loosely aligned with the military and intelligence communities—recognized which way the wind was blowing in American culture and decided to hoist their sails.

Torture and American Religious Freedom

While these arguments made *Deliver Us from Evil*'s content unique, Dooley's work was not the sole state effort highlighting Catholics' plight in Vietnam. It was not even the only one featured in *Reader's Digest*: Dooley's editor, Commander Lederer, had published his own foray into the Vietnamese religious freedom genre the year before.[62] Still, Dooley's was the most effective—and the most popular. Even with the government-supported public relations blitz, it is doubtful Dooley's work would have been as successful if the book itself was not engrossing to read.

Deliver's persuasive power lay in its effective use of torture stories. Ironically, one of the most effective ways to ease anti-Catholic sentiment in the United States was to circulate fabricated reports of anti-Catholicism elsewhere. To do this, Dooley and Lederer took poetic license with the plight of North Vietnamese Catholics, often exaggerating or inventing acts of oppression designed to pull on American heartstrings. For many of Dooley's readers who were familiar with neither Vietnam nor its history of French colonialism, the internecine conflict between Vietnamese factions competing for scarce resources—horrendous as it was—was stripped of any political or economic context and rendered as little more than a question of religious belief. Whether the torture involved the Viet Minh jabbing chopsticks in children's ears for listening to the gospel or Communist mutilation of priests who had the audacity to preach it, Dooley's allegations of torture imbued the book with high moral stakes.

The problem with Dooley claiming firsthand knowledge of anti-Catholic torture is that, according to many who served with Dooley, these things never happened.[63] One American who served with Dooley later reflected: "Frankly, I thought *Deliver Us from Evil* was a piece of shit. When I read it I almost threw it across the room I was so mad. I kept finding inaccuracies and he really laid on that Communist stuff."[64] The media's focus on the torture stories put Dooley's teammates—who hadn't spoken up about the apparently egregious torture—in a tough position. Why hadn't they said anything, written anything? Why had they not told anyone? One navy corpsman who assisted Dooley during Operation Passage to Freedom explained, "If I'd found a priest hanging by his heels with nails hammered in his head, I'd have the whole camp hearing about it. If those atrocities had occurred, human nature would make you talk about it at the time."[65] Others who were involved in the process, like Dooley's editor Robert Giroux, may have had their suspicions but pressed on regardless. The important thing, as Giroux said, was that *Deliver Us from Evil* "had the essence of truth."[66] The most damning assessment likely came from William Lederer, who served as Dooley's editor, mentor, and *Reader's Digest* conduit: "Those things never happened." Asked about the tales of Catholic torture in 1991, Lederer did not mince words. "The atrocities described in the books either never took place or were committed by the French," Lederer recalled. "I travelled all over the country and never saw anything like them."[67] Fortunately for Dooley and those invested in his story, these criticisms did not become public knowledge for decades.

The allegations of tortured Catholics also drew on Orientalist themes, combining fears of godless Communism with Asian barbarity and Eastern primitivism. In Dooley's writings, the American intervention in Vietnam did not simply end Communist torture. It also brought Vietnam into the modern world. Dooley's letters are rife with these ideas, as when he describes a village before his arrival as having

> had nothing but black magic, necromancy, witchcraft, clay images, sorcery and betel juice. The villagers wallowed in monkey's blood, cobwebs, tiger's teeth, and incantations. They never had hope, much less help. Today the people of Muong Sing have good medicine, compassionate help, training and a fine little 25 bed hospital. Twentieth century.[68]

Despite Dooley's claim that "the purpose of this book is not to sicken anyone or to dwell upon the horror of Oriental tortures," the book did just that.[69]

Consider the anecdote about shoving chopsticks in Catholic children's ears. This story featured in various excerpts of the book, including most importantly the *Reader's Digest* condensed version that catapulted Dooley to national fame.[70] Yet the reality in Vietnam, as was so often the case, was more complicated. There was a consensus among those who served with

Dooley that this scene never took place. Howard Simpson, who arrived in Vietnam in 1952 as a press officer at the nascent American embassy, was one of the few Americans with Dooley on the docks in Haiphong during Operation Passage to Freedom and grew to know the CIA's Lansdale as well.[71] "At one point I remember arguing with Lansdale," Simpson recalled,

> over a propaganda story about village children whose eardrums had been ruptured by the insertion of chopsticks during a Vietminh torture session. There was something about the account that didn't ring true. I had seen and heard enough of torture by both sides during my time in the field. Chopsticks had never featured as a preferred instrument. There were many more direct, simple, and horrifying methods. Lansdale only flashed his all-knowing smile and changed the subject. The chopstick story soon spread through Haiphong and was picked up by the Saigon press and some Western correspondents. The veteran psywarrior obviously knew his business.[72]

That Asians would torture other Asians using chopsticks may have seemed self-evidently plausible to many Americans in the 1950s, especially considering chopsticks would have been one of the few items most Americans could reliably associate with "Asia." Lansdale's psychological operations were sensitive to target populations, regardless of whether they lived in San Francisco or Saigon.

Assessing "Dooleymania"

These stories made Dooley a living saint in the eyes of many American Catholics. His piety multiplied with each tale of Catholic pain eased by his modern American medicine. Dooley's Catholic supporters deluged the doctor with mail, with much of it piling up in his mother's home in St. Louis. Much of this fan mail celebrated having a forward-thinking Catholic hero, such as the letter Dooley received from Clare DuBrock. "While you continue to 'light a few candles' in Asia," Brock wrote to Dooley, "a candle will continue to burn for your intentions before a shrine of Our Lady back in the United States."[73] The Catholic celebration of Dooley's work extended beyond America's borders, too. South Vietnamese president Ngo Dinh Diem wrote Dooley about his hope "that many Americans will read and enjoy your book and through it, better understand Viet-nam."[74]

Much of the operation's success was rooted in how Dooley fit into a changing American Catholic culture. Dooley had the ability to shift between upstanding red-blooded American and ethnic Irish Catholic. This was part of Dooley's appeal to the US government, and part of what made his public relations campaign about Southeast Asia so successful. Dooley represented a different kind of American Catholicism, and American Catholic masculinity, that appealed to religiously diverse popular audiences. To Catholic Americans, Dooley was the apotheosis of their national dreams. To non-Catholics, Dooley came across first and foremost as a serviceman, as someone dedicated to serving his country and fighting religious persecution wherever it may be. Of course, it helped that Dooley himself was a funny, brave, and well-spoken advocate for red-blooded Americanism. It also did not hurt that Dooley was incredibly photogenic. As one former colleague recalled, "when his book came out I can remember people, particularly Catholic women, just about swooning."[75] In this regard, Dooley was different from other prominent American Catholics. There was no danger of mistaking Senator Joseph McCarthy for a sex symbol. And unlike the frumpy senator, Dooley was not seen as divisive or overtly political. He looked better in front of TV cameras, too. And unlike Cardinal Francis Spellman or Bishop Fulton Sheen, Dooley was not a priest, whose celibacy was still treated as "strange" in the popular imagination.

Given the political and religious context of the day, it was crucial that Dooley's ambiguously sectarian religious identity was mellowed by his concrete Americanness. The mixture gave him bipartisan appeal. During the presidential election of 1960, both John F. Kennedy and Richard Nixon sought to use Dooley despite the lingering "Catholic Question" around Senator Kennedy. When Kennedy proposed the Peace Corps (itself an organization with a complicated relationship to US church-state policy), he called upon Dr. Dooley as the model citizen.[76] "Americans have marveled at the selfless example of Dr. Tom Dooley in Laos," Kennedy said, and the United States needed more Dooleys if it was to withstand "the modern techniques of combat."[77] A few months earlier, Kennedy's challenger had relied upon Dooley in a similar way. The date June 15, 1960, was "Tom Dooley Day" at the US Capitol, and Vice President Nixon—in full campaign mode—presided over the ceremony. Nixon spoke of the plight of Laos, where Dooley had recently worked: "What we fail to recognize is that the peoples of Laos and other countries are not interested in being pawns in this world struggle. They are not interested in fighting our battles; they are only interested in fighting their own."[78] This is why, Nixon continued, American foreign aid programs must be presented to these people "in a way they can understand." According to Nixon, no one knew this better than Dooley, since Dooley represented "the real heart of America, the best motivations of our Government and its traditions."[79] In Tri-Faith America, Dooley was a model citizen.

Dooley's rapturous reception in popular culture helped sell the most outlandish parts of his story. The overwhelming success of the domestic propaganda campaign was striking. Newspaper coverage of *Deliver Us from Evil* was extensive: the *South Bend Tribune* carried a story entitled "Dooley Tells of Red Torture," while the *Pennsylvania Visitor Register* reported "Book by Doctor Tells Story of Red Cruelty in Vietnam."[80] The *Chicago Daily News* was more direct: "Exclusive: How Reds Tortured Catholics."[81] Dooley's publisher also worked with the US Information Agency to publish the books abroad.[82] The story was presumed so universally appealing that a variety of foreign editions (Arabic, Urdu, Tamil, Japanese, etc.) were printed. Seth Jacobs argues that *Deliver Us from Evil* was the "*Uncle Tom's Cabin* of the Cold War," since it helped frame the conflict as nothing had before.[83]

The intelligence community generally agreed that their efforts had paid off in Vietnam, too. As one CIA officer recalled, "The Agency's operation worked. It not only convinced the North Vietnamese Catholics to flee to the South, thereby providing Diem with a source of reliable political and military cadres, but it also duped the American people into believing that the flight of the refugees was a condemnation of the Viet Minh by the majority of Vietnamese."[84] When Dooley received an honorary doctorate from Notre Dame in 1960, Dooley upstaged both of the other invited guests: President Eisenhower and Cardinal Giovanni Montini, the future Pope Paul VI. Dooley was so popular that the president of the United States had to fight for face time with the young doctor. "Where's Tom Dooley?" Eisenhower asked Notre Dame president Father Hesburgh. "I want to meet him and have a talk."[85]

Living the Cultural Cold War

Dooley left the navy in 1956, shortly after *Deliver* was published. Observers could be forgiven for thinking the decision abrupt. Dooley told the press that he had left the navy to pursue a new career as a full-time humanitarian, establishing medical missions in Southeast Asia. In truth, navy brass had discovered Dooley's romantic liaisons with men. On navy-sponsored publicity tours around the United States, Dooley indiscreetly brought men back to his government-furnished hotel rooms.[86] In addition to being troubled by Dooley's behavior, the navy was concerned about the public relations fiasco that would ensue if Dooley was caught. Yet the navy found itself in a bind: it could not dismiss Dooley at the peak of his popularity, lest it jeopardize the propaganda gains painstakingly made through him. Dooley and his handlers had successfully managed his Catholicism, but it was unthinkable that an openly gay man could long remain a national icon and emblem of Christian piety in the 1950s.

There had long been rumors regarding Dooley's sexuality, and those who worked in positions of power seemed to know the truth well enough.[87] In the 1980s, Lansdale recalled how Dooley's sexual orientation posed difficulties for the CIA's efforts to elevate Dooley's public stature. "He had gotten in trouble with his team . . . ," Lansdale recalled. "He had homosexual tendencies and his team got mad at him personally, and there were fights and I had to straighten that out."[88] Other wings of the national security state were less sympathetic. FBI director J. Edgar Hoover missed little, and Dooley's sexuality was no exception: the Bureau was tracking Dooley's sexual activities by early 1957.[89] Internal FBI documents show that Dooley's sexual orientation led the FBI to decline an invitation for Hoover to join an event with the Reverend Billy Graham, since Dooley would also be on the program.[90]

Ultimately Dooley's sexuality mattered less in terms of public relations—like much else about the doctor, the truth would not emerge for decades—than it did for how he was managed by the government. Once the navy let him go, Dooley was a man with a secret. For professionals who dealt in secrets, this was an investment opportunity. Dooley quickly signed on with the International Rescue Committee, a charitable organization with many intelligence luminaries on its board, including former OSS director William Donovan. Through these relationships, the IRC had a working relationship with the CIA. An arrangement was reached in which Tom Dooley's humanitarian organization, MEDICO, would be funded and managed by the IRC. MEDICO would operate medical facilities in several developing countries, beginning with Laos. In return for support, Dooley would act as an observation post in areas of national security interest.[91]

Yet as Dooley's professional life came back together, he was diagnosed with the cancer that would eventually claim his life. Rather than slow his pace to allow for treatment, Dooley maintained a feverish work schedule in Laos. By nearly all accounts, Dooley was working with renewed vigor for the benefit of his destitute patients. This self-sacrifice made him even more popular among Americans, and there was an eager audience for the two additional books Dooley wrote after his diagnosis. In *The Edge of Tomorrow* (1958) and *The Night They Burned the Mountain* (1960), Dooley detailed the challenges of running MEDICO clinics in Laos. Anyone familiar with his first book's themes would find much in common with his later work. Each book focused on American goodness, Asian suffering, and the evils of Communism. And, just like his first publication, these books elided his connections to US intelligence.

Having gone from a no-name sailor to an international superstar, Dooley found himself with less than a year to live smuggling weapons and administering medicine to destitute Laotian villagers.[92] Dooley's cancer soon sapped his ability to take care of himself and, in his final days, he returned to the States. As Tom Dooley lay dying in New York's Memorial Hospital, prayer vigils were organized by Americans around the country. Dooley even received a final bedside visit from Cardinal Spellman.[93] The night before he passed, President Eisenhower sent Dooley a telegram that read in part: "It must be a source of heartened gratification to realize that in so few years you have accomplished so much for the good of distant peoples and have inspired so many others to work for humanity."[94]

Tom Dooley died in his sleep the following day, January 18, 1961. In true Dooley fashion, and with a flair for marketing that DeWitt Wallace and *Reader's Digest* would have appreciated, Dooley arranged for a portion of his final letter to Father Hesburgh, president of Notre Dame, to be published after his death. "I have monstrous phantoms . . . as all men do," Dooley wrote. "But I try to exorcise them with all the fury of the middle ages. And inside and outside the wind blows."[95] Dooley's story veered between comedy and tragedy until the end. On the same day Dooley died in New York, his MEDICO clinic in Laos was overrun by the Communist Pathet Lao.[96]

Back home, Dooley's death was front-page news. Agnes Dooley was overwhelmed with sympathy letters, receiving over one thousand per day, some addressed simply to "Dr. Dooley's Mother, St. Louis, MO."[97] Upon hearing of Dooley's death, the Dalai Lama—himself a beneficiary of CIA aid—wrote about his sadness at Dooley's passing: "His heroic example has been a source of inspiration to us Tibetans."[98] Another such letter was from Angier Biddle Duke, an American diplomat and IRC bigwig who had worked with Dooley. Tom Dooley was more than a simple physician, Duke wrote Agnes: "He was, in fact, a cause, and a cause in which I believed most deeply."[99] Even those Americans who did not know the full story saw Dooley as part of something bigger. When Dooley died, his Christlike aura was still intact. At Dooley's funeral in St. Louis Cathedral, the Rev. George J. Gottwald reflected on Dooley's history of self-sacrifice and service, saying simply, "The greatest life that was ever lived in thirty-three years. Dr. Dooley was thirty-four."[100]

Dooley's death did not end the CIA's interest in Catholicism. The

Agency continued to push the Vietnam-Catholic connection, building on Dooley's tales to develop a larger genre of "Catholic Vietnam" and "Vietnamese religious freedom" stories.[101] A few months after Dooley's death, the *Saturday Evening Post* ran a remarkable story about a group of upstart Catholic guerilla warriors in South Vietnam. It was penned anonymously by "An American Officer," and titled "The Report the President Wanted Published." As the *Post*'s editors explained, President Kennedy had been so moved by this intelligence report that he ordered the file be declassified and widely published. The article told the story of Father Nguyen Loc Hoa—a Catholic priest, guerilla fighter, and former member of Chiang Kai-shek's Chinese Nationalist Army—who had led hundreds of "Christian refugees" from China to South Vietnam, seeking religious and political freedoms under a non-Communist government. But their new village of Binh Hung was beset by constant harassment from the Viet Cong (VC). Armed with whatever they could scrounge, they defended their lives, and their right to worship freely, each night the VC attacked. "Freedom is precious to them," the anonymous officer noted, recalling how many times the villagers of Binh Hung "asked me for assurance that the United States would stand firm in its policy in Asia."[102] These "Christian refugees" had risked everything in their journey to the religious and political freedoms of South Vietnam, the anonymous author explained, but now their very livelihood was under threat from the same Vietnamese Communists arrayed against US interests.

The anonymous author was, of course, Edward Lansdale.[103] As with Dooley, Lansdale had another winning story on his hands. Yet, unlike with Dooley, this story needed less massaging. The sheer quantity of human misery in Vietnam meant that not every report of Vietnamese Catholic suffering had to be fabricated. Catholics in Vietnam faced many struggles, as did their fellow Vietnamese of other religious groups. Father Hoa and Binh Hung were real, and their conflict with the Viet Cong was lethal. The stirring story of Binh Hung quickly captured national attention. KCRA San Francisco went to Binh Hung and made a documentary about the village that came to be known as *The Village That Refused to Die*.[104] Lansdale was thrilled about the story's reception, and he screened the documentary at the Pentagon for anyone interested in the "real spirit of counterinsurgency." The powerhouse Desilu production company picked up the story and aired a special on Binh Hung as part of their "Window on the World" series.[105] Concerned about the plight of Father Hoa's Catholic warriors, anxious Americans sent money to the *Saturday Evening Post* for the village's defense.[106]

Despite the story's commercial success, the story of Binh Hung marked the end of an era in America's involvement in Vietnam. Tom Dooley's tales, William Lederer's "Bayfield," and Lansdale's Father Hoa had a limited shelf life. The early 1960s were high tide in the American effort to Catholicize Vietnam in popular depictions back home. Even after Dooley's death in 1961, his books remained best-sellers and his name commanded respect and admiration. But the façade was crumbling. Vietnamese Buddhists increasingly protested the heavy-handed religious repression at the hands of the Catholic minority government. In the summer of 1963, the Buddhist monk Thich Quang Duc walked to the middle of a busy Saigon intersection and lit himself on fire. International news media recorded his perfectly still body as it was consumed by flame. As the situation unraveled, the South Vietnamese president Diem—America's "Joan of Arc" in Vietnam—was dragged from a Catholic Cathedral in Saigon and murdered in the back of an American-made M113 armored personnel carrier. Within a few weeks, America's own Catholic president would be murdered. The days when Americans would hear "Vietnam" and think "Catholicism" were over.

As the 1960s progressed, the CIA was forced to confront the reality that the Church was changing, too. To compound the Agency's confusion, they had to make sense of these changes amid an increasingly chaotic domestic political scene and a deteriorating war in Vietnam. Sixteen American soldiers were killed in Vietnam in 1961, the year Dooley died. The following year, Pope John XXIII opened the Second Vatican Council, a historic event that transformed Roman Catholic ideas and practice. American Catholics followed dramatic changes coming out of Rome even as they lived through dramatic changes at home in the United States. Pope Paul VI closed the council in 1965, a year that saw 1,928 Americans killed in Vietnam. Three years later, a desperate President Johnson sent Lansdale back to Vietnam as the number of Americans killed in action skyrocketed to 16,899.[107]

Whereas Dooley spoke to a familiar Americanness—a celebration of religious freedom and apple pie—new ideas emerged that fundamentally challenged what it meant to be both American and Catholic. In response, the Agency privileged older forms of Catholicism with which it was more familiar, and looked to new changes—in both the Church and America as a whole—with a wary eye.

The CIA's Preferred Brand of Catholicism

The CIA's investment in Catholicism made anything that could threaten its stability, like the Second Vatican Council, more troubling. The Vatican had been a reliable source of anti-Communist ideology, and the Agency was quick to study changes stemming from the Council to see if they might portend broader changes in the Vatican's approach to the Cold War. In 1963, CIA director John McCone—himself a Catholic—provided President Kennedy with intelligence on the state of the Church and the Council in advance of Kennedy's historic trip to Rome.[108]

The CIA was particularly worried about the papal encyclical *Pacem in Terris*. A month before DCI McCone briefed Kennedy, the Agency assembled a nuanced study that reflected a sophisticated understanding of the Vatican's place in world politics. While the Agency eventually concluded that the recent papal encyclicals avoided any radical changes, the Agency did note that the carefully chosen language of the documents left open the door to more substantial shifts in the Vatican's future relationship with the USSR. The Agency worried that the modern Church might not understand the true threat posed by the Soviets: "The Vatican's grasp of broader international problems," one CIA memo explained, "may be something less than comprehensive."[109]

Much of the CIA's focus was on the man behind the Council, Pope John XXIII. Some in the defense-intelligence community looked suspiciously on the Pope's outreach to the Soviet Union. The fear that the new Pope was soft on Communism dated back to World War II, when OSS eyes and ears in the Vatican had made note of then-Cardinal Angelo Roncalli (the future Pope John XXIII) for his overt friendliness to the Soviet ambassador—an uncommon sight at the Vatican, even during World War II.[110] In one CIA memo, Agency analysts sought to make sense of some of Pope John XXIII's seemingly liberal statements. Agency analysts could not rule out official relations between the Vatican and the USSR, a meeting between the Pope and Khrushchev, or new "concordats" between the two states—all of which were worrying possibilities for the Agency. Another memo explained:

> There is no reason to doubt that John, if he felt that good would result from such a meeting [with Khrushchev] or exchange [with the Soviets], would brush aside criticism thereof (even from within the Roman Curia), just as Christ dismissed criticism of His talking with Publicans and sinners.[111]

The CIA's portrayal of the Vatican in the early days of the Council paints a picture of an institution in the midst of great change. Young priests and laymen were excited about the liberalizing trends, with some even interpreting them to mean the Church now endorsed a "kind of socialism." Other Vatican insiders, meanwhile, were "deeply disturbed" at the possible consequences.[112] As changes spilled out from the Council and into the lives of American Catholics, the CIA began to be disturbed as well.

Few places symbolized the chaos and liberalizing trends unleased in both the Church and American culture as did *Ramparts* magazine. *Ramparts* began in California in May 1962, describing itself as a Catholic literary quarterly focusing on "those positive principles of Hellenic-Christian tradition . . . in an age grown increasingly secular, bewildered, and afraid."[113] According to Helen Keating, who co-founded the magazine with her husband Ed, *Ramparts* was designed to "present the ancient truths of the Church with intelligence and sophistication," but also to "stimulate the artists who had been stifled by the narrowmindedness of the Church in America."[114] *Ramparts* only lasted seven years, going out of business in 1969.[115] Even so, it had a remarkable impact, serving as a symbol of the changes to both the American Left and American Catholicism during the 1960s.[116]

Like other Americans, the magazine's staff was radicalized in large part by the Vietnam War and the civil rights movement. An early issue featured Thomas Merton challenging white liberals on racial issues. *Ramparts* defended a play, *The Deputy*, which charged Pope Pius XII with ignoring the Holocaust. Editorials criticized Cardinal James McIntyre, the archbishop of Los Angeles, for his insufficient support of the civil rights movement. The November 1964 issue excoriated Barry Goldwater. Merton cautioned the editors about their change in tone: "I do think that in certain areas a judicious restraint would perhaps do the magazine much more good than harm."[117] The magazine became increasingly strident, dancing on the border between Leftist activism and absurdism. Editor Warren Hinckle wrote that the Catholic Left was "the best thing that has happened to the Catholic Church since probably Jesus Christ."[118] The magazine's politics made it unpopular with the Church hierarchy, and in 1965 the magazine announced that it was now an ecumenical publication, aimed at Protestants and Jews as well as Catholics.[119] *Ramparts* had grown away from the Church even as its editors felt the Church had grown away from it. "The Church was a willing participant in the divorce," Hinckle later wryly observed.[120] The result was that, by the end of 1965, *Ramparts* was arguably more "Left" than "Catholic Left."

At the same time, a series of articles in *Ramparts* exposed the CIA on a number of fronts, including the Agency's activities during the early days of US involvement in Vietnam. First, *Ramparts* exposed Tom Dooley, revealing the Catholic superstar's fabrications and friendliness to the US government. In that time and place, and in that magazine, it was a damning indictment. In "Hang Down Your Head Tom Dooley" (1965), Robert Scheer cast Dooley as a well-meaning but naive individual used by dark forces within the American government, especially the CIA.[121] Scheer argued that Dooley foolishly believed the torture tales fed to him by Catholic sources, and that Dooley's depictions of Vietnam as a predominantly Catholic society could be nothing other than deceitful. The article illuminated Dooley's role in embroiling America in an anti-colonial war by selling American audiences a set of "myths" about Vietnam. However, Scheer's real critique was reserved for Cardinal Spellman, depicted as a moral leader complicit in the immoral dealings of America's early involvement in Vietnam. In the article's infamous conclusion, Scheer asked, "If the war continues, may it not one day be called Cardinal Spellman's final solution to the Vietnam question?"[122] Such voracious criticism of the Catholic hierarchy was unheard of in the Catholic press, and was one of *Ramparts'* most important contributions to 1960s American Catholicism.[123]

Ramparts followed up in July 1965 by dissecting the so-called "Vietnam Lobby," an informal group of lobbyists and decision-makers interested in pursuing interventionist US policy in Vietnam. The group included Cardinal Spellman, Edward Lansdale, and others. Scheer and Hinckle shed light on Operation Passage to Freedom, painting Dooley's Catholic humanitarian odyssey as little more than a strategic evacuation of civilians loyal to the old French colonial regime. In this view Tom Dooley was their unwitting, albeit well-meaning, stooge.[124] While the article did identify some important connections, it also slipped into conspiratorial theorizing by suggesting a nefarious network of Catholics in American politics shaping US policy in Vietnam. There were factual errors, too, but the argument's potency helped work it into popular memory.[125] As James Fisher has noted, it was a sign of just how unusual the times were that an ostensibly Catholic publication (albeit a far-left one) relied on nativist Protestant tropes to argue its point.[126] *Ramparts'* determination to demonstrate Catholic culpability for America's errors in Vietnam began, Hinckle later explained, "in an earnest attempt to hang something on the Catholic Church. We set out looking to lay some of the blame for Vietnam at the silken slippers of the Pope; we succeeded only in implicating Cardinal Spellman."[127] *Ramparts'* muckraking at CIA expense continued the following year when it published an exposé on the CIA–Michigan State University relationship, wherein the CIA paid MSU to train South Vietnamese in "covert police training."[128] *Ramparts* dropped another bombshell when it revealed, in 1967, that the CIA was funding the National Student Association and other ostensibly independent organizations.[129] For the CIA, the damage was done.[130] Future CIA director

Richard Helms later concluded that the *Ramparts* exposés were one of the contributing factors to the Congressional investigations of the CIA in the mid-1970s.[131]

In the moment, though, the Agency devised several strategies of dubious legality to counteract *Ramparts*. CIA director William Raborn ordered an investigation into *Ramparts*, in clear violation of the Agency's charter. CIA officers assembled dossiers on nearly two dozen *Ramparts* editors and writers. James Jesus Angleton, the Agency's counterintelligence expert, took over the investigation on the assumption that *Ramparts* was likely some form of Communist plot to weaken American resolve.[132] By 1967, Angleton had a dozen officers digging into *Ramparts*, and had investigated 127 employees and almost two hundred additional people with more tenuous connections to the magazine. In Angleton's own report on the investigation's findings, he made note of each time *Ramparts* had described things in ways the CIA deemed dangerous, such as the US government being "sick," or the Catholic Church being "reactionary," or the CIA being "evil."[133]

Meanwhile Desmond Fitzgerald, then CIA's deputy director for plans, tasked CIA officer Edgar Applewhite with finding covert ways to damage *Ramparts*. "I had all sorts of dirty tricks to hurt their circulation and financing," Applewhite later recalled.

> The people running *Ramparts* were vulnerable to blackmail. We had awful things in mind, some of which we carried off, though *Ramparts* fell of its own accord. We were not the least inhibited by the fact that the CIA had no internal security role in the United States.[134]

The CIA also investigated *Ramparts'* finances. In a meeting between the CIA and the Internal Revenue Service (IRS), the Agency made clear that it understood *Ramparts'* promise of future exposés as a threat, and as "an attack on CIA in particular, and the administration in general." The CIA proposed that the IRS "examine" the corporate tax returns of *Ramparts* in order to locate financial improprieties and identify the magazine's funders so the IRS could follow up by auditing individual supporters' tax returns. The memo makes clear the murky legal ground on which both agencies stood, and notes that any closer cooperation between the IRS and CIA would probably require a formal, and no longer deniable, agreement on paper.[135] The financial investigators hoped to find evidence of Soviet funding—which would have provided a more formal entry point for CIA's involvement—but they came up empty-handed. Two weeks later, the CIA decided there was not enough useful information to pursue a public investigation.[136] In the meantime, *Ramparts'* collapse from internal ideological disputes made further action unnecessary.

Just as OSS operations in World War II had sought out, maintained, and defended certain strands of American Catholicism, the CIA did much the same in its responses to the *Ramparts* exposés and the broader changes stemming from the Second Vatican Council. In trying to constrain liberal Catholic impulses, the Agency sought to ensure that the Church's anti-Communist bona fides remained intact. Too much had been invested to do anything else.

That the Church could be suspected of devious conservatism by left-oriented Catholic magazines like *Ramparts* while simultaneously being investigated by the CIA for its liberal leanings is but one mark of just how confusing the Church's place in American life was in the immediate aftermath of the Council. The controversy in and around *Ramparts* can be read as a contest to influence proper forms of American Catholicism. By the end of the 1960s, Dooley-esque Catholicism—clean-cut and authentically American—seemed a relic from a different time. And, in a sense, it was.

For the American involvement in Vietnam, there are two 1960s. The first half of the 1960s—a kind of "long 1950s"—witnessed an unironic confidence in American power held by men like Dooley, Lederer, and Lansdale. The latter 1960s, marked by assassinations, riots, and body counts, was the product of a society much less certain. The United States' ultimate defeat in Vietnam would wait until 1975, but the same strains of unbridled confidence heard in Lansdale's and Lederer's plans were echoed in Ambassador Graham Martin's refusal to evacuate the US embassy in Saigon even once its seizure was assured. The United States simply *did not lose*. The epistemic restructuring necessary to accept the second half of the decade after the success of the first half is the defining difference between these two 1960s. Dooley—the idea and the man—was created by the first America but judged by the second.

Remembering Tom Dooley

Memory of Dooley largely fell away by the 1970s, eclipsed by other cataclysmic changes in American culture. Once the toast of politicians and presidents, by the following decade even official navy histories mentioned Dooley only in passing.[137] Still, some Americans remained warm to Dooley, especially in Catholic circles.[138] After Dooley's CIA connections became public knowledge, one letter to the *Washington Post* read: "So Dr.

Tom Dooley has been unmasked! The man may have brought medical care and hope to half a million deprived souls, but he turns out to have been a damned American patriot. Very sad."[139]

Yet this effort paled in comparison to the veneration of Dr. Dooley when he was "Dr. America," the "celebrity saint."[140] This was due in part to the slow drip of scandal that emerged from Dooley's legacy — CIA contacts, homosexual activity — and then, in turn, those very scandals being overshadowed by the larger debacle of US involvement in Vietnam. Dooley's message was about the bonds of admiration that existed between Americans and Vietnamese and their common religious heritage. After the fall of Saigon, this read as if it was from another era. And, of course, it was. Vietnam was the last war of the 1950s. Dooley had the unfortunate duty of writing for the old guard at its peak, and he died just as they were being thrown out of the palace.

Dooley's story helps explain why the CIA deemed it in the interest of national security that the average American no longer view a crucifix apprehensively or think venerating the Virgin Mary and American patriotism were mutually exclusive. In this, the navy and CIA helped propagate a new type of American Catholic: someone religiously "different" enough from American Protestantism to qualify as a beneficiary of American pluralism, yet someone who could be reliably counted upon to support American foreign policy. When it came to Tom Dooley, the CIA's religious approach was applied to the home front just as much as it was in Vietnam.

The story of Tom Dooley helps explain how, in the early Cold War, US intelligence and American religion became further entwined in operations at home and abroad. Though forging that relationship involved a great deal of covert effort, the fruits of that relationship have always been, by design, in plain sight. In one of the early *Reader's Digest* articles about Vietnamese Catholics fleeing the North, a little girl was given a bath by a US sailor onboard a navy ship headed for South Vietnam. "Mama, the big American is a priest," she told her mother. "First he blessed me and then baptized me American."[141]

While Dooley may have instilled feelings of warmth toward Catholicism in some of his readers, the end goal of the propaganda machine built around him was to encourage anti-Communist intervention in places like Vietnam where non-white, non-Protestant peoples found themselves on the frontline of the Cold War. While Dooley succeeded at selling Catholicism to American audiences, it would be a mistake to view this outcome as anything other than incidental to more pressing national security concerns. Dooley's focus on Catholic practices at an individual, sympathetic level rendered Catholicism as apolitical ("religious") and, in an odd way, powerless. By muting the perceived church-state threat of Catholicism, Dooley's story provided a way for Americans to support their country's foreign policy and its Catholic citizens in the same breath, even if the larger institutional church remained off-putting.

In echoes of other Eisenhower administration initiatives like Militant Liberty, those involved in Dooley's story agreed that "religion" was the Free World's best defense (and, in many cases, best *offense*) during the Cold War. Operation Passage to Freedom and *Deliver Us from Evil* suggested not just that Americans attempted to alter the religious landscape of other countries, but that the new relationship between religion and national security necessitated covert government involvement in domestic American religion as well. Even when these arrangements were challenged by the Second Vatican Council or in new Catholic ideas in *Ramparts*, Dooley's story illuminates the relationship between American boots on foreign soil—whether worn by Tom Dooley, Edward Lansdale, or the 101st Airborne Division—and religion in America.

The final years of Tom Dooley's short life are one answer to the question put to William Donovan by his OSS colleagues during World War II: "What are we going to do with the religious approach?"[142] One could, it turned out, "do" just about anything one wanted. One person who lived that answer was Edward Lansdale. The arc of Lansdale's professional career mirrored the triumphs and struggles of Cold War American intelligence. Lansdale asked new questions about the role of religion and ideas in advancing and securing American power after World War II. From the Pentagon to Saigon—and many locations in between—Lansdale sought to incorporate the religions of the world into the craft of American intelligence, nationbuilding, and counterinsurgency. Lansdale's work with Tom Dooley and Catholicism was but one small piece of a career that, decades after his death, remains a puzzle.

Chapter Six

Counterinsurgency and the Study of World Religions

Lansdale would, of course, make a spectacular article—if you can get him
to cooperate. Allen Dulles could tell you a lot about him.
William Lederer[1]

Remember that generalizations are misleading.
US Navy's *Religions of South Vietnam in Faith and Fact* (1967)[2]

Retired intelligence officers receive strange mail. In 1976, a Catholic priest named Father John Ireland Gallery wrote Edward Lansdale with a plan for world peace. The great religious traditions of the West were squabbling among each other, Gallery thought. Turkish Muslims and Greek Christians were at each other's throats over Cyprus, and the Soviets were waiting to pounce. Gallery suggested a creative solution: get the North Atlantic Treaty Organization (NATO) to rebuild the ancient city of Ephesus along the Turkish coast. Using the Vatican's archives to figure out what ancient buildings existed in Ephesus, Father Gallery thought a "second Holy City (after Jerusalem)" could be rebuilt to "heal the 1000 year old Eastern schism and bring Greece & Turkey back together against the Reds—their real enemies." This "NATO Peace Project" might seem an odd suggestion, Gallery argued, but it had a lot going for it. Rebuilding Ephesus would supply the free world with a religious center of gravity, a place that major Western religious traditions could call home. This was existentially important because it was the West's religious backbone that enabled it to challenge Communism's godless aggression in the first place. As an added bonus, NATO would strengthen ties with Israel by rebuilding ancient synagogues. Gallery wanted Lansdale to know that the American taxpayer need not fear the costs of this plan, since it would be generously funded by the shah of Iran. Secretary of Defense Donald Rumsfeld had offered to set up a meeting with President Ford and, if the president gave his approval, the plan could get underway. "With your brains and my personality and the Shah of Iran's money, we could pull this off," Gallery wrote to Lansdale.[3]

If there was such a thing as a Cold War national security celebrity, Edward Lansdale was one. More than once Lansdale was compared to T. E. Lawrence, otherwise known as "Lawrence of Arabia."[4] He became so well known as an international man of mystery that his efforts to pretend otherwise verged on the comical. In the wilderness of mirrors that was American intelligence, Lansdale's cover took on an absurd edge, as the hubbub over his secrecy became a kind of cover in and of itself. Until near the end of his life, however, Lansdale insisted on keeping his relationship with the CIA a secret. Even after the Pentagon Papers leaked to the *New York Times* in 1971 (by Lansdale protégé Daniel Ellsberg, no less) and it was clear to the entire planet that Lansdale's career was anything but average, Lansdale stayed quiet. His memoir published a year later, *In the Midst of Wars*, is notable for how much it leaves out. Even his own family became puzzled by his obsession with obfuscation. Lansdale's brother, David, penned Ed a confused letter after reading the memoir, since "a review of the Pentagon papers makes it pretty clear to me that you were involved in activities that could make another completely parallel story."[5]

This parallel story connects Lansdale to some of the most important developments in the religious approach to intelligence during the Cold War. It also includes years of service to the CIA. Though Lansdale was never formally employed by the Agency, he often joked that everyone thought he was CIA: "Not only CIA, I was secretly head of CIA. I think they still think that out in Asia, all throughout."[6] He was the confidant of presidents, American and otherwise. He would fall out of favor just as Kennedy was assassinated, and he remains enduringly linked to conspiracy theories about the assassination. His legacy echoes in American popular culture, too: in Oliver Stone's *JFK* (1991), the scheming character of General Y bears more than a passing resemblance to Lansdale. These varied portrayals of Lansdale, combined with his links to the CIA, cemented Lansdale as a keystone holding together various Cold War conspiracies.[7] Yet it is what Lansdale actually accomplished—and why he did it—that make him worthy of consideration.

Over the course of Lansdale's intelligence career, he leveraged the religious beliefs of people around the world in the service of US national security. While the Ephesus Project never moved beyond the planning stages, others like it did. Lansdale's religious approach was rooted in his efforts to study and manipulate religious ideas in the service of American counterinsurgency programs in the Philippines and Vietnam during the 1950s and

1960s. Lansdale first rose to professional prominence by helping Filipino president Ramon Magsaysay resist a Communist rebellion in the 1950s. Lansdale attributed much of his success to his study of individual Filipino religious beliefs and a commitment to manipulate them for American ends. For Lansdale, counterinsurgency was about people and people were about religion. Americans had an intuitive understanding of religion, Lansdale thought, and this made them ideal communicators in a world in which religion was presumed to be a shared universal trait. American history would itself be the ideal guide. "I took my American beliefs with me to the Asian battlegrounds," Lansdale wrote, "as Tom Paine would have done."[8]

Lansdale's interest in unconventional ideas about counterinsurgency meant that opinion about him was split in the intelligence establishment. Many thought him a brilliant manipulator of the human mind—CIA director William Colby ranked him as one of the ten greatest spies of all time—while others thought him a kook and a crank.[9] Confident in his methods, Lansdale pressed on. In Lansdale's cache of reference materials, he kept an excerpt from the US Marine Corps' *Small Wars Manual* (1940): "Small wars are conceived in uncertainty, are conducted often with precarious responsibility and doubtful authority, under indeterminate orders lacking specific instructions."[10] It was an apt description for most of Lansdale's career.

Lansdale's specialty was psychological warfare: getting in the mind of the enemy, figuring out how they work, and understanding how to break them down. Even so, he had a romantic streak that sits uneasily with his legacy of covert American intervention in the developing world. Often brought in to teach special warfare tactics, Lansdale urged American intelligence officers and special forces to get to know people as a means of preventing conflict. "The biggest passport in the world is a smile," he explained.[11] During one class on counterinsurgency, he urged those in attendance to get invited into people's homes, share a meal with them, and befriend them. These were the marks of success in counterinsurgency, he taught: moments when it was most effective to "share what you believe in as American[s]."[12]

Lansdale's early career taught him to pay attention to religion and belief. Across several foreign postings, he had been struck by how important "superstition" and "folklore" were to the people with whom he was working, whether that was at the popular or diplomatic level. (It did not seem to occur to Lansdale that Americans had these beliefs, too, though they used names like "religion" or "common sense.") In both cases, Lansdale understood ideas to control actions. If one could control how someone *thought* about something—say, a Vietnamese peasant's ideas about his ancestors—

certain actions would necessarily follow. Lansdale firmly believed that by changing what people believed, you would change the world along the way.

Lansdale's career peaked before the irony of American empire, before Vietnam. When Lansdale worked with the CIA, many of the leading minds in the Agency were still a breed of liberal internationalist. His career testified to his conviction that people were ultimately more alike than different. Cultural differences, then, were like passwords that had to be discovered to access the essential human content within people. Lansdale's contribution to American religious history came about due to his curiosity on the front lines of the American empire in the twentieth century. Lansdale's study of human cultures, and the ends to which these studies were put, advanced the relationship between American empire, the study of world religions, and the Cold War.

Belief and Counterinsurgency in the Philippines

Lansdale got his professional start in OSS's analytical wing, the Research and Analysis Branch.[13] Lansdale's work dealt primarily with the peoples, cultures, and customs in East Asia. He was tasked with identifying cultural pressure points so East Asians would act in ways conducive to US policy. By directing the appropriate combination of words and symbols at just the right psychological fissure, the reasoning went, one could unlock desired behaviors in the target audience.[14]

This helped explain Lansdale's professional interest in unorthodox subjects, like Japanese proverbs. Lansdale's idea was that once the proverbs were properly understood, they could be tactically inverted and directed against the Japanese themselves.[15] For example, the Japanese proverb "the biggest serpent has no terrors for the eagle" was rich with propaganda potential. Lansdale argued that Allied propaganda could make use of this saying by casting Japan as the serpent and United Nations air power as the eagle. The Japanese would find such a picture "startlingly pertinent," Lansdale wrote. Lansdale took this seriously, arguing that proverb-based warfare was uniquely suited to challenge the Japanese (who "love proverbs") since "their literature—and their daily conversation—are interlarded with them."[16] Foreshadowing his later work, Lansdale viewed understanding a culture's closely held values as a necessary precondition to manipulating it.

Well before Lansdale led Cold War counterinsurgency campaigns in Southeast Asia, he was already learning to think of human cultures as discrete, unchanging phenomena. This strategy promised an easier way to understand foreign cultures, since they could be reduced to essential qualities and manipulated accordingly. This approach appealed to an intelligence community that was rapidly trying to make sense of much of the world. Like OSS as a whole, however, Lansdale understood the US victory in World War II as a vindication of his strategies in particular. The limits of this assumption would be made plain in the following decades, when he would apply these intelligence strategies as a panacea to America's woes in Southeast Asia.

When World War II ended, Lansdale moved to the Philippines with army intelligence. In 1947, Lansdale received a captain's commission in the newly created US Air Force, which would serve as his primary cover for the rest of his intelligence career.[17] Lansdale's first few years in the Philippines transformed his career: he entered the country as a young, successful intelligence officer and left it with his name on the lips of presidents. In the Philippines, his mission was to help restore order in an important Southeast Asian ally. The country was in disarray after the Japanese occupation, and American leaders wanted strong ties between the two countries. Lansdale was tasked with rebuilding the Filipino intelligence services.

As he worked, Lansdale developed close relationships with many Filipino leaders. As would be the case in South Vietnam a few years later, Lansdale's interest in and affection for local cultures and customs endeared him to Filipino colleagues. It helped that Lansdale favored national independence across Southeast Asia, though this made him less popular with some of his Western colleagues. "I was first of all an anti-colonial, I'd made that very plain," he later explained.[18] This occasionally put Lansdale in a difficult position, since the interests of the people he worked with did not always square with US policy. The contradictory nature of his position would sometimes blind him to the limits of his effectiveness by collapsing distinctions between American goals and the goals of the people with whom he was working.

This tension became clear when Lansdale's work in the Philippines was disrupted by an insurgency known as the Hukbalahap rebellion. While the US government saw the "Huks" as a Communist threat, the situation was not clear-cut: many of the rebels were peasants motivated by what they saw as unjust government policies. When violence broke out, American leaders viewed the Huks as threatening many of the security advances they had made in the Philippines since the end of the war, and Lansdale was thrust into the role of counterinsurgency advisor.[19] The fighting was brutal, and Lansdale became personally invested in the outcome of the struggle. The Huk rebellion, he said later, was a "very, very tough time."[20]

Lansdale developed a close working relationship with the Filipino secretary of national defense, Ramon Magsaysay. During the rebellion, Lansdale spent a lot of time with Magsaysay in the Filipino backcountry, where Magsaysay quickly earned Lansdale's respect as a leader and soldier. Comrades in arms, the two men grew to refer to each other as "brothers."[21] Yet Lansdale was surprised to find that Magsaysay, despite being an intelligent and gifted leader, also believed in Filipino folklore. With more than a touch of incredulity, Lansdale jotted down his realization that Magsaysay was "superstitious," that he "believed in the ghosts and ghoulies of the provinces."[22] Lansdale would later recall how surprised he had been to learn that Magsaysay believed in—and greatly feared—one creature in particular: the *kapre*, a large black humanoid said to hide in the fields and trees of the Philippines at dusk.[23] The knowledge that even educated Filipino leaders feared such things served as a practical confirmation of Lansdale's wartime theories about "Asian" belief systems.

US officials in the Philippines had a long history of manipulating Filipino belief in the service of American empire.[24] American colonial officials in the early twentieth century came to the same racist conclusions Lansdale eventually would: Filipinos were particularly gullible, and their credulity meant they were easily manipulated.[25] While the previous generation of American colonial leaders used this as evidence that Filipinos were unready for self-government, Lansdale enlisted this credulity in the service of fighting for Filipino independence—at least, the independence of the Filipino government America preferred.

Knowing what the Filipinos feared—knowing what they believed in and what they did not—proved to be an important element in Lansdale's deployment of psychological warfare operations against the Huks. Lansdale eagerly collected information about local folklore and religious belief, thinking it would produce the best psychological weapons. The "Eye of God" technique, for example, was a favorite from Lansdale's bag of tricks. At night, Filipino government soldiers would slip into rebel-held areas and paint big human eyes on every available surface: on houses, on businesses, on fences and walls.[26] "The 'Eye of God' technique," Lansdale explained, "when properly used, makes the target soldier feel that he is the helpless victim of an all-seeing and all-powerful enemy."[27] Lansdale was convinced that making the government's power felt, even in unconventional and subtle ways, was key to swaying the population in Huk areas.

One particularly brutal example involved Filipino tales of bloodsucking humanoids said to haunt the jungles of the Philippines. Local soothsayers called it the *asuang* and said that it preyed only on the morally devious. Lansdale thought of the *asuang* as many Westerners, or Hollywood film fans, would: that the Filipinos must be talking about vampires. Sensing an opportunity, Lansdale had Filipino government soldiers capture Huk rebels. Lansdale then ordered the Huks to be pierced twice at the neck, hung upside down, and drained of blood before dumping their bodies in the streets of Huk-controlled towns. The message, at least in Lansdale's mind, was clear: Filipinos who supported Communist rebels should expect the *asuang* to come knocking in the middle of the night. Lansdale reported drop-offs in rebel activity in areas where the drained bodies were left on display.[28]

How effective this plan was with its Filipino targets—and if it was effective for the reasons Lansdale thought—is unclear. There would be practical reasons for the rebels to avoid areas where prisoners of war were tortured, regardless of any regional superstition. For his part, Lansdale thought it a roaring success, and he would lecture about the vampire operation in many future talks to US intelligence and special forces units. Yet Lansdale was often mum about other, less dramatic parts of the plan he pursued, such as arranging for money and goods to be sent to Huk soldiers who agreed to lay down their arms.[29] Lansdale attributed much of his success in the Philippines to belief-manipulation operations. As he would later teach it, "the vampire evidence was compelling."[30] Of course, there is no evidence that Lansdale himself believed in the *asuang*, but he recognized Filipino beliefs as meaningful in a context where the end goal was the stabilization of US influence in the Philippines.

Lansdale explained that the key to successfully manipulating action was to find the right "activating idea": something that acknowledged the peculiarities of a target culture while recognizing the essential oneness of all humanity. Furthermore, Lansdale thought psychological operations must also have some sort of positive end for them to be effective. A good psychological operator should use the activating idea to push people to be *for* something.[31] This is where religion came in handy. Lansdale's list of requirements meant that psychological operations had to be based on a very specific kind of idea: something encouraging that was both locally relevant yet universally applicable. Religion, as it was increasingly understood by many Americans in the 1950s, was a positive and universal element of human culture. Most popular studies of it at the time presumed that everyone had it, and it was good. Western notions of "religion" and Lansdale's psychological operation were a natural fit.

It was in the Philippines that Lansdale began systematizing his religious approach to include "world religions" beyond local indigenous beliefs. One major influence was the working relationship Lansdale developed with the

Chinese-Filipino financier Albino Sycip, then chairman of the Board of Directors of the China Banking Corporation of Manila. Lansdale recorded in his notes that he and Sycip shared many "intense" discussions about how morality was understood differently in Eastern and Western cultures, and what might be done to bridge those differences. Lansdale saw religion as an operational asset, a social Rosetta Stone capable of universal cultural translation. Sycip and Lansdale developed a series of world religion flash cards containing their "findings." The cards were a kind of world religion cheat sheet, with a variety of religious traditions reduced to a single "golden rule" modeled on Jesus Christ's message at the Sermon on the Mount to "do unto others as you would have them do unto you."[32] The cards contained a list of ten traditions, each with "their" religion's golden rule: Jesus, Buddha, Confucius, Judaism, Mahomet, Parsee, "Hindu," Brahmanism, Taoism, and Zoroastrianism, with each tradition expressing a universal human idea in a unique way. So, for example, if your conversation partner knew Lao-Tzu ("Regard your neighbor's gain as your own gain, and your neighbor's loss as your own loss") but not Jesus ("Love thy neighbor as thyself"), you could try meeting in the middle at, say, the Buddha ("Hurt not others in ways that you yourself would find hurtful"). Each "golden rule" was phrased differently but carried the same meaning.[33]

The cards were useful tools, according to Lansdale: he called them a "practical key for understanding between the people of East and West." He claimed to carry one of the cards with him whenever he traveled around Asia. The world religion cards were valuable because they would allow anti-Communists (who were, naturally, pro-religion) to identify themselves to one another regardless of any other communication barriers, Lansdale explained: "The first step is for a person to believe in something and then to recognize fellow believers when he meets them, even in foreign countries or of alien skin and languages."[34] Having identified each other through a translated golden rule, freedom-loving peoples could then bond over their shared trait of living *for* something (freedom) rather than *against* something (Communism).

Like many other Cold War intellectuals, Lansdale presumed that each religion had anti-Communism at its core simply by virtue of being a religion. Thus, identifying "believers" was crucial to building anti-Communist alliances. This might manifest outwardly in different ways (such as different golden rules), but it reflected an inward sameness that crossed religious boundaries. As a result, religion could serve as an easily identifiable—and endlessly translatable—marker of "the good guys" to American psychological warfare specialists working far from home. Lansdale also thought that using religion as a means of alliance-building worked especially well for Americans, since they were already, as a nation, spiritually adept. Lansdale explained that

> the best American psychological operators I have known have had a deep spiritual kinship with our unpaid Continental troops at Valley Forge, with the men on both sides in the Sunday morning woods at Shiloh, and, yes, with the "Thomasites" of this century, the teachers sent by the War Department to start free public schools throughout the Philippines, often at risk of life.[35]

Understanding "religion" allowed American operators to translate human meaning across not just space but *time*, accessing the religious resonances in their own past to better conduct psychological warfare in the present.

Before leaving the Philippines, Lansdale helped his friend Magsaysay—the Filipino defense secretary with whom Lansdale had fought against the Huks—in his campaign to be elected president of the Philippines. Lansdale tried his hand at election sloganeering, adapting his psychological operations to write popular get-out-the-vote tunes like the "Magsaysay Mambo."[36] He also helped in more concrete ways by arranging financial assistance from the CIA. This made Magsaysay impressive to a Filipino electorate interested primarily in US guarantees of peace and financial assistance.[37] Magsaysay won the presidency in 1953 and ended the Huk rebellion the following year.

The two men stayed close even after Lansdale returned to the United States. During one particularly trying period, Magsaysay repeatedly phoned Lansdale and asked him to return to the Philippines. Lansdale, demurring, explained that he could not just leave his job on a whim, but Magsaysay kept calling. "My dad was visiting me, at the time," Lansdale later recalled, "and he said, 'Who's that fellow who keeps calling every night?' And I said, 'Oh, some guy out in the Philippines.'"[38] But Magsaysay would not be denied: after a direct call from Magsaysay to President Eisenhower, Lansdale found himself on a plane bound for the Philippines. Magsaysay did not get much time to work with Lansdale, however. Shortly after Lansdale touched down in Manila, the Geneva Accords were finalized and Lansdale was rerouted to Saigon. The US government wanted him to reproduce the "Magsaysay Miracle" with Ngo Dinh Diem in South Vietnam. Secretary of State John Foster Dulles instructed Lansdale to simply "do what you did in the Philippines."[39] After Lansdale's seeming success in Vietnam working with the

Catholic South Vietnamese president Ngo Dinh Diem and the US Navy doctor Tom Dooley, he was recalled to the United States in 1957 and went to work at the Pentagon.

Thinking about Religion at the Pentagon

Lansdale's return to the States concluded seven years of working closely with the CIA. Though he was no longer working with the Agency directly, his new position allowed him to stay abreast of life in secret intelligence.[40] He would spend most of the rest of his active duty career in the Office of Special Operations, where he worked as a liaison between the CIA, the National Security Agency (NSA), the State Department, and the White House.[41]

Lansdale's ideas about religion and psychological warfare made him something of an oddity at the Pentagon. Lansdale's colleagues had trouble describing him. He wasn't quite a hawk, and he wasn't quite a dove: "more like an owl," one later reflected.[42] Admiral Felix Stump, a friend of both Lansdale and the Agency, was once asked what it was that Lansdale *did*, exactly. "Oh," Stump quipped, "he just goes around preaching the gospel of love."[43] Not everyone was a fan of Lansdale's work or his outsized personality. Richard Helms, a future director of central intelligence, dismissed Lansdale's reputation as a miracle worker and suggested that Lansdale's true gift was self-promotion.[44] While some of Lansdale's more harebrained schemes certainly colored his colleague's impressions, easy dismissals of Lansdale's work also reflected doubts about the strategic importance of religious beliefs and ideas in modern war.

Lansdale's focus on the cultural and individualistic aspects of counter-insurgency butted up against the rigorous number-crunching of the new secretary of defense, Robert McNamara. While both men were employed by the Defense Department in the early 1960s—indeed, McNamara ran it—they represented two different approaches to American defense policy. One of the Ford "Whiz Kids," McNamara put his faith in numbers and quantitative projections. He held fast to the idea that anything of importance could be measured, reflected in the later fetishizing of enemy body counts in the Vietnam War. Conversely, Lansdale thought that "small wars"—such as Vietnam was in 1961 when McNamara became secretary of defense— were ultimately about something much harder to measure: people and their beliefs.

In both substance and style, McNamara and Lansdale were wildly different. Lansdale briefed the secretary on his first day in office. Lansdale began by placing a muddy weapon straight from a Vietnamese battlefield on the secretary's mahogany desk. Pointing to the weapon, Lansdale argued there was something missing in American aid to Vietnam: a non-material factor for which US training programs did not account. Lansdale's most important advice for the new secretary was "the need for something of the spirit, something of their own that the Vietnamese could believe in and defend."[45] It was a dramatic way to begin a briefing. For McNamara, it was also the wrong way. "Somehow, I found him very hard to talk to," Lansdale later recalled.[46]

Even as he watched from DC, Lansdale remained invested in the Vietnamese struggle. He had the chance to visit Vietnam from time to time, and he did not like what he saw. After a 1961 visit, he wrote depressingly that "Vietnam has progressed faster in material things than it has spiritually. The people have more possessions but are starting to lose the will to protect their liberty."[47] Good US aid—the kind of aid that the South Vietnamese truly needed—was spiritual in nature: "the U.S has filled their bellies but has neglected their spirit," he explained.[48] Spiritual aid strengthened South Vietnamese soft power by teaching about democracy and modeling republican ideals. Without spiritual aid, Lansdale thought, American forces would be increasingly limited to a reliance on hard power, a devil's bargain that promised statistical victories while forfeiting meaningful progress. All the napalm in the world would not help the Americans throw the Viet Cong out of Vietnamese villages if the villagers preferred the Viet Cong, Lansdale thought.

Yet Lansdale's push to supply spiritual aid clashed with McNamara's relentless attempts to computerize the war's progress. Lansdale remembered reviewing a list of categories that McNamara had mapped out on graph paper—body count, enemy casualties, and so on—and explaining to the secretary that he had left off the most important factor.

[McNamara] said, "What is it?" I said, "Well, it's the human factor. You can put it down as the X factor." So, he wrote down in pencil, "X factor." He said, "What does it consist of?" I said, "What the people out on the battlefield really feel; which side they want to see win and which side they're for at the moment. That's the only way you're going to ever have this war decided." And he said, "Tell me how to put it in [the graph]?" I said, "I don't think any Americans out there at the moment can report this to you." He said, "Oh, well," and he got out his eraser to erase it.

The "X factor" recalled earlier ideas in the Western study of religion that presumed there was something essentially inaccessible or ineffable about human religious activity.[49] In any case, Lansdale eventually came up with a way to quantify the "X factor" in order to please his boss. He devised a complicated system in which American soldiers would note how many children were present in each village, how many of the children were smiling, and to what extent they were smiling. Lansdale thought it a poor substitute for someone on the ground, *feeling* their way through local populations—but at least it could be quantified. This was the mistake the French made in Indo-China, according to Lansdale: not seeing the Vietnamese as real people.[50] He pleaded with McNamara to stop quantifying the war, telling the secretary that "You're going to fool yourself if you get all of these figures added up because they won't tell you how we're doing in this war."[51] Lansdale laughed about the incident years later, recalling how afterward McNamara "asked me to please not bother him anymore."[52] By late 1961, McNamara reined in Lansdale's involvement in Vietnamese policy.[53]

Looking for other places to get involved, Lansdale turned his attention to Latin America. The timing was ideal. President Kennedy was still smarting from the Bay of Pigs debacle, and he wanted to do something about it. Kennedy's interest in covert operations and special forces—as well as his lingering suspicion that the military brass had misled him on Cuba—made Lansdale an alluring option to lead the president's new task force. In what became known as Operation Mongoose, Lansdale developed plans to weaken and eventually overthrow the government of Fidel Castro. Once the rebellion was underway, Lansdale anticipated using Cuban Catholics to help lead the actual movement, as their religiosity made them particularly resilient to Communism's wiles. Lansdale built a tight timetable, with "open revolt and overthrow of the Communist regime" optimistically scheduled for October 1962.

Buried in a footnote in the US Senate's *Alleged Assassination Reports Involving Foreign Leaders* (1975) is one of the more audacious plans of Lansdale's career, in which he planned to use Christian eschatology to manipulate Cuban opposition to Castro. More simply, he wanted the CIA to simulate the Second Coming of Jesus Christ in Cuba. Under oath, CIA officer Thomas Parrott would later testify about the plan:

> I'll give you one example of Lansdale's perspicacity. He had a wonderful plan for getting rid of Castro. This plan consisted of spreading the word that the Second Coming of Christ was imminent and that Christ was against Castro (who) was anti-Christ. And you would spread this word around Cuba, and

then on whatever date it was, that there would be a manifestation of this thing. And at that time—this is absolutely true—and at that time just over the horizon there would be an American submarine which would surface off of Cuba and send up starshells. And this would be the manifestation of the Second Coming and Castro would be overthrown. Well, some wag called this operation—and somebody dubbed this—Elimination by Illumination.[54]

Harnessing people's religious beliefs to effect regime change might have been standard operating procedure for Lansdale, but many of his colleagues saw it as ridiculous. While the plan was never put into action, its publication as part of the Church Committee hearings in the mid-1970s caused substantial embarrassment. Lansdale wrote a curt letter to Senator Frank Church, chairman of the committee, in which he flatly denied involvement in any part of the plan.[55] While there is evidence that Lansdale may have been more involved than he acknowledged, it is also plausible that the story was included in the report as a bit of score-settling between old bureaucratic rivals.[56] Still, "Elimination by Illumination" differs from Lansdale's other operations in scale rather than scope. The management of Tom Dooley's Catholicism, Filipino "vampires," and simulated visits from Jesus all testify to Lansdale's firm understanding that belief motivated action.[57] Belief, properly stimulated, was a powerful thing: no less so in Havana than in Saigon.

Religious Studies and Counterinsurgency in Vietnam

Lansdale formally retired in 1963, but he could not retire his interest in Vietnam. He had been too connected to it for too long. Meanwhile, the situation in South Vietnam continued to deteriorate. Pressed for options, President Johnson asked Lansdale to come out of retirement and return to Saigon in 1965. Even after his retirement, Lansdale's name had such a strong "CIA" connotation that the State Department protested the appointment.[58] Nevertheless, Lansdale returned to South Vietnam as special assistant to the new ambassador, Henry Cabot Lodge Jr., from 1965 to 1968.[59]

Lansdale's return to Vietnam in the late 1960s saw him try to implement many of his old ideas about the importance of integrating Vietnamese culture into the war. Chief among these ideas was Lansdale's renewed interest in Vietnamese soothsaying, or fortune-telling. Lansdale had long been interested in the abundance of "prophets, astrologers, wizards, spiritualists, palmists, phrenologists, necromancers, geomancers, numerologists" and other "soothsayers" that were popular among both his friends and enemies in Vietnam.[60] Lansdale approached Vietnamese soothsaying as a possible psychological warfare asset. Much as he used Tom Dooley to sell "Vietnam" to Americans, he could use soothsaying to sell "Vietnam" to the Vietnamese. Since many Vietnamese put stock in the fortune-teller's predictions, Lansdale thought the United States would benefit if it could effectively influence the prophecies. "Have you ever wondered," Lansdale wrote to the ambassador, "what the soothsayers were advising the Vietnamese to whom you were giving your own pearls of wisdom?"[61] Lansdale did, and he made it his mission to find out.

The first step was to compile a list of influential Vietnamese soothsayers and astrologists. Lansdale cross-referenced each soothsayer with the Vietnamese officials they were known to advise as well as the types of prophecies they provided. The idea was to locate soothsayers who were not predicting sufficiently cheery results for America's efforts in Vietnam and get them to change their tune. "Most soothsayers are vulnerable to certain influences," Lansdale wrote to the ambassador, and he could think of "some folks" who "deserve a bit of influencing."[62] After doing some reconnaissance with local soothsayers, one of Lansdale's Vietnamese associates—who had previously disclaimed any belief in fortune-telling since he was "too good a Christian"—began to give the prophecies more credit. He tried to convince Lansdale to change his headquarters in Saigon to a location more pleasing to his soothsayer's sense of geomancy. ("I gave him a firm no," Lansdale told the ambassador, because he "hardly wanted to discommode the many secret agents who had found by now some really comfortable places to keep my house under constant surveillance for a whole host of suspicious Vietnamese masters."[63]) Though Lansdale made light of it, this was exactly the type of information he was interested in acquiring: where the Vietnamese believed auspicious sites for American military bases might be, or improving the internal geomantic layout of the embassy to instill confidence in Vietnamese visitors. Lansdale argued that US planners should organize new construction projects around dates and times that Vietnamese viewed as "superstitious." As part of his investigation into Confucian numerology (what he sometimes referred to as "old Chinese lore"), Lansdale sent a memo to Ambassador Bunker in which he listed dates to avoid in 1968.[64]

Lansdale's interest in soothsaying led him to investigate the origins of fortune-telling in Vietnamese culture. In particular, Lansdale was intrigued by the presence of the numbers three and five, and how they seemed to show up repeatedly in various Vietnamese beliefs and prophecies. As Lansdale dove into research on the Buddha, Mencius, Confucius, and Lao-Tzu, he began making wide-ranging descriptions of foreign religious cultures, similar in scope to early scholars of world religions. Lansdale assumed that the name of the thing—the text—would be fixed, as would its importance. Yet separating Buddhist, Confucian, and Taoist ideas into distinct categories was (and remains) a difficult task, in no small part because those traditions' practitioners have not always understood them as distinct in the way presumed by Western observers. Lansdale's confusion grew as he tried to distill Vietnamese "folk" belief into what he assumed was its constituent parts: Buddhism, Confucianism, and Taoism. For example, he noted in his memos that "threes" showed up in many places in these religions, and he endeavored to list every example he could find. The result reads like a disorganized world religions textbook. There were the Taoist "three principles" ("essence, breath, spirit"), the Taoist "three primordial powers" ("heaven, earth, water"), the Buddhist "3-fold division of the Universe" ("desire, form, formlessness"), and so forth. Anticipating critics who would dismiss these findings as useless, Lansdale cautioned that the Communists were already well aware of the power of "threes" and "fives" in Asian religions and were busy reformulating Communist precepts according to this numerology. So, for example, Lansdale noted how Chinese Communists talked about the "3 good things for youth: work, study, health" and the "3 assessments: of class origin, of fulfillment of duty, of fighting spirit."[65] Lansdale saw Communist adaptation of Confucian numerology as both clever and threatening, and he advised American leaders to that effect.[66]

Lansdale's Orientalist views also played a role in his attraction to indigenous Vietnamese traditions like soothsaying. Lansdale understood Asians—and particularly Vietnamese—as having a kind of social superpower for sensing what other people think of them, especially Westerners. He occasionally referred to this as "Asian Radar."[67] Lansdale attributed this to Confucian influence, and wrote memos outlining the key points of Confucianism for his fellow Americans. Lansdale encouraged American operatives in the field to prepare for what he called the "empty rituals" of Confucian social life—small talk, indirectly approaching the desired topic of discussion, teatime after business is conducted, and so on.[68]

As the war continued, Lansdale's interest in "applied" religious studies was reflected in other US government publications. One 1966 Civil Affairs Group publication, "Indigenous Religious Beliefs and Practices of Vietnam," argued that Americans needed to familiarize themselves with all forms of religion in Vietnam, however foreign they seemed. This was important not least because, the report claimed, the Communists were beginning to use false religion to subvert true religion in Southeast Asia.

Citing an academic research paper from the 1965 conference of the International Association for the History of Religions (IAHR), the report detailed how Communist propagandists were mastering the art of taking religious ideas and refashioning them to support Communist political goals. One example already occurring in Southeast Asia, it claimed, was how Communists were studying "ancient Burmese writings" and using this knowledge to "associate the temporal concept of Nirvana with the socialist state they are proposing."[69] Thus it was important to understand anything the Vietnamese thought of as religious, and the report had distinct sections on things like "lights," "flowers," "drums," "robes," and "lotus blossoms."

Of course, such one-for-one translations overlooked larger problems of cultural translation plaguing American understanding of Vietnamese religious practices. Even Lansdale, an official unusually attentive to life "on the ground," often understood religious practices to be deterministic, linking belief and action in an ironclad causal relationship. The issue was that what counted as "religious"—as documents like the Civil Affairs Group's publication made clear—was up for debate. The Vietnamese did not have a native category of "religion" equivalent to what the Americans meant by the term: a roped-off area of cultural life presumed to be devoid of political concerns while also being of the utmost cosmological importance.

US government attention to Vietnamese "folk" religion continued into 1967 when the Chaplaincy Corps released *The Religions of South Vietnam in Faith and Fact*, a handbook produced by the US Navy's Southeast Asia Religious Project. While America's buildup in Vietnam continued, military planners discovered that existing research on Vietnamese religious and social traditions in the West was "insufficient" and sought to remedy it. Managed by the navy's chief of chaplains, *The Religions of South Vietnam in Faith and Fact* was the product of this research. The authors explained that

> Americans cannot really understand the Vietnamese, nor work harmoniously with them, without an awareness of these religious beliefs and the ways in which they affect everyday attitudes and practices. Only when their seemingly strange and puzzling behavior is seen as reasonable and logical in its environmental context can it be fully appreciated.[70]

These publications were part of a larger change in approaching the war, in which the national security community leaned on academic specialists to offer alternative paths forward in the Vietnam War.[71]

Most importantly, the book argued that a lack of Vietnamese religious information could lead to an increase in American casualties. The introduction listed the values of increased cultural knowledge, allowing for greater respect of the Vietnamese among US military personnel in-country. The book itself had sections on Animism, Vietnamese Taoism, Confucianism in Vietnam, Hinduism in Vietnam, Buddhism in Vietnam, Islam, Roman Catholicism in Vietnam, Protestantism, Cao Dai, Hoa Hao, and finally a curiously titled chapter on "Religion in Everyday Life." This latter section contained the classificatory jetsam that researchers could not place anywhere else, including things like astrologers, fragrances, ancestor worship, and "women." This division echoed many of the problems of the world religions textbooks it tried to emulate. The other chapters on Islam, Buddhism, and Christianity did not exist in "everyday life," for example, seemingly because those systems made sufficient sense that their impact did not have to be explained.[72] While the book certainly pushed for more awareness than had previously existed, these types of oversights risked undercutting the book's efficacy by still placing indigenous Vietnamese traditions as self-evidently strange and exotic.

In both its promise and its problems, this work echoed Lansdale's conviction that the religious approach should be central to American counterinsurgency plans. He had seen firsthand how intra-Vietnamese propaganda rooted its claims in those who could see the future, for example, or who had access to Confucian and Taoist deities. Lansdale became convinced of its value, especially in rural areas of Vietnam where he understood "superstition and animistic belief" to still play a decisive role in shaping people's behavior.[73] Yet for all of Lansdale's interest in Vietnamese religion—and his determined, if flawed, efforts to understand its particularities apart from stock Oriental generalities—he still struggled to understand that the big questions about Vietnamese freedom (like the protests of the Buddhists against the US government) were not locked up in numerological puzzles requiring consultations with the *I Ching*, but were instead political and social grievances with less arcane causes. Lansdale once became disheartened when, sifting through various soothsayers' work, he could not find a single prophecy that cast American involvement in Vietnam in a positive light. At long last, he was relieved to find a happier prediction and shared it with the ambassador: "Americans will stay in South Viet-Nam, in spite of everything," it read, "for a longer period than expected."[74]

The World Religions Paradigm and the Cold War

Reimagining Lansdale as a Cold War intellectual, rather than solely as a spy or psychological warfare specialist, helps make sense of his interest in the religious approach. For Lansdale, this was a religious knowledge arms race in which people's beliefs were the battlefield. Lansdale recognized that knowledge of your opponent's beliefs, and the ability to manipulate them, could bring hard power to bear just as much as soft power. As he explained during a lecture to a special warfare class, "Just remember this. Communist guerrillas hide among the people. If you win the people over to your side, the Communist guerrillas have no place to hide. With no place to hide, you can find them. Then, as military men, fix them . . . finish them!"[75] If manipulating belief did not help you persuade someone, it could help you kill them.

Lansdale's interests corresponded with a research area in the burgeoning academic field of religious studies. Scholars of religious studies described a unified system for the study of world religions, in what became known as the "world religions paradigm" (WRP).[76] This idea held that while religious traditions displayed external differences, they shared an essence that made them functionally similar. The upside of this approach for academic researchers was the same as it was for Lansdale: it made it possible to organize an overwhelming amount of diverse human ideas and practices into easily classifiable terms.[77] While the idea may seem uncontroversial and even banal today, that is only because the idea has been so successful. While academic and popular authors increasingly critiqued this framework in the late twentieth and early twenty-first centuries, the WRP has become foundational for the modern academic study of religion as it is practiced across the United States and much of the Western world.[78]

Lansdale was no academic, but his philosophy of national security was informed by these new ideas about world religions as they entered American popular culture. The year before Lansdale and the CIA helped arrange publication for Tom Dooley's *Deliver Us from Evil* (1956), for example, the editors of *LIFE* published a major study of world religions for American audiences. Glossy and eye-catching, the *LIFE* series made clear that each tradition was fundamentally equal, even if some were more exotic than others.[79] There were many cultural factors encouraging this idea, not least of which was growing religious pluralism in the United States after World War II. The idea of a pantheon of world religions—theologically equal and equally deserving of First Amendment protections—drew strength from this increased religious pluralism. Lansdale's career coincided with new American approaches to managing "religion" across its global influence, and Lansdale is important precisely because he generated useful religious data for the American state.

Many of Lansdale's "discoveries" echoed the academic study of world religions and the WRP. Lansdale was already familiar with applying a form of religious studies through his development of the "golden rule" psychological operations cards in the Philippines. Listing each religion's "golden rule"—indeed, presupposing that each religious tradition *had* a golden rule—compressed each tradition into a one-sentence Christian theological mold. While the idea of "world religions" proved popular (and remains so), by the early 1960s critics of the idea noted how equating global religious traditions as different versions of the same thing rested on dubious assumptions.[80] Lansdale's work in the Philippines is part of a larger intellectual trajectory that understood European and Christian ideas as foundational for making sense of all human experience, one that sacrificed analytical complexity for a neat classification system. While this has its own problems in the academy, it posed unique problems for people like Lansdale who wished to use it to anticipate and control human behavior. If the WRP's sweeping generalizations could not be trusted, this promised challenges for those like Lansdale who based their operations on its assumptions.[81]

An intelligence officer had no use for a "universal history" if it did not add up to useful information about a target area. Lansdale is an important figure through whom to trace the development of world religions discourse precisely because he was professionally predisposed to recognize the danger of overgeneralizing local information. In theory, this provided a real-world "check" on his work that separated Lansdale from armchair theorists. After all, it was one thing to presume that religion functioned in similar ways across national boundaries but quite another to presume that propaganda appeals in the Philippines would work the same as they would in Vietnam. At times Lansdale was sensitive to this concern. Lansdale's career makes clear his understanding of the need for local, relevant knowledge. No detail was too small or seemingly insignificant: for example, Lansdale once chronicled how Vietnamese understood colors. Colors "meant" certain things to the Vietnamese, he noted: blue ("hope, peace, youth"), pink ("happiness"), and purple ("death").[82] This came in handy when Lansdale advised President Diem to print Vietnamese election ballots in particular colors, in the hope that Vietnamese voters would be drawn to Diem's party by the color of its ballots.[83]

For guidance in making these decisions, Lansdale trusted his sense of "feeling" rather than any fancy academic work. In other words, he went with his gut. Once one could "feel" their way around a foreign belief system or culture, it rewarded the practitioner with practical benefits. For example, Lansdale bragged about feeling his way into important friendships and alliances. "I really don't speak foreign languages. A few words and phrases only," he explained. "On substantive matters, I use an interpreter. Mostly, it was a matter of deep empathy that communicated itself, not requiring words."[84] Authentic knowledge about foreign religions came only from firsthand experience, according to Lansdale. He was dismissive of experts on Asian culture who did not share meals with Asians, or sleep at night in Asian homes.[85] Even Lansdale's methodology was one recognizable in the historical development of religious studies. Intelligence offices like Lansdale practiced "lived religion" before it became popular in the ivory tower.

Yet Lansdale's approach to "feeling" makes clear that while he was invested in the successes of programs built on recognizing cultural differences, he too fell into the universalizing trap highlighted by Masuzawa.[86] While scholars of religion developed a variety of theoretical explanations for why religion was a universal human experience, Lansdale's answer was simple: religion was Communism's opposite, and Communism was inhuman. Any "true American," according to Lansdale, would thus recognize the validity of all the world's religious traditions:

> The Free World does not claim that the specific European tradition of Graeco-Latin humanism, fused as it has been with Judaeo-Christianity, is the only pattern for the formation of Man. It sees in the worldwide variety of spiritual and ethical disciplines—including some, like Confucianism, which are now being perverted by Communism—the embodiment of the truth expressed by Christ, "In my Father's house there are many mansions." But it cannot reconcile itself with the Orwellian doctrine that rampant materialism can issue in the true spiritual dignity of Man.[87]

However important these belief systems were, they were still wrapped up within a predominantly Christian perspective. The reason *for* these belief systems' importance lay in a Christian understanding of the importance of toleration, recasting religions like Confucianism as one of the Christian God's "many mansions."

It is not coincidental, then, that Lansdale's approach reflected many of the same shortcomings as the academic study of religion. Lansdale's interest in world religions also reinforced an overtly racist attitude toward Asians, for one: "Asians," as a coherent category of people, could be analyzed and studied just as their beliefs were. Lansdale understood both the Asian (as individual) and the Asian's belief (as idea) to be mechanical, following certain predictable routines that made it easier to manipulate once one understood its inner workings. As Lansdale would explain to Ambassador Bunker after the latter arrived in South Vietnam:

As an aside, it is worth remembering that an Asian usually is "situation centered" and never separates himself from his surroundings. He does not look inward to his conscience, as we do, but outward to the possible effect of his actions on his environment. In this respect, he is like an actor, continually "on," keenly conscious of performing for an audience.[88]

Lansdale was far from the only member of the national security community to essentialize Asian thought and behavior. Director of Central Intelligence Richard Helms, who would oversee the CIA during the height of American combat operations in Vietnam, also thought in terms of the world religions paradigm but did so in a markedly less sympathetic way than Lansdale. When asked about Thich Quang Duc, the Vietnamese Buddhist monk who self-immolated at a Saigon intersection in June 1963, Helms was exasperated at how Americans had foolishly assumed that the monk was protesting the US action in Vietnam:

> Americans are so untutored in the cultures, religions, and social manifestations of so many foreign peoples, that we make a lot of mistakes, and this was one of those mistakes. That if we had really understood about the Buddhists, and all this business of burning themselves, etc., etc., we would have taken it far less seriously than [President John F.] Kennedy and [Assistant Secretary of State W. Averell] Harriman seemed to think. I mean, after all, Buddhist monks did things like this. It wasn't all that important.[89]

For Helms, a rudimentary understanding of Buddhism provided a means by which Buddhist critiques of US power could be dismissed out of hand simply because they were religious: "Buddhist monks did things like this." In so doing, Helms echoed a long-practiced pattern in the study of religion in which seemingly aberrant behavior could be explained as irrational or illogical simply by being labeled as religious. This was part of a broader shift in which the national security state drew on academic expertise in the field of religious studies. This relationship would continue developing during the Cold War in increasingly formal ways, as when the CIA visited the annual conferences of the International Association for the History of Religions (IAHR).[90]

While the field of religious studies did not see government intervention on the scale of other academic fields like anthropology or international relations, the academic study of religion—and particularly the study of world religions—was shaped by the Cold War in important ways.[91] Public funding sources like the National Defense Fellowships (as part of the federal government's National Defense Education Act) and private institutions like the Danforth and Ford Foundations encouraged growth in humanities departments, including early religious studies, to develop both strategic knowledge and contribute to public morality.[92] Histories of various academic fields have noted how even popular methodologies of the period mirrored earlier imperial practices and discourses.[93] National security intellectuals like Lansdale were already doing work quite similar to religious studies because of "religion's" perceived benefits to American culture during the Cold War—conclusions that were themselves reinforced by government-funded academic work.

Part of the growth in religious studies—whether accomplished in the academy or the Agency—is rooted in the political atmosphere of the Cold War's anti-Communist crusade.[94] Jacob Neusner, one of the most prominent and productive American scholars of religion, noted the newfound importance of religious studies after World War II because of the discipline's value in US foreign policy. The study of religion, Neusner explained, was useful because

> We had to make sense of other people's nonsense. The study of religion, formerly centered (where it flourished at all) on the truth or falsity of religious beliefs, on the one side, and the description by native believers of their personal beliefs, on the other, now began to ask the questions of social description and cultural analysis that now preoccupied the country.[95]

Indeed, the Supreme Court case that is widely credited with expanding the secular instruction of religion in public education, *Abington School District v. Schempp* (1963), struck down state-sponsored Bible reading in schools while lifting up the further study of the Bible and "comparative religion" as an academic good in and of itself.[96] While *Schempp* is often understood as part of an uplifting story of progress and the growth of American religious freedom, it should not be forgotten that the Court reached this conclusion at the height of the Cold War, hearing arguments just a few months after the Cuban Missile Crisis.[97] These challenges were likely what Neusner had in mind when he explained that "What now was needed was the research, translated into teaching, to make the country great and strong: atomic bombs of ideas which would win the Cold War."[98]

Neusner was not alone in seeing religious studies' applicability to national security. In the first edition of his best-selling *The Religions of Man* (1958), Huston Smith—arguably the twentieth century's most popular proponent of the world religions paradigm—described the US military's interest in religious information:

> Recently I was taxied by bomber to Air Command and Staff College at the Maxwell Air Force Base outside Montgomery, Alabama, to lecture to a thousand selected officers on the religions of other peoples. I have never had students more eager to learn. What was their motivation? Individually I am sure it went beyond this in many cases, but as a unit they were concerned because someday they were likely to be dealing with the people they were studying as allies, antagonists, or subjects of military occupation. Under such circumstances it would be crucial for them to predict their behavior, conquer them if worse came to worst, and control them during the aftermath of reconstruction.[99]

Huston Smith is clear that the world religions paradigm, as a kind of applied religious studies, lent itself to imperial languages of control.[100] Smith argued that learning about foreign religions was "one reason for coming to know people. It may be a necessary reason; certainly we have no right to disdain it as long as we ask the military to do the job we set before it."[101] Both Smith and Lansdale saw studying world religions as valuable because of that knowledge's geopolitical value. To see people like Huston Smith or Jacob Neusner as engaged in religious studies, but not people like Edward Lansdale or institutions like the CIA, misses much of the development of the religious approach and the WRP after World War II.

An Unshakable Confidence in America

If religion was an asset in counterinsurgency programs—and religious belief was understood by most American Christians to be ultimately individualistic—then it made sense that Lansdale focused on the individual as the primary target of counterinsurgency. In the early 1950s, his work developing Tom Dooley's Catholicism for public consumption drew strength from the rise of "Tri-Faith America." Lansdale's plans dealing with "foreign" or "world" religions in the 1960s followed major changes in domestic American life, such as the 1965 Immigration Act that increased the population of non-Christian religious groups in the United States. Lansdale's career is the national security parallel to those changes, reflecting a shift from the religious approach rooted in Tri-Faith America to a national security culture that was informed by the awareness and study of world religions. For those in the intelligence community interested in the religious approach, Tri-Faith America might have been a necessary ingredient in winning World War II, but the study of world religions was a necessary ingredient in winning the peace that followed. "The old formula for successful counterinsurgency used to be 10 troops for every guerilla," one American operator explained in 1967, but "now the formula is ten anthropologists for each guerilla."[102]

For intelligence officers like Lansdale, then, the battle for Vietnam was never only about Vietnam. It was never just about the Philippines, or even Asia. These battles were, instead, tests of American ideas in a world riven with false prophets and false prophecies. "The World of Freedom is an ecclesia," he wrote, and

> It stands opposed to another church which is unique in history because it is the embodiment of a "secular religion." Communism is impelled by a false materialist faith, but it is a faith that "moves mountains," even as it poisons the air and the waters and the souls of men. The church militant of Freedom must be visible.[103]

To be sure, the battle itself was not a foregone conclusion — Lansdale fought hard in Vietnam and elsewhere, taking nothing for granted — but he thought American ideas of progress would prove irresistible, even to its critics, once Americans had properly made their case. It was not supposed to be possible for America to lose in Vietnam, as it did in 1975.

After Saigon fell, Lansdale and his fellow church militant led a kind of ideological government-in-exile. As they re-evaluated this position after the war, they forged a creative compromise in which the defeat of South Vietnam was a bump on the road to fulfilling freedom's promise. They argued that by linking American religion to religious traditions around the world, American soldiers, diplomats, and spies left a noble legacy throughout the Cold War. In 1981, years after the vampire attacks, world religion flash cards, Diem's assassination, and the fall of Saigon, Lansdale found himself trying to explain this to a skeptical interviewer. "A lot of spiritual values are still there, even though we didn't work at it," Lansdale said about Vietnam. "We lived a lot of our ideals over there."[104]

It may seem odd to posit a sometime-CIA asset and psychological warfare specialist as a key figure in twentieth-century American religious history. Lansdale was not a missionary or member of the clergy. He did not claim for himself the title of prophet. He did not spend a single day working in a university. His own personal engagement with organized religion was brief and fleeting.[105] In much the same way that William Donovan's career took place alongside changing relations with Catholicism, Edward Lansdale's career coincided with new American approaches to managing the world's religions. Lansdale's ideas are an early example of what Elizabeth Shakman Hurd terms "expert religion," a kind of religious expertise that is notable for being neither fully in power nor fully interested in the everyday concerns of those individuals who understand themselves as members of a religious community. It is, instead, religious knowledge created "by those who generate 'policy-relevant' knowledge about religion in various contexts."[106] It is this confidence in expert knowledge—particularly in the knowledge about other peoples and their beliefs—that profoundly influenced Lansdale's religious approach to counterinsurgency during the Cold War.

Lansdale's career coincided with the religious approach's shifting interest from Tri-Faith concerns—modeled on an understanding of religious dynamics within the United States—to one in which the full variety of world religions could plausibly be encountered by US forces or become relevant to US interests. When the United States asserted the *Pax Americana* after World War II, it ensured that specialists in the manipulation of belief, religion, and the human mind would be required. Not entirely coincidentally, Lansdale's interest in global religious systems coincided with the growing study of world religions across American universities and popular culture. For Lansdale, religious belief and one's actions were causally related, and by understanding the one, you could successfully manipulate the other. Edward Lansdale saw the national security value of religion and, drawing on the growing discourse of world religions, tried to capitalize on it.

It was no coincidence that Lansdale was confident in both America's appeal to the world and religion's universality. These assumptions bled into one another, rooted in a certainty about the march of history, about what was modern and what was not. As the CIA drew on the world religions paradigm to explain the world around it, the Agency opened itself to the same weaknesses of the paradigm: rendering foreign cultures understandable only through the terms of your own. The weakness of this religious approach was not immediately evident to either Landale or academic researchers, though it would soon surface dramatically in Iran.

Chapter Seven
Iran and Revolutionary Thinking

> ... The forerunner of the Ayatollah Khomeini [was] the Buddhist bonzes that
> burned themselves. Because I think that's an exact forerunner, total rejection of
> the changes going on, modernization, an idealistic return to some religious base
> which, if you ever talk to any of these people you really see that it's all words and
> no content. I mean, very, very strange. Then the effect, however, of the Buddhist
> thing — again, I'm a little contentious about this because I believe that the Bud-
> dhist revolt, which blew up in June of 1963, had its major impact not in Vietnam
> but in the United States.
> Former Director of Central Intelligence William Colby (1981)[1]

A decade after 1979's Iranian Revolution, Richard Helms — who had served
as both director of central intelligence and US ambassador to Iran — made
a remarkable comment. "We don't understand Islam," Helms explained in
an interview, "we don't know anything about it."

> It's idiotic the way Americans react. The other day somebody was saying to
> me, "Were you surprised at that extraordinary outpouring at Khomeini's
> funeral?" And I said, "Not at all, if you know anything about Shiism, if you
> know that that's the kind of religion it is." So, we've got a lot better educa-
> tional process to do in our Government departments if we're going to really
> run a sensitive and sensible foreign policy.[2]

Helms argued that Americans failed to understand Shiism because they
did not realize it was essentially one thing: an unchanging, easily identified tradition. Rather than recognizing religious traditions as complex social
organizations with any number of internal differences, Helms understood
religions to be free-floating *sui generis* systems. Echoing long-standing
assumptions in the Western study of religion and the world religions paradigm (WRP), Helms and other American intelligence officers based their
analysis on Christocentric ideas of religion, politics, and society. From this

perspective, it was not possible to interpret the Revolution as part of a contest for authority within Shiism, or as a theological conflict about who gets to speak authoritatively in government, and why.

Helms was not alone. Among American political and intelligence leaders, the takeaway about Shiism seemed to be that the Iranian Revolution was actually evidence in favor of the Cold War thesis that Islam functioned as a social support for the status quo, since in this view the Iranian Revolution was the exception that proved the rule. One measure of how unexpected the Iranian Revolution was for the American intelligence community is the degree to which, even in the decades following the Revolution, there remained widespread disagreement about what went wrong and why. In this, the CIA was not alone: failed prophecies have long been sore spots for prophets.

The Iranian Revolution represented a major interpretive challenge for the religious approach to intelligence. After more than a year of civil unrest and mass demonstrations, the US-backed shah of Iran Mohammad Reza Pahlavi fled the country. Ayatollah Ruhollah Khomeini soon filled this power vacuum, overseeing the country's transformation into the Islamic Republic of Iran with himself as its new supreme leader who was sharply critical of the United States. Widespread Western assumptions about secularism, modernism, and the trajectory of "religion" in the modern world influenced the CIA's understanding of the Revolution. Certainty in the demise of religious power and confidence in the unity of so-called "world religions" guided the CIA's strategy toward religious movements around the world. While these assumptions were certainly not unique to intelligence officers, the CIA's teleological confidence—a confidence in where the world was going and what it would look like when it arrived—shaped the US response to international religious actors. These assumptions, crafted in and commonplace in the West, had for decades prepared analysts to disregard the prospect of religion as a serious challenge to US interests.

In the religious approach to intelligence, religious individuals, ideas, and institutions were largely assumed to be anti-Communist and pro-US by default. By the mid-twentieth century, much of Western scholarship agreed, deeming religion naturally anti-Communist. Equipped with this intellectual framework, the CIA underestimated the complex motivations of Iranian Muslim actors during the Iranian Revolution because they were "religious." Before Ayatollah Khomeini became the face of the Iranian Revolution, US observers struggled to imagine a coordinated effort by religious actors to overthrow the shah. Instead, they presumed that any such effort would be irreligious—and thus, by definition, would have been organized by the United States' atheist foes in the Kremlin.

Recasting this intelligence debacle through the lens of the CIA's early Cold War relationship with Islam and Muslims, as well as the broader religious approach to intelligence pursued since World War II, makes clear that CIA assumptions about the universal nature of religion occasionally prioritized collecting religious information over interpreting it. Intelligence officers assumed that Islam—which struck them as foreign yet more understandable than other world religions like Buddhism or Confucianism—functioned like Christianity, since both were monotheistic, Abrahamic traditions. These assumptions about religion and Islam were also widely shared in American popular and academic culture, which in turn helped confirm pre-existing assumptions about the accuracy of intelligence regarding religion's place in the modern world.

Reliant upon an overly simplistic understanding of Islam, CIA analyses encouraged a secular analytical hubris that did not fully account for the history, context, or intentions of Muslim actors. Focusing on whether something was "religious" or "political" blinded analysts to complicated intelligence about religion which, in turn, made them unable to anticipate actors like Iran's Ayatollah Khomeini. Since the US government evaluated religious practices through a Cold War prism of national security, it was difficult for these same analysts to counter religious movements—which were, presumably, automatically in line with US interests. American understandings of Islam during the early Cold War shed light on the increasingly central role that Islam played in US conceptions of its own national security.

For many Americans, the memory of US-Iran relations begins with the hostage crisis in 1979. They do not remember Iran as the site of struggles between the great powers during World War II, nor the American and British coup against the democratically elected Iranian government of Mohammad Mossadeq in 1953. They do not remember American training and support for SAVAK, the shah's brutal secret police.[3] This popular memory is itself a measure of how antiquated Western ideas about Islam and Muslims were predisposed to see events in Iran as evidence of Islam's dramatic re-emergence in the modern secular world. The history of US-Iran relations, and of how the United States sought to understand Iran and Iranian Muslims, is part of the larger story of how the US intelligence community sought to understand the "Muslim World." To collapse a 1,400-year-old tradition that crossed ethnicities, languages, and cultures into a cohesive and easily analyzed whole required a certain amount of analytical hubris.[4]

Yet just as OSS saw the "Muslim World" in World War II as an ancient and unchanging monolith, American postwar culture reinforced this perception through a variety of pop culture portrayals and academic studies. This terminology contributed to the idea of an essential Islam that informed US intelligence work before 1979.

Iran was a keystone of this worldview. It was part of the US effort to balance support for both Saudi Arabia and Israel, navigating between ultraconservative Islam and Jewish self-determination. If Iran fell apart, National Security Advisor Zbigniew Brzezinski warned President Carter in 1978, it "would be the most massive American defeat since the beginning of the Cold War, overshadowing in its real consequences the setback in Vietnam."[5] Iran was the geopolitical reminder that what Western analysts understood as the shackles of the past—superstition, theocracy, backward thinking—could be overcome through a disciplined, secular, technocratic government, even in the "Third World." Ironically, Khomeini came to power explicitly rejecting this argument (and in a published book, no less).[6]

Just as US intelligence identified Islam as an ally in World War II, Islam was again viewed favorably in the early Cold War as an anti-Communist asset.[7] Yet the intelligence community presumed Islam was resistant to Communism in part because they viewed Islam as backward and ancient. Islam did not fit well into teleologies of the future. Despite support in the early Cold War for the Muslim Brotherhood in Egypt or Ayatollah Abol-Ghasem Kashani in Iran, American thinkers tended to see Islam as not particularly relevant for the modern world.[8] The year 1979 was a major shock.

Confusion about the Revolution was not limited to the Americans. Many Iranians were themselves surprised as events unfolded.[9] Soviet scholars of religion also saw Islam as a roadblock to major social changes, and the Revolution caught them off guard. Like their American counterparts, they assumed that Islam would impede (rather than encourage) revolution.[10] The Revolution, then, is one of the most potent reminders that the Cold War was a competition for the "society of the future."[11] The academic study of religion in the West has always been, in some sense, an attempt to make sense of the modern world. These threads intersected in Iran, where the religious approach to intelligence was found wanting.

The Roots of the Agency's Analysis

After World War II, US intelligence remained relatively inexperienced with Muslim cultures. While OSS operated in North Africa and Southwest Asia during the war, intelligence officers did not give it the priority they gave to Western Europe. Early Cold War crises, including the Berlin Blockade, the Italian elections of 1948, and the Korean War, did not argue for more attention to Islam. This is not to say that religion generally was unimportant: indeed, the Italian elections fostered a relationship between the newly created CIA and the Roman Catholic Church.[12] Yet these crises did not offer a clear rationale for allocating resources to understand Islam or Muslim-majority countries.

For many Americans in the early Cold War, the importance of religion was not limited to specific traditions but extended to a supposed universal dimension.[13] Some intelligence officers, like Edward Lansdale, mirrored these assumptions in their work, understanding religion as a unique species of human thought that was inherently, incorruptibly, anti-Communist. In this view, the specter of Communism threatened American ideals not simply because of its contrasting economic systems or labor policies but because it was an irreligious—and, for many US officials, anti-religious— philosophy.

This approach toward the Soviet Union's official atheism illustrates how for both the CIA and the academy, the separation between "religion" and "politics" was natural and self-evident. This assumption underpinned larger Western knowledge about "world religions," a group of the "major" or "great" religious traditions operating around the world, most often including Judaism, Christianity, Islam, Hinduism, and Buddhism. The "fact" that five religions constituted the "main" traditions of the world supported the notion that studying one could also give insights into others. Thinking of religion in this way, as holding a set of essential characteristics interchange-able among traditions (like sacred texts, creation stories, deities, rituals, and so forth), was a product of the Enlightenment attempt to categorize and order human culture.[14] One of the most distinctive characteristics American analysts expected all religions to hold was a fundamental disinterest and aloofness toward politics and the state.[15] American observers tended to see developing nations at a crossroads between a path toward the modern West (publicly secular yet privately religious) or toward godless Communism (entirely irreligious) with no "third way" in between. Even if a religious worldview seized the levers of government, this line of reasoning went, it would be unlikely that this government would be anti-American (since, being religious, they would naturally identify with American values). A popular 1950s world religions reader produced by *LIFE* magazine explained that, whatever their differences, the world's religions all necessarily rejected

Communism since they "stand united against an alien view which finds nothing in existence but the play of material forces."[16]

These shared assumptions about religion were problematic generally, but particularly so with respect to Islam and Muslim-majority nations. Since analysts were well trained in viewing religion as an anti-Communist public good, Islam—as the predominant religion of much of the globe—was also less of a concern. What little official attention the CIA gave to Islam and Muslims was warm. Prior to 1953, the Agency was largely sympathetic to Arabs, Muslims, and the Palestinian cause.[17] An early CIA assessment of the Israel-Palestine conflict, for example, stressed the dangers of creating a Jewish state, predicting that support for Israel would bleed US support in the Middle East and upset relations with the USSR.[18]

Along with Judaism and Christianity, Islam was supposed to be uniquely resistant to Communism's seductive charms. This kind of thinking about religions paralleled long-standing Eurocentric assumptions in the academic study of religion. Conventional wisdom suggested, or at least implied, that religious traditions evolved over time. In this view, monotheistic Abrahamic religions represented the most advanced and "civilized" form of religious thought and practice, while polytheistic religions represented more modest development, and animistic or "tribal" religions represented the most "primitive" forms of religion. For example, a popular American study of world religions in the 1950s claimed that Buddhism, superior to polytheistic Hinduism, was a "potent civilizing force in the Far East." Other "Eastern" traditions further down the scale fared worse than either Buddhism or Hinduism. Taoism, for example, had "hordes of nearly illiterate, rapacious priests" whose teachings are hard to reduce to "coherence."[19] Yet Islam held a curious position in the WRP because although it was a monotheistic tradition, it often resided in geographic areas where polytheistic, atheistic, and animistic traditions dominated.

Echoing popular Western scholarship on Islam, US intelligence concluded that Islam was timeless. The best contemporary scholarship claimed that Islam encouraged tradition, authority, and respect for the status quo. In what would become the most influential and popular study of world religions for decades, Huston Smith's *The Religions of Man* (1958) introduced Islam by explaining its essential quality as submission to authority.[20] Yet American understandings of Islam were disproportionately filtered through centuries of Orientalism and racism, and so Islam was both valorized as an obstacle to Communism while racialized as the product of a lesser culture.[21]

In popular culture, literature, and public discourse, Arabs and Muslims (terms often mistaken as interchangeable) were disproportionately portrayed as obsessed with authority and social conservatism. Echoing traditional Orientalist ideas, Americans assumed that Muslims possessed a timeless way of life that had done little to adapt to the modern world.[22] Islam was racialized in an Orientalist way, too: Muslims, as religious people in the Orient, were presumed unfit to govern themselves in the modern world because they belonged to a timeless past. Popular studies of Islam reinforced these ideas by situating Muslim intellectual thought in the literal past, as did *LIFE* magazine when it explained that 1950s Muslim intellectuals were at the same point in their development as Christian intellectuals were during the publication of *On the Origin of Species* (1859).[23] Huston Smith agreed, explaining to his millions of readers that Islam was "emerging from its partial stagnation" of the last few centuries.[24] Another reason for this perception was that Christian missionaries produced a significant amount of American knowledge about Islam.[25] According to CIA officer Duane R. Clarridge, Washington was still "terribly dependent on the missionaries and the oil crowd for firsthand knowledge" in the early Cold War.[26]

The information accessible to Western analysts pursuing the religious approach to intelligence reflected the Orientalist and racist assumptions of nineteenth- and twentieth-century anthropologists and theologians that Islam was religious—and even Abrahamic—while somehow still deficient. In CIA analyses, the deficiency most often manifested itself in terms of whether Muslims were a risk to US national security. Academic work focused on how and whether Muslims could be trusted in the fight against Communism. The prominent Orientalist and defense intellectual Bernard Lewis, perhaps the most famous Western postwar expert on the Middle East and Islam, took up this question early in his career. In a 1954 essay, "Communism and Islam," Lewis attempted to figure out what in the Islamic tradition "might facilitate or impede" the advance of Communism in Muslim countries.[27] For Lewis, it was a mixed bag. He concluded that Muslims would like the brute strength and efficiency of Communist rule, since Muslims were used to autocratic dictatorships. Furthermore, many Muslims could find Communism appealing because they associate the West with racism and colonialism. While acknowledging that this could apply to other religions, Lewis argued that Islam was different because it held a uniquely "formative and determinative" power over its adherents. Both the Muslim *ulema* (religious leaders) and the Communist Party prize a "totalitarian doctrine," Lewis contended, since they both offer "complete and final answers to all questions on heaven and earth."[28] Lewis did not address how, precisely, this differed from other religions.

Yet Lewis did not think the cause of Islamic anti-Communism was lost. "It is, however, fortunate, both for Islam and for the Western world," he wrote,

> that the choice is not restricted to these two simple alternatives, for the possibility still remains for the Muslim peoples of restoring, perhaps in a modified form, their own tradition; of evolving a form of government which, though authoritarian, and perhaps even autocratic, is nevertheless far removed from the cynical tyranny of European-style dictatorship.

Lewis's argument reflected a remarkable analytical confidence in interpreting the religious traditions and political motivations of other people. In this view, Western scholars understood other traditions so well that they hoped other traditions *could restore something about themselves* in order to inoculate themselves against Communism. Lewis argued that the act of restoring "essential" Islam would necessarily strengthen Islamic anti-Communism—perhaps because, in line with the assumptions of the world religions paradigm, all religions shared an anti-Communist essence.[29]

Lewis's work was part of the broader arc of Western interpretations of Islam and the so-called Muslim world during the early Cold War. Then as now, the study of religion was used to frame issues of national security and the security of the "West." When the United States first paid significant attention to Muslims during World War II, the interest was a tactical one: to what extent could Muslim actors be motivated to challenge German and Japanese forces? OSS presumed that religion was the most efficient method to motivate Muslims. After the war, long-standing Orientalist ideas about Islam came to the fore as the dominant interpretation. But, as Lewis's article indicated, it was unclear precisely how Muslims would identify with either Communism or nationalism in the chaos of decolonization. The history of the 1950s convinced US observers that nationalism outpaced religion as the dominant influence in the politics of Muslim-majority nations. Analysts also seemed to understand the "secular" dictatorships in Arab and Muslim countries, resulting in large part from the chaos of decolonization, as self-evidently normal for both Arabs and Muslims. CIA analysts thought Sunni countries' most potent force was secular nationalism rather than religion, and they understood both Anwar Sadat's strength and Turkey's secularism through this prism.[30]

Conversations in the CIA's in-house journal, *Studies in Intelligence*, illustrate how these long-standing academic ideas influenced intelligence theory. In 1959, Francis Hollyman wrote "Intelligence Gathering in an Unlettered Land" as a guide for Americans attempting to develop intelligence contacts in Arab and Muslim countries. According to Hollyman, Americans must first recognize the difficulty in attempting to recruit people molded by "the peculiarities of an anachronistic society." In so doing, Hollyman both drew from and reinforced the idea that Islam was unchanging—what might be termed the timelessness thesis—as he considered the practical difficulties of intelligence work in Arab and Muslim countries.[31]

Hollyman argued that it was difficult to recruit well-placed officials in Muslim societies because, even if cultural obstacles could be overcome, many Muslims are not particularly intelligent. According to Hollyman, Muslim leaders who have an "important place in commerce or government cannot read a map, and he may not even be aware that the world is not flat!"[32] Education was poor, since what little they received as children focused on the "Koran." If intelligence officers wished to understand the Muslim mind, the road to true understanding was long and frustrating:

> Aside from wanting to be a proper Arab and a good Muslim, he has no strong aims or convictions. His experience is too little, his ignorance too great, to provide a foundation for opposition to Communist imperialism as his motive force. He has no strong sense of socio-political responsibility, no felt need for thinking, for making a political choice. The idea of subscribing to a positive ideological program or doctrine, except as it incorporates his immediate Arab interests, is beyond him. He does not like to generalize about the world, because all he knows is his home, the marketplace, the desert, and the edge of the sea. Very often his attitude is that of the merchant, even if he is not engaged in commerce. His aims and desires are very simple ones, and he does not want to change them.[33]

All the Orientalized and racist assumptions about Arabs and Muslims are present: the affection for autocracy and force, the intellectual deficiencies, the wistfulness for centuries past, and a desire to disengage from the modern world.[34] In this view Muslims are not evil, but rather simple, unintelligent, and staid ("he is essentially gentle, not belligerent"). The Muslim, continued Hollyman, "respects force partly because it is simple and within his comprehension." Crucially, the author interprets the outdated nature of Islam as the very thing that helps insulate Muslims from Communism's charms, since the Muslim mind was too antiquated to fully appreciate the supposed benefits of Communism. While Communism might be evil, it was also modern. The essay begrudgingly acknowledges that it still required some level of intelligence to understand dialectical materialism. Hollyman's Arab Muslims are fragments of the past, characters from an earlier time and place who have persisted into the twentieth century and now must be dealt with by civilized intelligence services.

A few years later, another CIA publication outlined the importance of "face" in Arab and Muslim culture. Written by Peter Naffsinger, the essay was a guide to working with Arab Muslims who, in Naffsinger's view, refuse personal responsibility and avoid acknowledging errors. Naffsinger opens with a story familiar to his American readers:

> George Washington, American children are told, having cut down his father's favorite cherry tree, showed his sterling character by confessing to the deed. An Arab hearing this story not only fails to see the moral beauty of such behavior but wonders why anyone would ever compromise his integrity by admitting thus his guilt. As to Washington's explanation that "I cannot tell a lie," the Arab asks how a man could rise to the presidency if he were not suave enough to use a well-concocted falsehood as a tactic in emergency behavior.[35]

In Naffsinger's explanation, this is a "universal" feature among Muslims and Arabs because their religion encourages a fatalistic view of life. While Christianity teaches that guilt must be acknowledged so that sin can be forgiven, Naffsinger argued that Islam had no such compulsion. US intelligence officials must recognize that in contrast to Christian theology, Islamic theology "conveys the feeling that God is so all-pervading and at the same time so far above and removed from the individual that all human actions and their consequences are but the sequels of God's doings: the individual is merely an animate pawn." (The author, we can assume, was not a Calvinist.) Allah, "this supremely impersonal God, above and beyond rather than within a person, impresses on the individual no requirement to accept guilt or personal responsibility for anything or to develop a conscience differentiating between intrinsic right and wrong."[36]

The intelligence community would not appreciate the flaws of this intellectual model until the late 1970s, when the foment preceding the Iranian Revolution began to reveal weaknesses in the Agency's analysis. By January 1979, however, Khomeini and other revolutionaries had already identified and exploited this analytical blindness.

The 1953 Coup

The CIA's early attention—or inattention—to Islam was evident decades before the Revolution. Iran's democratically elected government, led by Prime Minister Mohammad Mossadeq, decided to nationalize the petroleum industry in 1951. The sale of oil was a major source of Iranian revenue, even though the lion's share of the profits went to the Anglo-Iranian Oil Company (later renamed British Petroleum [BP]) under earlier colonial agreements. Unable to stomach the loss of oil profits and fearing that Iranian oilfields would gravitate toward the Soviet orbit, American and British secret services encouraged a coup in 1953. The power vacuum allowed Mohammad Reza Pahlavi, the shah (Persian for "king") of Iran, to increase his political power and rule as a monarch. The lessons of the coup—and whether religion mattered—were important for both the CIA and Khomeini. The CIA's involvement, though widely known for the better part of the twentieth century, was not officially acknowledged by the US government until 2013.[37]

Among the few religious figures the CIA considered in their coup planning was Ayatollah Abol-Ghasem Kashani. As religious figures went, Kashani was an important one: he was a *marja*, among the highest living authorities in Shiism, whose eminence was second only to the Holy Quran and the line of prophets. When the CIA and State Department tried to learn about Kashani's sympathies, they received mixed messages from their officers in the field. The problem, as one CIA memo put it, was that Kashani was an "opportunist" and the Agency had no sense of his true feelings.[38] State Department memos planning for a possible coup worried that Kashani could ally himself with the Iranian Communist party Tudeh, wedding Kashani's sizeable popular support to a USSR-backed organization.[39] While some American officials in Iran assumed that Kashani could never ally himself with Tudeh—as Communism and religion were mutually exclusive—the CIA and State Department received troubling reports of Kashani defending Tudeh as a "loyal Muslim organization" while conspiring to use the party to overthrow Mossadeq.[40] Secret British and American meetings even considered acting against Kashani as a test run for a possible coup of their own against Mossadeq, though this plan was never put into motion.[41]

Yet if Kashani could be swung the right way, his value as a religious leader would be invaluable. State Department official Loy W. Henderson met with Kashani multiple times, each time making a religious appeal to Kashani's sense of himself as a Muslim leader. Henderson stressed that the fate of Soviet Muslims in Central Asia—sending their children to atheist schools and losing their Islamic heritage—could befall Iranian Muslims if the United States and Iran did not work well together. The image of Kashani that emerges from these memos is of a religious leader aware of his political power, and playing the great powers against one another. Henderson quotes Kashani as explaining that he is "not an ordinary person. I am leader of Moslem world and Moslem world will soon be force to be reckoned with. It is in interest of good people everywhere that Moslem world and US cooperate."[42] As planning for a possible coup progressed, the CIA kept track of Kashani, noting his increasingly anti-Communist statements.[43] Kermit Roosevelt noted "friendly meetings" between Ayatollah Kashani and Fazlollah Zahedi, an Iranian general who would eventually depose Mossadeq in a coup d'état.[44] Though Roosevelt and other coup plotters may have later taken too much credit for their role in motivating the Shia clergy (and their larger role in the coup in general), they did appreciate the potential for the Shia clergy to turn out large crowds in the streets.[45]

Notably for an ayatollah, Kashani formally entered politics as speaker of the Iranian *majles* (parliament). Though a critic of British colonialism and an advocate for oil nationalization, Ayatollah Kashani turned against Mossadeq, apparently because the ayatollah thought he was owed more political favors by Mossadeq than he received.[46] The finer details of Shia clergy's eventual swing of support away from Mossadeq and back to the shah may have been lost on Western observers, however, tied up as it was with complicated processes of decolonization, Shia authority structures, and Iranian nationalism. For US intelligence analysts who believed that Islam and Muslims prized an authoritarian status quo and resisted dramatic political changes (e.g., the argument put forward the following year by Bernard Lewis and echoed by Western observers of Islam), it would make sense that Ayatollah Kashani opposed Mossadeq. In this view, Mossadeq represented a change to the status quo away from the firm, authoritarian power of the shah. Kashani, as a religious leader, would support the shah because he upheld a strong political and social order. It appears that Kashani did indeed grow to oppose Mossadeq, though for entirely different reasons than what American analysts would expect. It was nothing timeless in Islam, but instead Mossadeq's refusal to acquiesce to Kashani's newfound temporal political power.

Kashani's political trajectory influenced Ayatollah Khomeini's later choices. Khomeini's main criticism of Kashani was that "instead of trying to Islamize politics, he politicized Islam."[47] Kashani's participation in the formal Iranian political system as speaker of the *majles* rendered Islamic authority secondary to democratic structures, which in Khomeini's view was unacceptable. While both Shia leaders were interested in achieving proper governance, Khomeini rejected Kashani's decision to work within the system.[48] The system, instead, required a revolutionary rethinking. Because the CIA did not understand the inner workings of the Shia clergy, they were analytically blinded to how the future Ayatollah Khomeini would interpret the events of 1953.

Rather than adapt the mullah to the *majles*, Khomeini adapted the system of government to the mullah. To do this, Khomeini wanted to undo the stigma attached to the "political mullah." He saw religion and politics as never separated to begin with and resisted the Western-imposed division between cleric and state. Khomeini became an outspoken opponent of the shah during the 1963 riots, further raising him to prominence. The following year, he critiqued the shah's decision to grant US military personnel in Iran extraterritorial rights. Khomeini interpreted this as a cessation of Iran's sovereignty, and said so publicly. He would be exiled the following year, an exile he would famously return from in 1979 at the head of the Revolution.[49]

Khomeini's lessons were not a high American priority after 1953, however. The Battle of Dien Bien Phu the following year began a tectonic shift in American involvement in Southeast Asia, committing the United States to another poorly understood decolonization struggle. Vietnam soon monopolized the CIA's attention, freeze-framing its Orientalized picture of Islam during the 1960s and 1970s.[50] When the American involvement in Vietnam ended in 1975, the shah's days were numbered. Much of the CIA's resources, long devoted to counterinsurgency in Southeast Asia, were initially a poor fit to interpret Shia dissatisfaction with the shah's technocratic government in the late 1970s. Intelligence failures in Vietnam were themselves a precursor to the Agency's experience in Iran. Anthony Lewis, writing in the CIA's in-house journal in 1973, argued that post-Vietnam intelligence improvements should be rooted in overcoming "unconscious assumptions that our views and convictions about the world, as well as our more basic beliefs, values, and norms, are held by reasonable and educated people everywhere"[51] The Agency's troubles stemmed from a lack of cultural understanding, or more accurately, an inability to imagine the legitimacy of other cultures and beliefs. Lewis critiqued the idea that the CIA could reduce foreign cultures and peoples to easily digestible categories native to American culture. To universalize American experience and assumptions was not simply an academic error, Lewis insisted, since it also complicated the analytical and interpretive work of intelligence professionals. Around the same time, scholars of religion started making similar moves. In what became the opening volley of the critical turn against the world religions paradigm, Wilfred Cantwell Smith wrote in *The Meaning and End of Religion* (1963) that "to understand the world, and ourselves, it is helpful if we become critical of the terms and concepts that we are using."[52]

Interpreting the Iranian Revolution

Although it was not yet clear to American observers, this same critique applied to the situation in Iran. As the shah's government weakened during the 1970s, US intelligence noted the government's struggles without fully appreciating the causes. Six weeks before the shah would flee into exile, Brzezinski warned President Carter that the Middle East was on the verge of a major crisis, but presented it largely in terms of the Soviet Union's possible gains.[53] The CIA's mind-boggling 1978 assessment that "Iran is not in a revolutionary or even a prerevolutionary situation" was wrong in part because of what the CIA assumed about Islam, Muslims, and religion in general.[54] It also reflected misleading assumptions in CIA thinking that the Agency's journal had warned about five years previously. The CIA's teleological confidence heavily influenced their assessments of the shah's hold on power. The CIA, and the Carter administration it informed, imagined the shah as the endpoint of Western liberalism. Wearing Western dress and promoting Western ideas, the shah looked and sounded like a leader of the future was supposed to look and sound.[55] The secular, technocratic nature of the Iranian government was just what a modern country was supposed to look like.

This teleological confidence made basic curiosity difficult, blinding US intelligence operatives to what should have been red flags in the lead-up to the Revolution. When Iranian students seized the US embassy in 1980, they had trouble identifying CIA employees among the embassy workers, since the intelligence personnel did not speak Persian. The Iranians were in disbelief that the mighty CIA could be so disorganized and seemingly ineffective.[56] In this context, the two most important CIA analytical assumptions about Islam, made under the influence of the world religions paradigm, were about the nature of Shiism as a species of Islam and the motivations of Ayatollah Ruhollah Khomeini.

Declassified documents suggest that the Agency began producing assessments of Shiism only in the late 1970s. Previous CIA reports had dismissed the threat of religious opposition to the Shah as unserious, deriding it as "mere sociology."[57] This changed as the shah began facing serious clerical opposition. Memos and briefings connected the shah's plight to detailed histories of Shiism and an appreciation for the role of martyrdom in Shia culture. One assessment noted how memories of the Battle of Karbala, a formative event for Shia Muslims, were used to link the shah to a history of foreign (Sunni) authority.[58]

The CIA's first comprehensive report on Iranian Islam was not completed until after the Revolution, in early 1980. The report's explanation of Iranian history, and the relationship between Shia and Sunni Muslims, is important because it became intelligence officers' first significant introduction to Iran and Islam. The history told was not substantially different from Bernard Lewis's essay written decades previously: Iranian Islam was an antiquated religion stuck in a modern world that had no place for it. The CIA's analysis of Iran's problems runs for nearly one hundred pages, summarized in the Agency's thesis that radical Shiism could not be rolled back until "Shia Islam makes its peace with the modern world."[59] While the report was clearly rushed as the shah's government crumbled and Khomeini rose to power, this overarching understanding of Iran led to two specific conclusions about the nature of Shiism.

First, the Agency concluded that Shiism itself was uniquely revolutionary. This argument stemmed from their observation that Shia theology and authority structures were more resistant to institutional authority than Sunni thinking. Whereas earlier analysis viewed Islam as resistant to change, Shiism was seen as the exception that proved the rule. Conveniently, this meant that the Revolution's cause was something particular to Shiism rather than anything uniquely problematic about the shah's government.[60] At the same time, the Revolution was presumed to have little traction in Sunni countries where secular nationalism still held sway. Another contributing factor in interpreting Shiism as revolutionary was its presumed affinity for emotional outbursts, which—to the American observers—were visible in public outpourings of emotion during holidays like Moharram, where self-flagellation was not uncommon.[61] Second, American leadership presumed that since Shiism was uniquely predisposed to revolution and emotionalism, it was also irrational. President Carter himself conflated Ayatollah Khomeini in Iran and the Religious Right at home as fundamentalist because they mixed religion and politics.[62] "It's almost impossible to deal with a crazy man," Carter wrote of Khomeini in his journal.[63]

The CIA rooted their conclusions about Shiism in Iranian history, arguing Iran's religious troubles began when Iranians imported European ideas "to modernize the corrupt, unwieldy, and inefficient oriental bureaucracy that had developed through the centuries." Yet this policy of "European and American-inspired modernization" troubled relations between emerging political leaders like the shah, and the Shia clerics who had exercised authority in the past. The clergy's opposition was simple, since from their perspective "what had not already been provided for by Islam could only be harmful."[64] Consequently Iran never had the chance to modernize, such as developing a proper separation of "church and state." In this view, Muslim leaders like Khomeini were asserting a "rejuvenated" Islam as the source of all possible answers since they wanted to avoid the embarrassment of adapting "Islam to a world it did not make."[65]

In the CIA analysis, Islam was described as another world.[66] Of the everyday Iranian Muslims who had joined Khomeini's government, "most of these are caught between two worlds," the CIA explained. "They usually have a modern education, often received abroad, but unlike the early Western-educated class, they have not rejected traditional Islam. They try to reconcile the two worlds, not always successfully."[67] The CIA's understanding of Iranian Shiism offered little space for genuine Iranian frustration with the shah. In this view, the "new" ideas Iranian Muslims claimed to be concerned about—such as imperialism and colonialism—were not the product of legitimate concerns but rather the "half-assimilated" understandings imposed upon them by foreign Marxists.[68] This interpretation represented more than just the CIA's narrative. With few additions, this would also prove to be the narrative that Americans took away from the Revolution: that Islam (and particularly Iranian Shiism) was an ancient relic standing in the way of positive change. This echoed centuries of Orientalizing studies assuring Western readers that what was strange about "the East" was unique *to* the East. For the Agency, the person who embodied all of Shiism's strangeness was Ayatollah Ruhollah Khomeini.

By 1978, the CIA recognized Khomeini as an important figure in Iranian politics, but also as someone whose efficacy would be limited by his religiosity. In the CIA's assessment, governing a "modern" state would likely prove too difficult for someone wedded to religious principles like Khomeini. Within a few years, though, that perspective would change. In 1983, the CIA concluded that the Revolution would have been impossible without Khomeini. In the CIA's view, the ayatollah and his ideology— which the Agency termed Khomeinism—became uniquely responsible for the Revolution.[69] In the interim, however, Khomeini confused the Agency because he did not conform to the Islam imagined by the scholarship and analysis the United States had at its disposal.

This was apparent not only in the formal intelligence analysis, but also in the on-the-ground experience of US intelligence officers and soldiers in pre-Revolutionary Iran. One American trainer later recalled how, while working with Iranian soldiers in 1978, American confidence in the inevitably of the shah's rule sometimes blinded them to the threat posed by his opponents. "In my conversations with people in the embassy," they explained, "there was no indication anything was wrong." Yet in interactions with Iranian soldiers and during travel to outlying areas, it was clear things were not so simple. "We could tell that Iranians from the 23rd [Iranian Special Forces Brigade] were nervous—they would make comments like 'can we buy your rifle? Can we buy your ammunition?' We couldn't do that, of course." Once, after noticing an increase in graffiti around Tehran, they took pictures of it—no one in the unit read Persian—and translated it upon return to Ft. Bragg. "It didn't mention Khomeini," the officer later recalled,

> but it was Islam-Islam-Islam. That didn't fit and we weren't sure what to make of it. Combined with guys from the 23rd trying to buy our weapons . . . this didn't add up. We concluded there were big problems in Iran. So we wrote a report about it, saying there are problems here and we need to look into this Islam thing, and sent it up the chain. It took months to hear back, and we got it just before Khomeini's return to Iran. I'll never forget the response. "Well prepared. Well written. However, [the author] should keep his personal opinions to himself. The Shah is as solid as a rock."[70]

Even as some Iranian and American observers noted changes in Iranian attitudes, US intelligence presumed Communist ideology, not "religion," to be the real source of problems.[71] As the Revolution unfolded, some even remained convinced the USSR was behind the shah's opposition.[72] Ultimately, their argument went, Muslims would not overthrow the shah because this would strengthen Soviet atheism. Communism, they thought, was fundamentally incompatible with all religions, including Islam. Imagining a "middle space" between the United States and Communism presented analysts with a striking degree of difficulty because their worldview left little space for religious motivations that did not line up with familiar Cold War ideological divides.

By November 1978, the CIA's assessment of Ayatollah Khomeini was that he was irrational, unpredictable, but also representative of long-standing trends in Shia Islam. "In place of the Shah," one CIA report noted, "Khomeini advocates the creation of a vaguely defined 'Islamic Republic' to be guided only by the principles of Shia Islam. This concept is not Khomeini's alone; it is a doctrine firmly embedded in Shiism."[73] Yet Khomeini's articulation of "the guardianship of the Islamic jurist" (*Velayat-e faqih*) arguably departed from traditional Shia theology. While many Shia thinkers placed authority in jurists to guide people in certain aspects of life, they disagreed about the jurist's proper jurisdiction. Some Shia leaders were hesitant to engage in formal politicking. Grand Ayatollah Khoei, for example, said that a "jurist" could not provide "guardianship" over a whole nation.[74]

Khomeini disagreed at length in his book *Islamic Government* (1970).[75] In its most concise form, Khomeini's argument was that government should be subject to the law of God, not the other way around. Nearly twenty-five years after Ayatollah Kashani lent his religious authority to a Western-backed government, Ayatollah Khomeini would avoid making the same heretical mistake. Khomeini's innovation would eventually be established as a new Iranian and Shia orthodoxy through the Revolution. The office of the supreme leader, which Khomeini was the first to occupy, embodied his vision. These disagreements among Shia thinkers were lost on the American public, which learned of Shiism through news reports and presented Khomeini as a leader whose authority was already settled among his people.

The Agency's problematic understanding of Khomeini's ideas about the jurist (i.e., the role of religion in government) is significant because it reflects larger challenges in understanding both Khomeini and Shia ideologies. This problem was not unique to the CIA. Labeling Khomeini a "fundamentalist," for example, appealed to different groups for various reasons. Western analysts and government officials associated the word with the chaos of the Revolution (and eventually the hostage crisis). Yet marking Khomeini as a "fundamentalist" also appealed to many academic specialists, since these Orientalists could denounce Khomeini as an outlier—someone who ruptured their tidy classification of Islam as "timeless"—which effectively obscured how the very knowledge produced by academic Orientalists failed to anticipate Khomeini's ideas.[76] Ironically, Khomeini's success during the Revolution seemed to reinforce his orthodoxy to the CIA. Yet by interpreting Khomeini's new ideas as long-standing settled doctrine, American analysts lost the opportunity to understand the importance of Khomeini's ideas, including his specific critiques of the West, secularism, and modernism.

Even as the CIA struggled to understand Khomeini's motivations, the ayatollah's ideas proved persuasive to a great many Iranians who saw the shah's government as equal parts corrupt and brutal. While the Revolution itself had roots stretching back decades, the late 1970s witnessed an accelerating cycle of protests, which were subdued by increasingly violent government crackdowns, which in turn caused more protests. In one particularly egregious event, scores of protesters were killed by government forces in Tehran in September 1978. In what became known as "Black Friday," the shah's increasingly desperate and violent attempts to maintain power were on display for the entire world. Rocked by government instability and a strained relationship with the military, the shah left the country the following January. On the first of February 1979, Khomeini returned to Iran and began consolidating power. A year after the CIA assessed Iran as not in a revolutionary situation, Khomeini became supreme leader of the Islamic Republic of Iran. After the Revolution, there was a brief period in which American leaders considered their options. Brzezinski wondered whether the new Iran could be used as part of an "arc of Islam" along the southern flank of the Soviet Union. Hearkening back to earlier Cold War American understandings of Islam, Brzezinski posited that the shared religiosity of Christians and Muslims meant that they would make for natural allies against Communism.[77] It was not to be.

The November 1979 hostage crisis disrupted cautious assessments of the Revolution and profoundly shaped American perceptions of the new Islamic Republic. Held for 444 days, the American hostages—and the failed American military operation to rescue them—became a symbol of American weakness for the Carter administration even as they strengthened Khomeini's hand in Iran. In American popular media, the hostage crisis amplified the voices of pundits and politicians intent on painting Islam as backward, violent, and uniquely prone to terrorism. American media's portrayal of Islam as monolithic also encouraged a revival in American Christian nationalism.[78] These trends would accelerate alongside the election of Ronald Reagan—an event heavily influenced by the hostage crisis—and the rise of the Religious Right.

The Iranian Revolution and the World Religions Paradigm

In a remarkable 1983 assessment that reflected the CIA's changing religious approach to Iran, the Agency noted that "[Khomeini] and his supporters have created a doctrine so radical that, as one Western scholar has written, if Khomeini lives long enough to preside over its institutionalization, Shiism as it has been known in Iran will come to an end."[79] Curiously, this mirrored Khomeini's own argument. For Khomeini, the Western scholars of religion were "servants of imperialism" because they portrayed Islam as uninterested in politics. Khomeini critiqued the classic assumptions of the world religions paradigm that prioritized colorful differences between religions while ignoring temporal challenges like governmental policy or authoritative claims to power. This Western picture of Islam was content to opine solely on seemingly inconsequential issues (which for Khomeini meant ritual purity and gender roles) that made it easier for Westerners to compare Islam to other religions.[80] For Khomeini, Islam was always about politics and how to order society. In trying to make Islam fit the Western category of religion and the world religions paradigm, Western scholars had started from the assumption that religion *cannot* be about politics, and so ended with an inaccurate portrait of Islam. That the CIA cited a "western scholar" arguing that Khomeini's success would end Shiism as they knew it—well, Khomeini would likely have agreed.

To be sure, Khomeini's concern was not the Western study of religion so much as the ideas it produced and took for granted. These ideas influenced Western culture and seeped into Iran, where they could shape impressionable Muslim youth.[81] Instead of imbibing a "Western" understanding of Islam, Khomeini argued that Shia leaders must "present Islam to the people in its true form,"

> so that our youth do not picture [clerics] as sitting in some corner in Najaf or Qom, studying the questions of menstruation and parturition instead of concerning themselves with politics, and draw the conclusion that religion must be separate from politics. This slogan of separation of religion from politics and the demand that Islamic scholars should not intervene in social and political affairs have been formulated and propagated by the imperialists; it is only the irreligious who repeat them. Were religion and politics separate in the time of the prophets?[82]

For Khomeini, the Western study of Islam was closely connected to the imperial project. Like Western scholars a generation later, Khomeini argued that the study of foreign religions was inseparable from attempts to control that religion's adherents.[83] Writing almost a decade before Edward Said's groundbreaking *Orientalism* (1978), Khomeini would attend to many of the same points, including how power is the precondition for knowledge and how colonial knowledge production said more about those producing the knowledge than those being studied.[84]

Khomeini recognized Western understandings of Islam as inaccurate precisely because Islam was measured against the Western category of "religion," itself formatively shaped by Western understandings of Christianity.[85] In his 1970 book, Khomeini lamented that Muslims accept the erroneous notion that Islam is limited to certain spheres of human life when they accept Western views of Islam. Specifically, they internalize an understanding of Islam as "man's relation to God" rather than an all-encompassing worldview. Muslims who think this, Khomeini argues, "will imagine that Islam is like Christianity."[86] Later Western academic critiques of the world religions paradigm would take a similar approach, noting that the production of religious knowledge in the West was long mediated through Christian categories, mistaking uniquely Christian developments—such as an ostensibly self-evident separation between religion and politics—for universal religious attributes.[87] Indeed, geopolitical earthquakes like the Iranian Revolution helped show Western scholars that all was not well with their models of "religion."

Yet rather than consider whether their model was correct, the Agency (and many American scholars at the time) simply placed Khomeini outside of it. For his part, Khomeini recognized that the model was bunk, and that Christianity (at least as it had evolved in the West) and Islam (as Khomeini understood it to be) were apples and oranges. The Western attempt to place Islam and Christianity in the same category did not make sense to Khomeini; it did not reflect his understanding of Muslim history or practice. In turn, the Agency's confidence in this model limited their ability to understand Khomeini. They could not predict his strategy or eventual success, because the CIA began with the assumption that Islam, as a world religion, was fundamentally *not about politics*. The Agency's analytical weakness on Islam was not actually about Islam at all, but about religion more broadly. It was not rectified in part because it was never identified as a weakness in the first place.

The CIA and other American observers struggled to extricate themselves from Americentric notions about the relationship between religion and modernity. An American military trainer who served in Iran in 1978 later noted that "We didn't understand that Islam was more than a religion, as we understood religion."[88] The CIA, in its formal intelligence assessments, also struggled to appreciate Khomeini's motivations. "Khomeini's ambiguity reflects a lack of interest in a specific political program," the CIA concluded in 1978, since "for him Shia Islam is a total social/political/economic system that needs no further explanation."[89] For Khomeini, of course, Shia Islam *was* a specific political program: it provided a transcendent claim to authority that opposed, in all times and places, illegitimate or corrupt governments.

The Agency's analysis is a relic of the CIA's teleological confidence in the trajectory of religion in the modern world. The world religions paradigm is fundamentally about modernity—a single direction in which the world was moving: *toward* progress, *toward* secularism, *toward* moderniza-tion.[90] It came of age with other grand narratives of the European Enlight-enment, born of a confidence that all human behavior and thought could be rationally understood. Within months of the Revolution, that inter-pretation had suffered a body blow. "Islam is better understood as an all-encompassing ideology than as a religion in the Western sense," one CIA report explained in 1980. "There is not even a suitable word in Arabic, Per-sian, or other Islamic languages for 'temporal' or 'secular.'"[91] This was taken as a sign of how inconceivable these things were to Muslims, Arabs, and Persians rather than how culturally particular these same things were to the "West." For some, hope still lingered that the Revolution might be an aber-ration, an exception that would prove the rule rather than break it. A few pages later in the same report, the Agency concluded that "It is too early to know if recent developments mark a genuine long-term return to Islam or are merely a temporary setback in the general trend toward complete secularization"—a trend that, by the Agency's own assessment, Muslims had no word to describe.[92]

For the CIA, the consequences of the Iranian Revolution were not lim-ited to the Agency's approach to Islam. The hostage crisis dragged on for 444 days, dominating media coverage and serving as a painful reminder of just how off the mark the CIA's analysis had been. In this atmosphere, the Agency became markedly more open-minded about the broad possibilities of religious movements around the globe. Gone were the days when reli-gious movements were assumed to be anti-Communist and pro-American by default. If the seemingly unassailable government of the Shah could be brought down, what else was possible when confronting these new revolu-tionary forms of religion?

The Iranian Revolution was an intelligence failure, to be sure, but it was also a failure of imagination. The inability to imagine religion's role in the Revolution stemmed from the same secular certainties that would be over-turned by the rise of the Religious Right in the United States. Analysts failed to see popular Western ideas as an ideology with values that might not be universal for everyone. Influenced by the world religions paradigm and the religious approach to intelligence, the CIA believed in the intelligibility and universality of human experience. The CIA's teleological confidence about religion in the modern world led to confusion about Khomeini, delaying the realization that he was more powerful and more effective than first imagined. Intelligence analysts and scholars underestimated the appeal of Shiism as an alternative value system and worldview. In the imaginations of Western scholars, to be modern was to be secular, Westernizing, and technocratic. Khomeini's Shiism was none of these. For the CIA, Khomeini's ideas were so foreign as to be unrecognizable in the modern present in which secularism had triumphed. Underestimating Khomeini reflected American overconfidence in their own models, and in the stories they told themselves about religion in the modern world.

Conclusion

A New Wilderness

I am still not clear on our terminology. However, I know we are referring to the same thing.
   OSS officer Alan Scaife (1944)[1]

A little more than a year after Ayatollah Khomeini returned to Iran, Archbishop Óscar Romero offered Mass in El Salvador. The popular archbishop of San Salvador had become an outspoken critic of the ruling military junta. Romero was associated with "liberation theology," a Christian worldview that called for radical empathy for and solidarity with the poor and oppressed. Distraught at the killings of civilian protesters, Archbishop Romero's sermon appealed to the Salvadorian soldiers enforcing the junta's orders. "No soldier," he preached, "is obliged to obey an order against God's law."[2] While Romero celebrated Mass the following day, a man walked into the chapel and shot Romero through the heart.[3] Romero's death did not end the chaos. Supported by the Carter and Reagan administrations, El Salvador's military government would wage a twelve-year civil war against Communist-backed forces. Archbishop Romero's assassination dramatically illustrated the violence and brutality wracking the lives of everyday people in Latin America, and why many in the region were drawn to liberation theology.

In 1968, the Peruvian priest Gustavo Gutiérrez formalized the idea of liberation theology in his book *A Theology of Liberation* (1971). Gutiérrez explained liberation theology as "theological reflection born of the experience of shared efforts to abolish the current unjust situation and to build a different society, freer and more human."[4] Rooted in the gospels and in the experience of poverty, liberation theology focused on the liberation of the poor from all sources of oppression. While these ideas certainly reflected global concerns—James Cone and other thinkers were articulating Black liberation theology in the United States around the same time—Gutierrez and his colleagues were rooted in what they saw as the unjust political and economic context of Latin America. Stressing solidarity with the poor, these thinkers wanted to "do" theology by making it responsive to the needs of the most vulnerable. Given the focus on poverty and the action of "liberation," this theology was frequently criticized as a wolf in sheep's clothing, a Communist plot to leverage Christian theology for its own vision of class warfare. Even within the Catholic Church, liberation theology was a contentious movement, drawing both popular adulation and official censure.[5]

The Reagan administration and the papacy of John Paul II shared concerns about these developments in Latin America. Liberation theology threatened doctrinal purity and Church unity, as well as the economic and political arrangements in this US sphere of influence. Cardinal Joseph Ratzinger, the future Pope Benedict XVI, issued a condemnation of liberation theology in 1984 when he headed the Vatican's powerful Congregation for the Doctrine of the Faith, which policed doctrine and heresy.[6] For the Americans, the Reagan administration position was shaped by foreign-policy thinkers deeply suspicious of liberation theology. Several Reagan advisors argued that the US government should "confront" liberation theology as an explicitly Communist threat.[7]

The Agency's new focus on liberation theology owed much to the shock of the Iranian Revolution. After the shah's downfall, there was a marked increase in the CIA's attentiveness to religious groups and their potential anti-American politics. In Khomeini's shadow, much of the Agency's attention focused on Islam. The CIA produced voluminous studies about individual Muslim countries ("Egypt: Islamic Cults, Crisis, and Politics") that reflected these new analytical priorities.[8] At the same time, the Agency produced broader geopolitical syntheses of Muslim movements to act as a kind of early warning system for religious fundamentalism. Running well over 100 pages, "Islam and Politics: A Compendium" (1984) is a remarkably ambitious country-by-country assessment of every nation-state with a sizeable Muslim population.[9] The document reviewed an extensive range of information about each country, assessing how religiously "fundamentalist" certain things appeared, including schooling, courts, government policies, popular Muslim organizations, and popular understandings of religious establishment.

Renewed attention to liberation theology and Islamic fundamentalism meant that, by the early 1980s, the Agency understood both as radical movements empowered through the "overall religious revival." They were dangerous precisely because they did not obey the religious norms the Agency had come to expect, like support for capitalism and the free market.

Warning of Islamic fundamentalism's susceptibility to Communism, for example, the "Compendium" noted that Islamic fundamentalists "want society restructured to protect the underprivileged and to institutionalize an equitable distribution of the fruits of labor."[10] These concerns paralleled fears about liberation theology in the context of the Church's social teachings. As the CIA quickly learned, liberation theology had some of its roots in the liberalizing changes made at the Second Vatican Council, and seemed to be just the sort of left-leaning outcome that the CIA had worried about as it watched the Council unfold.[11]

Reflecting growing concern within the Reagan administration, the CIA tracked developments in liberation theology throughout the 1980s. A 1985 Agency conference on "Liberation Theology and Communism" featured a keynote address by CIA director William Casey.[12] The following year, the CIA produced a major study of liberation theology, which it identified as both "anti-West" and anti-American. The Agency viewed liberation theology as opening a door for increased Soviet involvement in Latin American countries, as well as an opportunity for Cuban president Fidel Castro to "export the Cuban revolution."[13] In countries like Nicaragua—where the CIA supported right-wing forces seeking to overthrow the democratic-socialist Sandinistas—the Agency saw liberation theology working against US Cold War goals in Latin America.[14] Worryingly for the Agency, however, many of the movement's adherents were there not because of Soviet propaganda but because they understood the movement as part of a persuasive Christian framework. The "preferential option for the poor," long a feature of Catholic social teaching and raised to prominence within liberation theology, acted as a powerful influence on Latin American Catholics. This included members of the clergy, who the CIA noted had in some cases cooperated with violent extremist groups. While the Agency was heartened to see Vatican condemnation of liberation theology for "its misuse of the Bible to justify political acts," it was clear that liberation theology would continue despite official criticism.[15] The CIA tried to reverse-engineer liberation theology's popularity so it could be anticipated and countered. The Agency concluded that a combination of repressive government policies, religious participation in government, a high percentage of Catholics, and socio-economic insecurity offered the ideal situation in which liberation theology took hold.[16]

The Agency's specific concerns about liberation theology can be seen in individual country assessments, such as in a 1988 study of Haiti. By the late 1980s, Haiti was reeling from a series of coup d'états and military rulers. Seeing many of the indicators the CIA had discovered in other Latin

American countries rife with liberation theology, the Agency noted how all the ingredients were present in Haiti for a turn toward religious radicalism. Complicating the assessment of Haitian religion, however, was the presence of Haitian Vodou, a syncretistic religious system that drew from West African, Catholic, and indigenous religious traditions. (The CIA noted that most adherents saw "no contradiction" between practicing both Vodou and Christianity.[17]) Drawing on unnamed academic studies, the CIA concluded that while Vodou was not normally political, it did tend to reinforce troubling aspects of Haitian society such as "nationalism, xenophobia, and acceptance of arbitrary authority." "Voodoo"—as the CIA called it—operated as a "social glue" in Haitian society, and this made it a potential partner for Catholic liberation theology. Haitian society was secretive, they thought, which meant that "radical catholic and voodoo elements" had a chance to organize with clerics favorable to liberation theology and accomplish "leftwing Catholic subversion." In a heavily redacted section of the 1988 report, the Agency gave special attention to the "leftist priest" Jean-Bertrand Aristide, Haiti's most prominent champion of liberation. Three years later, Aristide would become Haiti's first democratically elected president.[18]

The Haiti memo and others like it reflected the Agency's renewed efforts to provide careful, nuanced analysis of religion's role in foreign societies. The world religions paradigm was confounded by Iran, and new approaches were needed to understand liberation theology. In the case of Haiti, religion was assessed through the lens of both Haitian politics but also Haitian society more generally. Attention was given to Catholicism's anti-Vodou campaigns, the uneasy place of Protestantism in Haitian life, and even Vodou itself, which—while not treated evenhandedly—received markedly more serious engagement than other smaller religious groups had in decades past. Far from ignoring religion, by the late 1980s CIA analysis reflected considerable attention to religious movements and their ability to impede US policy.

These CIA studies stand in marked contrast to the easily generalizable studies of religion predating 1979. Just as the Iranian Revolution had pushed the CIA to produce detailed, qualified studies of Muslim diversity, the Agency produced similar work in order to understand liberation theology. In one particularly telling exchange, Agency analysts critiqued a proposed White House statement on liberation theology for not thinking sufficiently critically about the movement they were analyzing. When the White House document described priests favoring liberation theology as atheistic and put their Catholicity in quotation marks, an Agency analyst scratched it out and wrote: "This is grossly inaccurate: radical clergy is Catholic; no one challenges that."[19] These corrections got to the heart of the mistakes made in the lead-up to the Iranian Revolution: recognizing the diversity of religious ideas within a tradition and understanding that, contrary to popular opinion, a religious group's opposition to US policy did not make it non-religious—particularly so for its many religious followers.

The CIA's approach to liberation theology made sense in a post–Iranian Revolution world. Having seen their analytical models crumble in Tehran, Agency analysts understood that the old assumptions—about the United States and religious actors making natural allies, or religion's resistance to Communism—could no longer be taken for granted in a world where a seventy-seven-year-old imam could topple one of the United States' most crucial allies, or a Peruvian priest could persuasively indict US foreign policy on the global stage. The rise of liberation theology, coinciding as it did with the aftermath of the Iranian Revolution, seemed to confirm these new suspicions. Its sudden debut on the Latin American scene was another reminder that the "world religions" that made up the world religions paradigm were fragmented, diverse social groups that did not easily conform to any one set of rules.

*　*　*

The study of other people's beliefs is a difficult task. Whether it is pursued in the world of intelligence or academia, success requires self-reflexivity. Poking holes in your own ideas and trying to understand a novel concept in different ways are crucial skills when your job is making sense of new and unfamiliar information. This seemingly straightforward task is challenging since, in order to make the strange familiar, the strange has to be interpreted through pre-existing categories and ideas.[20] The most successful intelligence work appreciated this methodological tension, and the most consequential analytical failures reflected overconfidence in one's own understanding of the world without appreciating how one's ideas—just like those of your opponents—are shaped by a cultural milieu that might make you more likely to act and think in specific ways. The OSS and the CIA, as US intelligence organizations, reflect the challenges of the United States becoming self-reflexive about its place in the world after World War II just as the academic study of religion attempted to do the same at American universities. Both attempted to shape public knowledge and discourse about America's place in the world.

Informed by popular ideas in US culture, OSS and the CIA pursued a religious approach that understood "religion" as a coherent dimension of human life and society, as an object that could be identified and generalized in universal terms. Echoing the academic study of religion, intelligence officers saw religion as something that everyone everywhere possessed all the time. This made it a profitable avenue to understand foreign cultures and peoples, since every culture had religion. Religion's ostensibly universal presence and structure would also make it easy to use the knowledge of one tradition to interpret another. Over time, a pattern emerged in OSS and CIA analysis of local religious groups: while "religion" writ large might share certain qualities (such as key figures, rituals, and beliefs), each specific tradition in different locations had unique qualities that had to be understood in order for officers to anticipate—and possibly control—the motives and behaviors of practitioners. These imperial concerns were reflected in how this information was collected, analyzed, and operationalized.

While dramatic operations and adrenaline-pounding stories dominate depictions of intelligence on both screen and page—a critique rarely leveled at religious studies—this overlooks the real value of studying intelligence history, which provides a window onto how US intelligence officers understood human nature, how they imagined foreign people, their ideas, and the places in which they lived. The intelligence operations chronicled in this book were born of the belief that history was moving in one certain direction, toward toleration, progress, and the American way. What emerges from this study is not a simple lesson that the intelligence community thought or acted uniformly. To study OSS or the CIA means looking at the collective actions of tens of thousands of specialists across several decades who followed different protocols and thought different things yet presented themselves as if they were moving in lockstep toward shared goals and objectives. Recognizing this helps us see how intelligence officers' teleological confidence plastered over conceptual holes in the religious approach since, even when the specific elements of the religious approach were in doubt, the overarching value of "religion" was rarely questioned.

In this way, studies of the intelligence community mirror studies of religious communities: actors present their actions and their ideas as shared across rank-and-file members when, upon greater scrutiny, it becomes clearer that they exist in a field not unlike a wilderness of disparate actions and ideas. The value is not in determining that the CIA *thought one thing*, but that the collected experiences presented here illustrate Americans' tendency to think themselves expert on religion no matter their expertise. Intelligence officers had to make sense of conflicting, confusing, and sometimes contradictory religious information—and make decisions about what counted as religion in the first place—in the service of what they understood as the security of the United States.

The ultimate irony of the religious approach was that religion was not special at all. It was not the universal Rosetta Stone its advocates hoped it would be, unlocking the mysteries of human behavior in every society and culture. It sometimes marked a set-apart area of human society. Other times it did not. This is a familiar conundrum for those of us who study religion. The lesson is not that religion does not matter, but instead that religion may matter in unexpected ways—such as, for example, presuming "religion" itself to be a useful tool to study foreign cultures. In this methodological overlap, the history of American intelligence and the history of American religion have much to say to one another. This book has tried to show that religion and national security share a genealogy in the twentieth-century American imagination, and neither of their stories can be told without reference to the other. The study of US intelligence work and American religion then becomes a way to understand how the United States changed as it asserted itself as a global superpower with a new errand, and what that meant for people around the world.

Acknowledgments

I started this project because I wasn't sure I would have a chance at another one. I stumbled into the tale of Tom Dooley and wound up with a story about religion, psychological warfare, Vietnam, the history of the study of world religions, anti-Catholicism, several psychics, two intelligence agencies, and at least one simulated return of Jesus Christ. That these unwieldy topics have fused into a book is a testament to the friendship, generosity, and patience of many people.

The Religion Department at Florida State University was a wonderful place to train, in large part because of Amanda Porterfield's mentorship. As is often the case, she understood this project's value before I did. When I feared my topic would not pan out—perhaps only yielding invitations to appear on the History channel in programs concerning extraterrestrials— she encouraged me to stay the course. I am grateful that she did. The intellectual freedom and flexibility she fostered is the reason why readers may find value in this book. Classes and conversations with Amanda Porterfield, John Corrigan, Mike McVicar, Martin Kavka, and Adam Gaiser sharpened my thinking and work. G. Kurt Piehler and Neil Jumonville provided a warm welcome in the History Department. I would not be a professor without Amy Koehlinger, who showed me I had a place in the community of scholars. This book would not exist without Matthew Day, who taught me to ask better questions.

Moving to the University of Northern Iowa, I traded a steep drop in average annual temperature for a new community of wonderful teacher-scholars. Working with and learning from my colleagues in the Department of Philosophy and World Religions has been a pleasure. Thank you to Susan Hill, John Burnight, Yasemin Sari, Mike Prophet, and Brittany Flokstra for enriching the everyday. Coffee runs with Abby Helgevold were treasured opportunities to reflect on the craft of teaching, and why it is that we do what we do. Special thanks to Helen Harrington, who makes it so much easier for me to do my job. Thanks also to my UNI students, especially Courtney Post, for reminding me why I love to get up and go to work in the morning.

Beyond my own campus, colleagues far and wide made innumerable contributions to my work and life without which this book would not have been possible. Participation in the Society for Historians of American Foreign Relations (SHAFR) Summer Institute at the University of Cambridge was an intellectual turning point for this project. I owe a debt to Andrew Preston, Mario del Pero, and all of the participants who encouraged me to lean into the interdisciplinary potential of this book. Thanks also to SHAFR for supporting these activities and for including adjunct faculty. Paul Dafydd Jones and Charles Mathewes graciously welcomed me into the Emerging Scholars workshop at the University of Virginia, and I thank them and my fellow participants for their feedback. I'm also grateful for so many people who provided fruitful conference responses, took time out of their busy schedules to meet with me, or provided support and encouragement over email, including Brent Nongbri, William Inboden, James Fisher, Lerone Martin, John Modern, Roy Domenico, Kevin Schultz, Russell McCutcheon, Hugh Urban, Edwin A. Martini, John C. Seitz, Charles Gallagher, Sylvester Johnson, Zareena Grewal, Flagg Miller, Finbarr Curtis, Ray Haberski, Hugh Wilford, and Merinda Simmons. Dianne Kirby was generous with her time and feedback, and the manuscript is much improved for her efforts. Matt Sutton was always helpful, keen to swap ideas and sources, and modeled collegiality to a junior scholar working on a similar topic. An earlier version of chapter 1 was published in the *U.S. Catholic Historian*, 33 no. 4 (2015), and I am grateful for their permission to adapt it here. Thanks also to the external readers whose comments greatly improved the manuscript.

These colleagues would have had little to read if it hadn't been for the hard work of many archivists and librarians who helped make this project possible. John Waide, of the Pius XII Library at the Saint Louis University Archives, went above and beyond the call of duty in helping me track down Tom Dooley's scattered papers. When I could not afford the trek myself, Danielle Kovacs at the University of Massachusetts–Amherst Special Collections graciously located and copied some of William Lederer's papers. Katherine Graber of the Billy Graham Center Archives at Wheaton College and Valoise Armstrong at the Dwight D. Eisenhower Presidential Library helped me access archival materials and were patient and helpful. Carol A. Leadenham and the staff at the Hoover Institution Archives made my trip to Stanford particularly fruitful. Thanks also to Dr. Mary Elizabeth Curry of the National Security Archive, and the staff at the National Archives at

College Park. A Florida State University Dissertation Research Grant made these trips possible, and for that I'm grateful. I am in awe of the Interlibrary Loan Staffs at the University of Northern Iowa and Florida State University for always managing to locate whatever material I requested, no matter how strange or obscure. A sincere thank you to all of the archivists and librarians who helped me piece this project together.

At the University of Chicago Press, Tim Mennel graciously met with me when this project was little more than a series of interesting ideas. He was patient and supportive as I completed the project. Thanks to Susannah Engstrom for guiding me through the production process, and to everyone else at Chicago who made this book possible.

My friends and colleagues from the FSU Religion program are an embarrassment of riches, without whom I could not have conceived this book's central questions. Conversations with Brad Stoddard and Tara Baldrick-Morrone ignited my curiosity in the world religions paradigm. Adam Park is as smart as he is humble, and modeled intellectual generosity in the seminar room when I most needed to see it. Charles McCrary is one of our field's indispensable scholars, and will forever be my favorite flag football QB. Meredith Ross is equal parts fantastic colleague and excellent wedding DJ. Jeffrey Wheatley is kind and brilliant: the sort of colleague you sometimes get but never quite deserve. I spilled tacos on Sarah Dees the first time I met her, which she graciously overlooks each time she provides her generous and brilliant feedback on my writing. Cara Burnidge did her best to dissuade me from graduate school, which didn't quite work, but we did talk until closing time and eventually got married. Others who have enriched my life and work while this project marinated include Andy McKee, Haley Iliff, Stacy Stoddard, Jenny Collins-Elliott, Zac Johnson, Randy Tarnowski, Molly Reed, Haley McCrary, Tim Colletti, Emily Clark, Anna Amundson, Shem Miller, and the staffs of Bird's Aphrodisiac Oyster Shack and the Tennessee Street Waffle House. Jeff, Sarah, Charlie, and Cara read and commented on parts of this manuscript more than anyone in their right mind would ever care to, and for that I thank them.

Closer to home, I was sustained by friends who enriched my life during this process. Marco and Maria are the kind of friends who usually only exist in movies, except that they are real and come to visit you after the birth of a new baby to make you soup. Tim, Jason, and the kids are a delight. Dillon has been my good friend for a very long time, across continents, countries, and innumerable internet dragons. Alex only sweetens the deal.

Last but not least, thanks to my family for their support. In the process of writing this book, Tom welcomed me into his family and shared the best places to find fried chicken in town. I am grateful for both. The presence and humor of my brother, Paul, is a gift. That you hold this book in your hands is a testament to my parents' enduring support for me: this work is dedicated to them. Cara is simply the best. To Rose, I say: be quick, but don't rush.

Notes

Introduction

1   Bruce Lincoln, "Theses on Method," *Method and Theory in the Study of Religion* 8 (1996): 225–28.

2   "Full Text: Bush's National Security Strategy," *New York Times*, September 20, 2002, sec. Politics, https://www.nytimes.com/2002/09/20/politics/full-text -bushs-national-security-strategy.html.

3   Jim Schnabel, *Remote Viewers: The Secret History of America's Psychic Spies* (New York: Dell Publishing, 1997). This was part of the same program that was popularized through Jon Ronson, *The Men Who Stare at Goats* (New York: Simon & Schuster, 2009).

4   "Project Sun Streak," October 18, 1988, CIA-RDP96–00789R001400180001–7, National Archives (CREST Database).

5   Jonathan Z. Smith, *Relating Religion: Essays in the Study of Religion* (Chicago: University of Chicago Press, 2004), 389.

6   For the religious aspects of NSC-68, see the introduction in Dianne Kirby, ed., *Religion and the Cold War* (New York: Palgrave Macmillan, 2002); For more on NSC-68 in general, see Ken Young, "Revisiting NSC 68," *Journal of Cold War Studies* 15, no. 1 (2013): 3–33.

7   "A Report to the National Security Council by the Executive Secretary on United States Objectives and Programs for National Security," April 14, 1950, Harry S. Truman Presidential Library, https://www.trumanlibrary.gov/library/research -files/report-national-security-council-nsc-68.

8   Ferdinand Mayer to William Donovan, July 17, 1945, RG 226, Entry 210, Box 338, Folder 1, National Archives at College Park, College Park, MD.

9   Office of Strategic Services, "Morale Operations Field Manual," January 26, 1943.

10 By "empire," I do not mean that the United States constituted itself in any legal sense as an empire. Instead, I have in mind Said's definition of empire as "the practice, the theory, and the attitudes of a dominating center ruling a distant territory." Edward W. Said, *Culture and Imperialism* (New York: Vintage, 1994), 8.

11 Allen Dulles to W. G. Wyman, April 10, 1956, CIA-RDP80B01676R0012000600 36-6, National Archives (CREST Database). Until the 2004 Intelligence Reform and Terrorism Prevention Act that restructured the intelligence community, the DCI also served as the director of the Central Intelligence Agency. After this restructuring, the director of the Central Intelligence Agency reported to a new position, the director of national intelligence (DNI). While the DCI was the formal title for the head of the CIA and wider intelligence community between 1946 and 2005, this position was widely known as "CIA director" in American popular culture. While post-9/11 usage may differ, this book is concerned with a time period in which "CIA director" was used interchangeably with DCI. Consequently, this book mirrors this usage.

12 In making this argument, I draw on important work about the changing relationship between religion and the state after World War II, including Kevin M. Schultz, *Tri-Faith America: How Catholics and Jews Held Postwar America to Its Protestant Promise* (New York: Oxford University Press, 2011); David Sehat, *The Myth of American Religious Freedom* (New York: Oxford University Press, 2011); Winnifred Sullivan, *The Impossibility of Religious Freedom* (Princeton, NJ: Princeton University Press, 2005); Zareena Grewal, *Islam Is a Foreign Country: American Muslims and the Global Crisis of Authority* (New York: NYU Press, 2013); Wendy L. Wall, *Inventing the "American Way": The Politics of Consensus from the New Deal to the Civil Rights Movement* (New York: Oxford University Press, 2008); Kevin Kruse, *One Nation Under God: How Corporate America Invented Christian America* (New York: Basic Books, 2015).

13 On the simultaneous familiar-foreign tension in American Catholicism, see John T. McGreevy, *Catholicism and American Freedom: A History* (New York: W. W. Norton, 2003); James T. Fisher, *Dr. America: The Lives of Thomas A. Dooley, 1927-1961* (Amherst: University of Massachusetts Press, 1997); Peter R. D'Agostino, *Rome in America: Transnational Catholic Ideology from the Risorgimento to Fascism* (Chapel Hill: University of North Carolina Press, 2004); Maura Jane Farrelly, *Papist Patriots: The Making of an American Catholic Identity* (New York: Oxford University Press, 2012); John C. Seitz, "The Mass-Clock and the Spy: The Catholicization of World War II," *Church History* 83, no. 4 (December 2014): 924-56, https://doi.org/10.1017/S0009640714001176; Robert A. Orsi, *History and Presence* (Cambridge, MA: Harvard University Press, 2016); Katherine D. Moran, "Catholicism and the Making of the U.S. Pacific," *Journal of the Gilded Age and Progressive Era* 12, no. 4 (October 2013): 434-74, https://doi.org/10.1017/S1537781413000327; Elizabeth Fenton, *Religious Liberties: Anti-Catholicism and Liberal Democracy in Nineteenth-Century U.S. Literature and Culture*, 1st ed. (New York: Oxford University Press, 2011).

14 For broad coverage of religion and the "Cultural Cold War," see Jonathan P.

Herzog, *The Spiritual-Industrial Complex: America's Religious Battle against Communism in the Early Cold War* (New York: Oxford University Press, 2011); William Inboden, *Religion and American Foreign Policy, 1945–1960: The Soul of Containment* (Cambridge and New York: Cambridge University Press, 2008); T. Jeremy Gunn, *Spiritual Weapons: The Cold War and the Forging of an American National Religion* (Santa Barbara, CA: ABC-CLIO, 2008); Raymond Haberski, *God and War: American Civil Religion since 1945* (New Brunswick, NJ: Rutgers University Press, 2012); Seth Jacobs, *America's Miracle Man in Vietnam: Ngo Dinh Diem, Religion, Race, and U.S. Intervention in Southeast Asia, 1950–1957* (Durham, NC: Duke University Press, 2004); Seth Jacobs, "'Our System Demands the Supreme Being': The US Religious Revival and the 'Diem Experiment,' 1954–55," *Diplomatic History* 25, no. 4 (2001): 589–624; Andrew Preston, *Sword of the Spirit, Shield of Faith: Religion in American War and Diplomacy* (New York: Anchor Books, 2012); Jonathan Nashel, *Edward Lansdale's Cold War* (Amherst: University of Massachusetts Press, 2005); Robert Dean, *Imperial Brotherhood: Gender and the Making of Cold War Foreign Policy* (Amherst: University of Massachusetts Press, 2003); Andrew Preston, "Monsters Everywhere: A Genealogy of National Security," *Diplomatic History* 38, no. 3 (June 1, 2014): 477–500, https://doi.org/10.1093/dh/dhu018; Kirby, *Religion and the Cold War*; Dianne Kirby, "The Religious Cold War," in *The Oxford Handbook of the Cold War*, ed. Richard H. Immerman and Petra Goedde (New York: Oxford University Press, 2013), 540–64; Odd Arne Westad, *The Cold War: A World History* (New York: Basic Books, 2017); K. H. Gaston, "The Cold War Romance of Religious Authenticity: Will Herberg, William F. Buckley Jr., and the Rise of the New Right," *Journal of American History* 99, no. 4 (March 1, 2013): 1133–58, https://doi.org/10.1093/jahist/jas588. For an excellent example of these trends in the study of religion itself, see Lucia Hulsether, "The Grammar of Racism: Religious Pluralism and the Birth of the Interdisciplines," *Journal of the American Academy of Religion* 86, no. 1 (March 5, 2018): 1–41, https://doi.org/10.1093/jaarel/lfx049.

15 On the world religions paradigm, see Christopher R. Cotter and David G. Robertson, "The World Religions Paradigm in Contemporary Religious Studies," in *After World Religions: Reconstructing Religious Studies* (New York: Routledge, 2016), 1–20. For important work on the history of this idea, see Tomoko Masuzawa, *The Invention of World Religions: Or, How European Universalism Was Preserved in the Language of Pluralism* (Chicago: University of Chicago Press, 2005); Jonathan Z. Smith, "Religion, Religions, Religious," in *Critical Terms for Religious Studies*, ed. Mark C. Taylor (University of Chicago Press, 1998); Brent Nongbri, *Before Religion: A History of a Modern Concept* (New Haven, CT: Yale University Press, 2013). One early critical response to this idea is Wilfred Cantwell Smith, *The Meaning and End of Religion* (Minneapolis: Fortress Press, 1962); For other excellent work informed by this critical attention, see Elizabeth Shakman Hurd, *Beyond Religious Freedom: The New Global Politics of Religion* (Princeton, NJ: Princeton University Press, 2015); Nicholas B. Dirks, *Castes of Mind: Colonialism and the Making of Modern India* (Princeton, NJ: Princeton University Press, 2001); Donald S. Lopez, *Curators of the Buddha: The Study of Buddhism under Colonialism* (Chicago: University of Chicago Press, 1995); Jason Ananda Josephson, *The Invention of Religion in Japan* (Chicago: University of Chicago Press, 2012).

16 W. G. Wyman to Allen Dulles, March 30, 1956, CIA-RDP80B01676R0012000 60037-5, National Archives (CREST Database).

17 The Staff of *LIFE*, ed., *The World's Great Religions, Volume 1: Religions of the East* (New York: Time Incorporated, 1955). On religion at Henry Luce's publications, see Eden Consenstein, "Religion at Time Inc.: From the Beginning of Time to the End of Life" (PhD diss., Princeton University, 2021); Chaplain Corps Planning Group, "The Religions of South Vietnam in Faith and Fact" (US Navy Bureau of Naval Personnel, 1967), Edward Geary Lansdale Papers, Box 62, Folder 1619, Hoover Institution Archives. For other examples of national security interventions in Cold War American religion, see Hugh B. Urban, *The Church of Scientology: A History of a New Religion* (Princeton, NJ: Princeton University Press, 2011); Sylvester A. Johnson and Steven Weitzman, eds., *The FBI and Religion: Faith and National Security before and after 9/11* (Oakland: University of California Press, 2017); Kirby, *Religion and the Cold War*; Hugh Wilford, *The Mighty Wurlitzer: How the CIA Played America* (Cambridge, MA: Harvard University Press, 2008); Matthew Dunne, *A Cold War State of Mind: Brainwashing and Postwar American Society* (Amherst: University of Massachusetts Press, 2013); Lori L. Bogle, *The Pentagon's Battle for the American Mind: The Early Cold War* (College Station: Texas A&M University Press, 2004); Inboden, *Religion and American Foreign Policy, 1945-1960.*

18 David Chidester, *Savage Systems: Colonialism and Comparative Religion in Southern Africa* (Charlottesville: University of Virginia Press, 1996); Chidester, *Empire of Religion: Imperialism and Comparative Religion* (Chicago: University of Chicago Press, 2014). In a specifically US context, see Johnson and Weitzman, *The FBI and Religion.* Many of the chapters in this edited volume speak to this theme, but see especially Michael Barkun, "The FBI and American Muslims After September 11," in *The FBI and Religion: Faith and National Security Before and After 9/11*, ed. Sylvester A. Johnson and Steven Weitzman (University of California Press, 2017), 244-55; Sylvester A. Johnson, "Dreams and Shadows: Martin Luther King Jr., the FBI, and the Southern Christian Leadership Conference," in *The FBI and Religion: Faith and National Security Before and After 9/11*, ed. Sylvester A. Johnson and Steven Weitzman (University of California Press, 2017), 168-90.

19 Jonathan Z. Smith makes this point about the study of world religions more generally: "It is impossible to escape the suspicion that a world religion is simply a religion like ours, and that it is, above all, a tradition that has achieved sufficient power and numbers to enter our history to form it, interact with it, or thwart it . . . All 'primitives,' by way of contrast, may be lumped together, as may the 'minor religions,' because they do not confront our history in any direct fashion. From the point of view of power, they are invisible." See Jonathan Z. Smith, "Religion, Religions, Religious," 280.

20 Chakrabarty argues that "the phenomenon of 'political modernity'—namely, the rule by modern institutions of the state, bureaucracy, and capitalist enterprise—is impossible to think of anyway in the world without invoking certain categories and concepts, the genealogies of which go deep into the intellectual and even theological traditions of Europe." See Dipesh Chakrabarty, *Provincializing Europe: Postcolonial Thought and Historical Difference* (Princeton, NJ: Princeton University Press, 2007), 4. Also see Chidester, *Empire of Religion*; Bruce Lincoln, *Discourse and the Construction of Society: Comparative Studies of Myth, Ritual, and Classification* (Oxford: Oxford University Press, 1992); Mary Douglas, *Purity and Danger: An Analysis of Concepts of Pollution and Taboo*, 1st ed. (Milton Park, UK: Taylor & Francis, 1966); Jonathan Z. Smith, *Imagining Religion: From Babylon to Jonestown* (University of Chicago Press, 1982); Peter Harrison, *"Religion" and the Religions in the English Enlightenment* (Cambridge and New York: Cambridge University Press, 2002); Talal Asad, *Genealogies of Religion: Discipline and Reasons of Power in Christianity and Islam* (Baltimore: Johns Hopkins University Press, 1993); Lopez, *Curators of the Buddha*.

21   Chidester, *Savage Systems*, 6. For more specifically American and/or transnational contexts, see Tisa Wenger, *Religious Freedom: The Contested History of an American Ideal* (Chapel Hill: University of North Carolina Press, 2017); Sylvester Johnson, *African American Religions, 1500–2000: Colonialism, Democracy, and Freedom* (New York: Cambridge University Press, 2015); David Hollinger, *Protestants Abroad: How Missionaries Tried to Change the World but Changed America* (Princeton, NJ: Princeton University Press, 2017); Jolyon Baraka Thomas, *Faking Liberties: Religious Freedom in American-Occupied Japan* (Chicago: University of Chicago Press, 2019).

22   For one specific example, see William Casey, "The Clandestine War in Europe (1942–1945): Remarks of William J. Casey on Receipt of the William J. Donovan Award at Dinner of Veterans of O.S.S.," December 5, 1974, William J. Casey Papers, Box 429, Folder 1, Hoover Institution Archives, 2.

23   Some of the many intelligence histories that influenced this book include Kenneth Osgood, *Total Cold War: Eisenhower's Secret Propaganda Battle at Home and Abroad* (Lawrence: University Press of Kansas, 2006); Christopher M. Andrew, *For the President's Eyes Only: Secret Intelligence and the American Presidency from Washington to Bush* (New York: HarperPerennial, 1996); Rhodri Jeffreys-Jones, *Cloak and Dollar: A History of American Secret Intelligence* (New Haven, CT: Yale University Press, 2003); Rhodri Jeffreys-Jones, *The CIA and American Democracy*, 3rd ed. (New Haven, CT: Yale University Press, 2003); John Prados, *The Family Jewels: The CIA, Secrecy, and Presidential Power* (Austin: University of Texas Press, 2013); John Prados, *Presidents' Secret Wars: CIA and Pentagon Covert Operations from World War II through the Persian Gulf* (Chicago: I. R. Dee, 1996); Dina Rezk, "Orientalism and Intelligence Analysis: Deconstructing Anglo-American Notions of the 'Arab,'" *Intelligence and National Security*, September 3, 2014, 1–22, https://doi.org/10.1080/02684527.2014.949077; Wilford, *The Mighty Wurlitzer*. For considerations of Vatican intelligence in particular, see David Alvarez, *Spies in the Vatican: Espionage and Intrigue from Napoleon to the Holocaust* (Lawrence: University Press of Kansas, 2002). For an example of a careful and meticulous study of OSS operations, see Timothy Naftali, "Artifice: James Angleton and X-2 Operations in Italy," in *The Secrets War: The Office of Strategic Services in World War II*, ed. George Chalou (Washington, DC: National Archives Trust Fund

Board, 1992). For considerations of intelligence in American popular culture, see Christopher Moran, "Ian Fleming and the Public Profile of the CIA," *Journal of Cold War Studies* 15, no. 1 (2013): 119–46; David Alvarez and Eduard Mark, *Spying Through a Glass Darkly: American Espionage Against the Soviet Union, 1945–1946* (Lawrence: University Press of Kansas, 2016). For an excellent example of the important revisionary work being done by scholars of intelligence, see Kaeten Mistry, "Re-Thinking American Intervention in the 1948 Italian Election: Beyond a Success–Failure Dichotomy," *Modern Italy* 16, no. 2 (May 2011): 179–94, https://doi.org/10.1080/13532944.2011.557224. This book was also influenced by Matthew Sutton's research as he wrote his study of missionaries and American intelligence during World War II. See Sutton, *Double Crossed: The Missionaries Who Spied for the United States During the Second World War* (New York: Basic Books, 2019).

24 For a persuasive historiographical argument on intelligence history in relation to other fields, see Kenneth A. Osgood, "Hearts and Minds: The Unconventional Cold War," *Journal of Cold War Studies* 4, no. 2 (2002): 85–107, 95.

25 Smith, *Imagining Religion*, xii.

26 Kaeten Mistry writes that "The scholarly task is to nuance understanding of the CIA in the wider context of American intervention. A fixation on Agency records detracts from this objective and implies a 'hidden truth' that lurks inside a dusty box on some far-flung archival shelf." See Mistry, "Approaches to Understanding the Inaugural CIA Covert Operation in Italy: Exploding Useful Myths," *Intelligence and National Security* 26, no. 2–3 (April 2011): 267, https://doi.org/10.1080/026845 27.2011.559318.

27 An earlier version of this chapter was first published in the *U.S. Catholic Historian* 33, no. 4 (2015), Catholic University of America Press.

28 Perry Miller, *Errand into the Wilderness* (Cambridge, MA: Belknap Press of Harvard University Press, 1956), 14.

29 Miller, *Errand into the Wilderness*, 14.

30 As Amy Kaplan wrote, "the field of American studies was conceived on the banks of the Congo." See Kaplan, "'Left Alone With America': The Absence of Empire in the Study of American Culture," in *Cultures of United States Imperialism*, ed. Donald E. Pease and Amy Kaplan (Durham, NC: Duke University Press, 1993).

31 Quoted in Rivka Maizlish, "Rethinking the Origin of American Studies (with Help from Perry Miller)," *U.S. Intellectual History Blog*, November 13, 2013, https://s-usih.org/2013/11/rethinking-the-origin-of-american-studies-with-help-from-perry-miller/.

32 "Perry Miller Personnel File," July 19, 1945, RG 226, Entry 224, Box 526, National Archives at College Park, College Park, MD.

33 "Perry Miller Personnel File."

34 Quoted in David Robarge, "'Cunning Passages, Contrived Corridors': Wandering in the Angletonian Wilderness," *Studies in Intelligence* 53, no. 4 (December 2009), https://www.cia.gov/library/center-for-the-study-of-intelligence/csi-publica tions/csi-studies/studies/vol53no4/201ccunning-passages-contrived-corridors 201d.html. Robarge's article provides a useful overview of scholarship on Angleton.

35 Angleton appears to have borrowed the line from Eliot's poem "Gerontion." See Loch K. Johnson, "James Angleton and the Church Committee," *Journal of Cold War Studies* 15, no. 4 (October 2013): 135, https://doi.org/10.1162/JCWS_a_00397. Angleton's paranoia caught up with him during the Congressional investigations of American intelligence during the mid-1970s, and he was forced to resign.

36 Miller, *Errand into the Wilderness*, ix.

37 Quoted in Kai Bird, *The Good Spy: The Life and Death of Robert Ames* (New York: Crown, 2014), 256.

38 John 8:32.

39 These numbers were accurate as of April 2020. Central Intelligence Agency, "CIA Pays Tribute to Its Fallen in Annual Memorial Ceremony," May 21, 2019, https:// www.cia.gov/news-information/press-releases-statements/2019-press-releases -statements/cia-pays-tribute-to-its-fallen-in-annual-memorial-ceremony.html.

40 The relative moral value of intelligence operations, even if they were the "lesser evil," was always understood against the "greater evil" of Communism (and, relatedly, its demonization). See Dianne Kirby, "Christian Anti-Communism," *Twentieth Century Communism*, no. 7 (Autumn 2014): 134.

41 Casey, "The Clandestine War in Europe (1942–1945): Remarks of William J. Casey on Receipt of the William J. Donovan Award at Dinner of Veterans of O.S.S.," 6.

42 Stanley Lovell, *Of Spies and Stratagems: Incredible Secrets of World War II Revealed by a Master Spy* (Englewood Cliffs, NJ: Prentice-Hall, 1963), 190. Emphasis original.

Chapter One

1 Richard Dunlop, *Donovan: America's Master Spy* (Chicago: Rand McNally, 1982), 375.

2 William J. Donovan, "The Need of Spiritual Recovery," *Brooklyn Central*, December 6, 1935, Folder No. 1—Letter and Clipping Publications and Papers, 1920–1935, William J. Donovan Papers.

3 Donovan was first appointed "Coordinator of Information" in July 1941. This office was restructured in June 1942 and renamed the Office of Strategic Services. See

Douglas C. Waller, *Wild Bill Donovan: The Spymaster Who Created the OSS and Modern American Espionage* (New York: Free Press, 2012), 69–72.

4   William Casey, "The Clandestine War in Europe (1942–1945): Remarks of William J. Casey on Receipt of the William J. Donovan Award at Dinner of Veterans of O.S.S.," December 5, 1974, William J. Casey Papers, Box 429, Folder 1, Hoover Institution Archives, 2.

5   "Pencils-Time Delay SRA-2," n.d., RG 226, Entry 215, Box 9, Folder 1, National Archives at College Park, College Park, MD.

6   Office of Strategic Services, "Arson: An Instruction Manual," May 1945, RG 226, Entry 215, Box 9, Folder 1–2, National Archives at College Park, College Park, MD.

7   Fernando Lujan, "Wanted: Ph.D.s Who Can Win a Bar Fight," *Foreign Affairs*, March 8, 2013, http://foreignpolicy.com/2013/03/08/wanted-ph-d-s-who-can-win-a-bar-fight/.

8   For more detailed assessments of OSS's legacy, see Christopher M. Andrew, *For the President's Eyes Only: Secret Intelligence and the American Presidency from Washington to Bush* (New York: HarperPerennial, 1996), 133–35; David Alvarez and Eduard Mark, *Spying Through a Glass Darkly: American Espionage Against the Soviet Union, 1945–1946* (Lawrence: University Press of Kansas, 2016), 11–15; Rhodri Jeffreys-Jones, *The CIA and American Democracy* (New Haven, CT: Yale University Press, 2003), 18–21; Jeffreys-Jones, *Cloak and Dollar: A History of American Secret Intelligence* (New Haven, CT: Yale University Press, 2003), 145–46. In addition to OSS's focus on research, Prados notes OSS's success with guerilla warfare. See John Prados, *Presidents' Secret Wars: CIA and Pentagon Covert Operations from World War II through the Persian Gulf* (Chicago: I. R. Dee, 1996), 15–18.

9   Louis Menand, "Wild Thing," *The New Yorker*, March 14, 2011, http://www.newyorker.com/magazine/2011/03/14/wild-thing-louis-menand. Menand's essay offers a different perspective than Eisenhower's, and is worth reading to understand many of the most common criticisms lobbed at Donovan and OSS.

10   Quoted in Walter L. Hixson, *Parting the Curtain: Propaganda, Culture, and the Cold War, 1945–1961* (New York: St. Martin's Press, 1998), 3.

11   Anthony Cave Brown, *The Last Hero: Wild Bill Donovan* (New York: Times Books, 1982), 2.

12   Ferdinand Mayer to William Donovan, July 17, 1945, RG 226, Entry 210, Box 338, Folder 1, National Archives at College Park, College Park, MD.

13   For this "long view" of the Cold War, see Odd Arne Westad, *The Cold War: A World History* (Basic Books, 2017).

14 Mayer to Donovan, July 17, 1945.

15 Chadwick provides a useful overview of many of the major players interested in the Vatican during the war. See Owen Chadwick, *Britain and the Vatican during the Second World War* (Cambridge: Cambridge University Press, 1986). Also see Michael Phayer, *The Catholic Church and the Holocaust, 1930–1965* (Bloomington: Indiana University Press, 2001); Alvarez and Mark, *Spying Through a Glass Darkly: American Espionage Against the Soviet Union, 1945–1946*; Charles R. Gallagher, *Vatican Secret Diplomacy: Joseph P. Hurley and Pope Pius XII* (Princeton, NJ: Yale University Press, 2008).

16 William Donovan, "Intelligence: Key to Defense," *LIFE*, September 30, 1946.

17 One important influence was the American imperial projects in the Philippines. See chapters 1 and 2 in Tisa Wenger, *Religious Freedom: The Contested History of an American Ideal* (Chapel Hill: University of North Carolina Press, 2017).

18 In the 1930s and 1940s, the Supreme Court heard dozens of cases involving the Jehovah's Witnesses. See Shawn Francis Peters, *Judging Jehovah's Witnesses: Religious Persecution and the Dawn of the Rights Revolution* (Lawrence: University Press of Kansas, 2002).

19 Michael Graziano, "Race, the Law, and Religion in America," *Oxford Research Encyclopedia of Religion*, September 2017, https://doi.org/10.1093/acrefore/978 0199340378.013.501.

20 Salvatore R. Martoche, "Lest We Forget: William J. Donovan," *Western New York Heritage* 6, no. 1 (2003): 6.

21 Waller, *Wild Bill Donovan*, 9–14.

22 Quoted in Cave Brown, *The Last Hero*, 29; Martoche, "Lest We Forget: William J. Donovan," 10–11.

23 For more on the thought/action divide in studies of ritual, see Catherine Bell, *Ritual Theory, Ritual Practice* (Oxford: Oxford University Press, 1992).

24 Quoted in Finbarr Curtis, "The Fundamental Faith of Every True American: Secularity and Institutional Loyalty in Al Smith's 1928 Presidential Campaign," *Journal of Religion* 91, no. 4 (October 2011): 519–44, https://doi.org/10.1086 /660925, 534. Judging from Smith's conversations with confidants, he offered this question seriously.

25 Cave Brown, *The Last Hero*, 31–35.

26 Waller, *Wild Bill Donovan*, 22–23. Daniel J. Sweeney, *History of Buffalo and Erie County, 1914–1919* (Buffalo, NY: Matthews-Northrup Works, 1920), 291–92.

27 Waller, *Wild Bill Donovan*, 21–22.

28 Waller, *Wild Bill Donovan*, 26–35. The citation in the Congressional Record is provided in full in Dunlop, *Donovan*, 106.

29 William J. Donovan, "Log of the Mediterranean Cruise," 1923, Diaries and Reports from 1920 to 1925, Box 132B, William J. Donovan Papers.

30 Donovan, "Log of the Mediterranean Cruise."

31 Donovan, "Log of the Mediterranean Cruise."

32 Martoche, "Lest We Forget: William J. Donovan," 23.

33 Richard V. Oulahan, "Three Quit Lowden Ranks," *New York Times*, June 11, 1928.

34 William J. Vanden Heuvel, "Donovan, William J. (Wild Bill)," in *The Yale Biographical Dictionary of American Law*, ed. Roger Newman (New Haven, CT: Yale University Press, 2009); "Hoover Pays Visit to Coolidge Again," *New York Times*, January 10, 1929; Richard V. Oulahan, "Morrow Pressed by Leaders to Head Hoover's Cabinet," *New York Times*, January 21, 1929.

35 L. C. Speers, "Problems That Confront President Hoover," *New York Times*, March 10, 1929.

36 Quoted in Robert A. Slayton, *Empire Statesman: The Rise and Redemption of Al Smith* (New York: Free Press, 2007), 309.

37 Cave Brown, *The Last Hero*, 124.

38 William J. Donovan, "Fellowship of Faith Speech," September 13, 1931, Folder No. 1—Letter and Clipping Publications and Papers, 1920–1935, William J. Donovan Papers.

39 Donovan, "The Need of Spiritual Recovery."

40 "Donovan Sees Need for Church Leaders: Holds Spiritual and Cultural Promotion Should Be on Nation-Wide Basis," *New York Times*, March 1, 1935.

41 The historiography on this subject is extensive, and important work includes Susan M. Griffin, *Anti-Catholicism and Nineteenth-Century Fiction* (Cambridge: Cambridge University Press, 2004); Tracy Fessenden, *Culture and Redemption: Religion, the Secular, and American Literature* (Princeton, NJ: Princeton University Press, 2007); William R. Hutchison, *Religious Pluralism in America: The Contentious History of a Founding Ideal* (New Haven, CT: Yale University Press, 2004); Elizabeth Fenton, *Religious Liberties: Anti-Catholicism and Liberal Democracy in Nineteenth-Century U.S. Literature and Culture*, 1st ed. (New York: Oxford University Press, 2011); Philip Hamburger, *Separation of Church and State* (Cambridge, MA: Harvard University Press, 2004); Peter R. D'Agostino, *Rome in America: Transnational Catholic Ideology from the Risorgimento to Fascism* (Chapel Hill: University of North Carolina Press, 2004); Wenger, *Religious Freedom*.

42 In his astute study of Al Smith's campaign, Finbarr Curtis observed the irony of these "worries" at a time when the KKK could be quoted as a reasonable source of information in the *New York Times*. See Curtis, "The Fundamental Faith of Every True American," 521. See also chapter 5 in Finbarr Curtis, *The Production of American Religious Freedom* (New York: NYU Press, 2016).

43 "Is There a Catholic Problem?," *The New Republic*, November 16, 1938.

44 Elizabeth Fenton's work traces the history of this exclusionary aspect of liberal democracy: "However natural it might seem to render religion a matter of personal conscience, within the context of Anglo-American politics the very idea of religious privacy derives from a Protestant ideal of private judgment that position the individual as a rational subject capable of fashioning his or her own conscience without the interference of a dogmatic clerical or governmental hierarchy." See Fenton, *Religious Liberties*, 6.

45 Waller, *Wild Bill Donovan*, 36–37.

46 "Col. Donovan Censured: Members of Irish Societies Ask His Removal From Post," *New York Times*, November 24, 1941.

47 William Donovan, "Discussion by Brigadier General Donovan, Director of Office of Strategic Services, at 11:00 A.M., May 1, 1943, Room 3-E-869," May 1, 1943, Document #CK3100563187, Declassified Documents Reference System.

48 Quoted in Stanley Lovell, *Of Spies and Stratagems: Incredible Secrets of World War II Revealed by a Master Spy* (Englewood Cliffs, NJ: Prentice-Hall, 1963), 21.

49 William R. Corson, *The Armies of Ignorance: The Rise of the American Intelligence Empire* (New York: Dial Press, 1977), 182.

50 "Alleged CIA Operation Gone Astray," May 13, 1985, CIA-RDP88-01070R000301700009-0, National Archives (CREST Database).

51 Quoted in Cave Brown, *The Last Hero*, 298.

52 Quoted in Dunlop, *Donovan*, 402; Clayton D. Laurie, "An Exclusionary Position: General MacArthur and the OSS, 1942–1945," *Studies in Intelligence*, n.d.

53 Quoted in Dunlop, *Donovan*, 321.

54 Francis Spellman to William Donovan, December 3, 1941, Director's Office Records, NARA Microfilm Publication M1642, Roll 105, National Archives at College Park, College Park, MD.

55 William Donovan to Fulton Sheen, November 2, 1943, Director's Office Records, NARA Microfilm Publication M1642, Roll 71, National Archives at College Park, College Park, MD; Fulton Sheen to William Donovan, October 7, 1943, Director's Office Records, NARA Microfilm Publication M1642, Roll 71, National Archives

at College Park, College Park, MD; Fulton Sheen to William Donovan, March 18, 1944, Director's Office Records, NARA Microfilm Publication M1642, Roll 106, National Archives at College Park, College Park, MD.

56 "Valerio Borghese Ci Serviva," *Epoca*, February 11, 1976, FOIA Electronic Reading Room.

57 Quoted in Steven Rosswurm, *The FBI and the Catholic Church, 1935–1962* (Amherst: University of Massachusetts Press, 2009), 44. Also see Dianne Kirby, "J. Edgar Hoover, the FBI, and the Religious Cold War," in *The FBI and Religion*, ed. Sylvester A. Johnson and Steven Weitzman (Berkeley: University of California Press, 2017).

58 See, for example, Kevin M. Schultz, *Tri-Faith America: How Catholics and Jews Held Postwar America to Its Protestant Promise* (New York: Oxford University Press, 2011); Kevin Kruse, *One Nation Under God: How Corporate America Invented Christian America* (New York: Basic Books, 2015); Wendy L. Wall, *Inventing the "American Way": The Politics of Consensus from the New Deal to the Civil Rights Movement* (Oxford: Oxford University Press, 2008).

59 The United States would not send an ambassador to the Vatican until the Reagan administration in 1984. See Marie Gayte, "The Vatican and the Reagan Administration: A Cold War Alliance?," *Catholic Historical Review* 97, no. 4 (2011): 713–36, https://doi.org/10.1353/cat.2011.0170; On FDR's personal representative, see Luca Castagna, *A Bridge across the Ocean: The United States and the Holy See between the Two World Wars* (Washington, DC: Catholic University of America Press, 2014); Gerald P. Fogarty, S.J., "The United States and the Vatican, 1939–1984," in *Papal Diplomacy in the Modern Age*, ed. Peter C. Kent and John F. Pollard (Westport, CT: Praeger, 1994), 230. There were other informal representatives, most importantly Father Joseph Hurley. Gallagher, *Vatican Secret Diplomacy*, 99–101.

60 William Donovan, "Memorandum for the President No. 265," February 18, 1942, Director's Office Records, NARA Microfilm Publication M1642, Roll 22, National Archives at College Park, College Park, MD.

61 Donovan, "Memorandum for the President No. 265."

62 William Donovan to Franklin Roosevelt, July 3, 1944, Director's Office Records, NARA Microfilm Publication M1642, Roll 30, National Archives at College Park, College Park, MD.

63 Quoted in Waller, *Wild Bill Donovan*, 258.

64 See Chadwick, *Britain and the Vatican during the Second World War*. For coverage of internal Vatican politics that shaped the institution's response to this outreach, see Phayer, *The Catholic Church and the Holocaust, 1930–1965*.

65 "Special Report #81, 'Ecclesiastical Contact with Allied Intelligence,'" March 6,

1945, RG 226, Entry 210, Box 311, Folder 2, National Archives at College Park, College Park, MD.

66 OSS Spec. Det. G-2, "The Military Significance of Political Conditions in Rome," February 21, 1944, RG 226, Entry 210, Box 313, Folder 5, National Archives at College Park, College Park, MD.

67 David Alvarez, *Spies in the Vatican: Espionage and Intrigue from Napoleon to the Holocaust* (Lawrence: University Press of Kansas, 2002), 274.

68 Vincent Scamporino to Director, Office of Strategic Services, "Malvina Report No. 54," October 9, 1944, RG 226, Entry 210, Box 461, Folder 4, National Archives at College Park, College Park, MD.

69 For these and other fascinating plans, see Lovell, *Of Spies and Stratagems*.

70 Lovell, *Of Spies and Stratagems*, 82–83.

71 William Maddox to Whitney Shepardson, "Vatican Coverage," January 13, 1945, RG 226, Entry 210, Box 373, Folder 9, National Archives at College Park, College Park, MD.

72 Vincent Scamporino to William Maddox, January 22, 1945, RG 226, Entry 210, Box 373, Folder 9, National Archives at College Park, College Park, MD.

73 Memos about the material gleaned from these communications can be found in "Current Conditions in Vienna," January 8, 1945, RG 226, Entry 210, Box 468, Folder 6, National Archives at College Park, College Park, MD.

Chapter Two

1 Quoted in William R. Corson, *The Armies of Ignorance: The Rise of the American Intelligence Empire* (New York: Dial Press, 1977), 182.

2 Central Intelligence Agency News and Information, "A Look Back . . . The Office of Strategic Services: Operation RYPE," April 30, 2013, https://www.cia.gov/news -information/featured-story-archive/2010-featured-story-archive/oss-operation -rype.html.

3 William Egan Colby and Peter Forbath, *Honorable Men: My Life in the CIA* (New York: Simon and Schuster, 1978), 55–56.

4 This assumption was influential in other parts of the government, too. See President Truman's struggles with outreach to the World Council of Churches in Dianne Kirby, "Harry S. Truman's International Religious Anti-Communist Front, the Archbishop of Canterbury and the 1948 Inaugural Assembly of the World Council of Churches," *Contemporary British History* 15, no. 4 (December 1, 2001): 35–70, https://doi.org/10.1080/713999430.

5   For scholars of religion, Protestantism is often seen as the standard around which the "world religions paradigm" was built. What is different about the situation with OSS and Catholicism, however, is that OSS found Catholicism well suited to modeling, with its clear lines of authority and institutionalization. For more on Protestantism's central role in understanding the WRP, see Tomoko Masuzawa, *The Invention of World Religions: Or, How European Universalism Was Preserved in the Language of Pluralism* (Chicago: University of Chicago Press, 2005).

6   For more on these relationships in specific academic fields, see David H. Price, *Anthropological Intelligence: The Deployment and Neglect of American Anthropology in the Second World War* (Durham, NC: Duke University Press, 2008); Peter Mandler, *Return from the Natives: How Margaret Mead Won the Second World War and Lost the Cold War* (New Haven, CT: Yale University Press, 2013); Robin Winks, *Cloak and Gown: Scholars in the Secret War, 1939–1961*, 2nd ed. (New Haven, CT: Yale University Press, 1996).

7   Dianne Kirby's work is particularly important for understanding this transnational context. See Kirby, "Britain and the Origins of the Religious Cold War, 1944–47," in *Britain in Global Politics Volume 2: From Churchill to Blair*, ed. J. W. Young, E. G. H. Pedaliu, and M. D. Kandiah (New York: Palgrave Macmillan, 2013). One specific example of this was Britain's "Religions Division." See Kirby, "The Church of England and Religions Division during the Second World War: Church-State Relations and the Anglo-Soviet Alliance," *Electronic Journal of International History*, no. 1 (2000).

8   Ferdinand Mayer to William Donovan, July 17, 1945, RG 226, Entry 210, Box 338, Folder 1, National Archives at College Park, College Park, MD.

9   The Research and Analysis Branch is one of the most interesting parts of OSS; it is also one of the parts least studied. For exceptions to this, see Rhodri Jeffreys-Jones, *Cloak and Dollar: A History of American Secret Intelligence* (New Haven, CT: Yale University Press, 2003); Barry M. Katz, *Foreign Intelligence* (Cambridge, MA: Harvard University Press, 1989).

10 Katz, *Foreign Intelligence*, 203.

11 Stanley Lovell, *Of Spies and Stratagems: Incredible Secrets of World War II Revealed by a Master Spy* (Englewood Cliffs, NJ: Prentice-Hall, 1963), 183–84.

12 Quoted in Katz, *Foreign Intelligence*, 1.

13 See chapter 11 in Max Hastings, *The Secret War: Spies, Ciphers, and Guerrillas, 1939–1945* (New York: Harper, 2016).

14 Quoted in Richard Dunlop, *Donovan: America's Master Spy* (Chicago: Rand McNally, 1982), 325.

15 Quoted in Mandler, *Return from the Natives*, 66.

16 Quoted in Katz, *Foreign Intelligence*, 4.

17 William H. Webster, "Remarks by William H. Webster, Director of Central Intelligence, At the Dedication of a Statue of General William J. Donovan, CIA Headquarters Building," October 26, 1988, Document #CK3100274754, Declassified Documents Reference System.

18 Quoted in Katz, *Foreign Intelligence*, 9.

19 Winks, *Cloak and Gown*, 495–98; Katz, *Foreign Intelligence*, 203.

20 Chief SICE to Chief SI, "Vatican Activities of Zsolt Aradi," December 17, 1944, RG 226, Entry 210, Box 373, Folder 9, National Archives at College Park, College Park, MD; SASAC VIENNA to SASAC AMZON, November 2, 1945, RG 226, Entry 210, Box 160, Folder 15, National Archives at College Park, College Park, MD.

21 Zsolt Aradi to Chief SI, "Intelligence Through the Vatican," November 27, 1944, RG 226, Entry 210, Box 327, Folder 3, National Archives at College Park, College Park, MD.

22 Aradi to Chief SI, "Intelligence Through the Vatican."

23 Aradi to Chief SI, "Intelligence Through the Vatican."

24 OSS valued Aradi's insights, retaining his services even after the war as a "Vatican specialist." See SASAC VIENNA to SASAC AMZON, November 2, 1945.

25 David Williamson to William Donovan, "Suggested U.S. Action to Combat Anti-Allied Sentiment Among Catholics Resulting from Vatican Bombings," March 23, 1944, Director's Office Records, NARA Microfilm Publication M1642, Roll 98, National Archives at College Park, College Park, MD.

26 Williamson to Donovan, "Suggested U.S. Action."

27 "Jocists Still Active in Belgium Despite German Occupation," *The Observer*, July 13, 1941.

28 Felix Morlion, *The Apostolate of Public Opinion* (Montreal: Fides, 1944), 18–19.

29 Morlion, *The Apostolate of Public Opinion*, 23.

30 Felix Morlion, "Rapport Sur Les Activities Du Reverend Pere Morlion Dans La Domaine de La Guerre Psychologique," July 4, 1942, Anna M. Brady Papers, Box 2, Folder 24, Georgetown University Manuscripts.

31 Waller estimates $2,000 per month, but OSS documents suggest the figure was likely higher. See Douglas C. Waller, *Wild Bill Donovan: The Spymaster Who Created the OSS and Modern American Espionage* (New York: Free Press, 2012), 257;

Frederic Dolbeare to John C. Hughes, October 31, 1944, RG 226, Entry 210, Box 311, Folder 2, National Archives at College Park, College Park, MD.

32 Morlion, "Rapport Sur Les Activities."

33 Morlion, "Rapport Sur Les Activities."

34 John C. Hughes to William Donovan, "Special Black Report," October 23, 1944, RG 226, Entry 210, Box 311, Folder 2, National Archives at College Park, College Park, MD; John C. Hughes to E. J. Putzell, November 4, 1944, RG 226, Entry 210, Box 322, Folder 2, National Archives at College Park, College Park, MD.

35 Frederic Dolbeare to Allen Dulles, November 9, 1944, RG 226, Entry 210, Box 363, Folder 4, National Archives at College Park, College Park, MD.

36 London Desk to Chief, S.I., "HJ Reports," June 30, 1944, RG 226, Entry 210, Box 414, Folder 4, National Archives at College Park, College Park, MD.

37 William Maddox to Whitney Shepardson, "HJ Memos," March 16, 1944, RG 226, Entry 210, Box 414, Folder 4, National Archives at College Park, College Park, MD.

38 This referred specifically to one of Pro Deo's correspondents, code-named "Hank Judah." Alan Scaife to Frederic Dolbeare, "H. J. Reports," October 23, 1943, RG 226, Entry 210, Box 414, Folder 1, National Archives at College Park, College Park, MD; London Desk to Chief, S.I., "HJ Reports," June 30, 1944; Maddox to Shepardson, "HJ Memos," March 16, 1944.

39 Dolbeare to Hughes.

40 International Services of the Center of Information Pro Deo, "Note on Broadcasts for Psychological Warfare in Religious Circles of Occupied Europe," n.d., RG 226, Entry 106, Box 062, Folder 312, National Archives at College Park, College Park, MD.

41 Felix Morlion, "Summary of the Collaboration with the Belgian War Effort of the International Center of Information Pro Deo (Itercip), Founded by Rev. Felix Morlion, O.P., Director of the Belgian Catholic Press Central," February 7, 1943, Anna M. Brady Papers, Box 2, Folder 21, Georgetown University Manuscripts. For more on the impact of the NCCJ, see Kevin M. Schultz, *Tri-Faith America: How Catholics and Jews Held Postwar America to Its Protestant Promise* (New York: Oxford University Press, 2011).

42 "Special Propaganda in Catholic Milieux of Latin America," n.d., RG 226, Entry 210, Box 388, Folder 1, National Archives at College Park, College Park, MD.

43 Dolbeare to Hughes.

44 Dolbeare to Hughes.

45 Office of Strategic Services to Ustravic, London, 1943, RG 226, Entry 210, Box 453, National Archives at College Park, College Park, MD.

46 Frederic Dolbeare to Alan Scaife, December 29, 1943, RG 226, Entry 210, Box 414, Folder 1, National Archives at College Park, College Park, MD.

47 Alan Scaife to Frederic Dolbeare, January 7, 1944, RG 226, Entry 210, Box 414, Folder 1, National Archives at College Park, College Park, MD.

48 Caserta, Italy, and Office of Strategic Services, "Cable #11774," November 4, 1944, RG 226, Entry 210, Box 311, Folder 2, National Archives at College Park, College Park, MD.

49 J. B. Montini to Felix Morlion, November 17, 1944, Anna M. Brady Papers, Box 2, Folder 11, Georgetown University Manuscripts.

50 Marie Gayte, "The Vatican and the Reagan Administration: A Cold War Alliance?," *Catholic Historical Review* 97, no. 4 (2011): 713–36, https://doi.org/10.1353/cat .2011.0170.

51 "Untitled CIP Planning Document," n.d., RG 226, Entry 210, Box 388, Folder 6, National Archives at College Park, College Park, MD.

52 Allen Dulles to George Bowden, October 10, 1942, RG 226, Entry 214, Box 7, National Archives at College Park, College Park, MD.

53 Felix Morlion, "Conclusions for Immediate Action in Fact of the Increased Social-Communist Threat," 1951, CIA-RDP80R01731R003300410030-2, National Archives (CREST Database).

54 Hughes to Putzell, November 4, 1944.

55 Allen Dulles to Gordon Gray, November 1, 1951, CIA-RDP80R01731R0033004 10030-2, National Archives (CREST Database).

56 Dr. Lilly to the Director and Mr. Taylor, "The Project of Rev. F.A. Morlion, O.P.," July 10, 1952, Document #CK3100085334, Declassified Documents Reference System.

57 Frederic Dolbeare to Earnest Brooks, June 30, 1944, RG 226, Entry 210, Box 414, Folder 4, National Archives at College Park, College Park, MD.

58 James Clement Dunn to Ferdinand Mayer, February 13, 1945, RG 226, Entry 210, Box 415, Folder 2, National Archives at College Park, College Park, MD.

59 Huntington Harris, "Field Report on the 'Pilgrim's Progress Project,'" November 15, 1945, RG 226, Entry 216, Box 3, Folder 1, National Archives at College Park, College Park, MD.

60 Harris, "Field Report."

61 Many of these reports (sometimes termed "Black Reports" or "Special Black Reports") bear such introductions. One such example is William Donovan to Franklin Roosevelt, February 16, 1945, Director's Office Records, NARA Microfilm Publication M1642, Roll 119, National Archives at College Park, College Park, MD.

62 For a helpful overview of the VESSEL affair, see Timothy Naftali, "Artifice: James Angleton and X-2 Operations in Italy," in *The Secrets War: The Office of Strategic Services in World War II*, ed. George Chalou (Washington, DC: National Archives Trust Fund Board, 1992).

63 Naftali, "Artiface"; Winks, *Cloak and Gown*, 387.

64 Winks, *Cloak and Gown*, 333.

65 Richard Harris Smith argued in 1972, and maintains in his 2005 reprint, that the source for VESSEL was none other than Cardinal Montini, the future Pope Paul VI. This account relies primarily upon Smith's interviews, however, and this interpretation is largely discounted by other histories of OSS. See Richard Harris Smith, *OSS: The Secret History of America's First Central Intelligence Agency* (Berkeley: University of California Press, 1972); Max Corvo, *Max Corvo: OSS Italy, 1942-1945*, rev. ed. (New York: Enigma Books, 2005), 243-44.

66 Importantly, OSS officer Max Corvo (who had experience working with VESSEL) made clear that Montini had no involvement in VESSEL. Still, Corvo argued that Angleton's interference was responsible for the popular portrayal of VESSEL as an intelligence failure rather than a success. See Max Corvo, "War-Time Controversy over Vatican-OSS Relations Renewed by 'Declassification,'" *Executive Intelligence Review* 12, no. 5 (February 5, 1985), 56-59.

67 For the piece largely credited with dispelling the myth of Cardinal Montini's involvement in VESSEL, see Robert Graham, "Notes and Comments," *Catholic Historical Review* 59, no. 4 (January 1974): 719-35; Naftali, "Artifice," 2; Jefferson Morley, *The Ghost: The Secret Life of CIA Spymaster James Jesus Angleton* (New York: St. Martin's Press, 2017), 33.

68 Winks, *Cloak and Gown*, 540.

69 Colonel Buxton to David Bruce, "Cable #04150," August 4, 1943, RG 226, Entry 210, Box 443, Folder 7, National Archives at College Park, College Park, MD.

70 Harris, "Field Report."

71 789 to Lester Houck, "Snapdragon Reports," August 18, 1945, RG 226, Entry 214, Box 7, Folder 7, National Archives at College Park, College Park, MD.

72 "Papal Order for Donovan: Former OSS Director to Get St. Sylvester Award Tonight," *New York Times*, January 30, 1946.

73 "For Distinguished Service to Humanity," *New York Times*, January 31, 1946.

Chapter Three

1 Quoted in Anthony Cave Brown, *The Last Hero: Wild Bill Donovan* (New York: Times Books, 1982), 252.

2 William A. Eddy, "The Moors Draw Their Knives in Tangier," 1942, William A. Eddy Papers, Box 17, Folder 1, Princeton University Library.

3 By "Orientalist," I refer to the argument that monolithic ideas of "Asia" or the "Orient" have long trafficked in specific systems of political and economic power. Perhaps the best summary of this position is the one given originally by Edward Said when he wrote, "I have been arguing that 'the Orient' is itself a constituted entity, and that the notion that there are geographical spaces with indigenous, radically 'different' inhabitants who can be defined on the basis of some religion, culture, or racial essence proper to that geographical space is equally a highly debatable idea." Edward W. Said, *Orientalism* (New York: Vintage, 1979), 322. For excellent work on the relationship between these ideas and intelligence work, see Dina Rezk, "Orientalism and Intelligence Analysis: Deconstructing Anglo-American Notions of the 'Arab,'" *Intelligence and National Security*, September 3, 2014, 1–22, https://doi.org/10.1080/02684527.2014.949077; Rezk, *The Arab World and Western Intelligence: Analysing the Middle East, 1956–1981* (Edinburgh: Edinburgh University Press, 2017).

4 "Why Are Japs Japs?," *Time*, August 7, 1944, http://content.time.com/time/magazine/article/0,9171,886212,00.html.

5 These ideas did not end with the war. See Brandon Seto, "A Defense of Faith: SCAP and Japan's Religious Rehabilitation in the Early Cold War," *Journal of American-East Asian Relations* 23, no. 4 (November 21, 2016): 368–93, https://doi.org/10.1163/18765610–02304002.

6 Vincent Scamporino to Whitney Shepardson and Earl Brennan, "Considerations on Reflections That Allied Victories over Germany May Have on Japanese Public Opinion," October 6, 1944, RG 226, Entry 210, Box 384, Folder 9, National Archives at College Park, College Park, MD.

7 On how US perceptions of Buddhism influenced this process, see Duncan Ryūken Williams, *American Sutra: A Story of Faith and Freedom in the Second World War* (Cambridge, MA: Belknap Press, 2020); Also see Anne M. Blankenship, *Christianity, Social Justice, and the Japanese American Incarceration during World War II* (Chapel Hill: University of North Carolina Press, 2016).

8 Clayton D. Laurie, "An Exclusionary Position: General MacArthur and the OSS,

1942–1945," *Studies in Intelligence*, n.d.; Irvin Molotsky and Special to the New York Times, "O.S.S. Lives Again at Spies' Reunion," *New York Times*, September 21, 1986, http://www.nytimes.com/1986/09/21/us/oss-lives-again-at-spies -reunion.html.

9   One excellent introduction to this history is Brent Nongbri, *Before Religion: A History of a Modern Concept* (New Haven, CT: Yale University Press, 2013). On the study of Shinto today, see Jolyon Thomas, "Big Questions in the Study of Shinto," *H-Japan*, November 13, 2017, https://networks.h-net.org/node/20904/discussions /837862/review-jolyon-thomas-studies-shinto.

10   See for example Jason Ananda Josephson, *The Invention of Religion in Japan* (Chicago: University of Chicago Press, 2012); David Chidester, *Empire of Religion: Imperialism and Comparative Religion* (Chicago: University of Chicago Press, 2014); Tisa Wenger, *Religious Freedom: The Contested History of an American Ideal* (Chapel Hill: University of North Carolina Press, 2017).

11   Nicholas B. Dirks, *Castes of Mind: Colonialism and the Making of Modern India* (Princeton, NJ: Princeton University Press, 2001); C. S. Adcock, *The Limits of Tolerance: Indian Secularism and the Politics of Religious Freedom* (Oxford and New York: Oxford University Press, 2013); Peter van der Veer, *The Modern Spirit of Asia: The Spiritual and the Secular in China and India* (Princeton, NJ: Princeton University Press, 2013). For similar examples in other locales, also see Donald S. Lopez, *Curators of the Buddha: The Study of Buddhism under Colonialism* (Chicago: University of Chicago Press, 1995); Josephson, *The Invention of Religion in Japan*; David Chidester, *Savage Systems: Colonialism and Comparative Religion in Southern Africa* (Charlottesville: University of Virginia Press, 1996); Chidester, *Empire of Religion*.

12   Jason Ananda Josephson makes this argument by, among other things, "read[ing] the seeming inconsistencies in the translation as tactical efforts on the part of Japanese diplomats to quarantine Christianity and forestall missionary activity." See Josephson, *The Invention of Religion in Japan*, 73. These debates continued into the twentieth century, and extend after the war, as Jolyon Thomas convincingly demonstrates. See Jolyon Baraka Thomas, *Faking Liberties: Religious Freedom in American-Occupied Japan* (Chicago: University of Chicago Press, 2019). See also Jolyon Thomas, "Religions Policies During the Allied Occupation of Japan, 1945–1952: Occupation Policy and Religion in Postwar Japan," *Religion Compass* 8, no. 9 (September 2014): 275–86, https://doi.org/10.1111/rec3.12117.

13   David Price's excellent study is indispensable for understanding the relationship between anthropology and intelligence work. See Price, *Anthropological Intelligence: The Deployment and Neglect of American Anthropology in the Second World War* (Durham, NC: Duke University Press, 2008). Also see chapter 4 in Peter Mandler, *Return from the Natives: How Margaret Mead Won the Second World War and Lost the Cold War* (New Haven, CT: Yale University Press, 2013). On Japanese religion, one of the most influential thinkers was a University of Chicago–trained PhD named Daniel Clarence Holtom. His work was widely read by American leaders in charge of Japan policy. See Holtom, *Modern Japan and Shintō Nation-*

alism (Chicago: University of Chicago Press, 1943). For more on Holtom, see Jolyon Thomas's excellent article: Thomas, "Religions Policies During the Allied Occupation of Japan, 1945–1952."

14 OSS personnel read Western experts including William McGovern and Kenneth Saunders. See "Plan for Psychological Warfare Against Japanese Government," n.d., RG 226, Entry 139, Box 110, Folder 1522, National Archives at College Park, College Park, MD.

15 "Plan for Psychological Warfare Against Japanese Government."

16 "P.P. Report #40, 'Japanese Problem Explained by Father Candeau,'" n.d., RG 226, Entry 210, Box 414, Folder 9, National Archives at College Park, College Park, MD.

17 The idea that "religion" (and specifically "bad religion") motivated irrational and often violent behavior has a long history. Jeffrey Wheatley's work examines this in relationship to histories of colonialism and racialization. See Wheatley, "Policing Fanaticism, Religion, and Race in the American Empire, 1830–1930" (PhD diss., Northwestern University, 2020).

18 "P.P. Report #40."

19 OSS, like many Americans, assumed the primacy of belief when it came to matters of religion. On the Christian influence behind this idea, see Donald Lopez, "Belief," in *Critical Terms for Religious Studies*, ed. Mark C. Taylor (Chicago: University of Chicago Press, 1998).

20 Edward Lansdale, "From the Serpent's Mouth," October 25, 1943, Edward Geary Lansdale Papers, Box 31, Folder 694, Hoover Institution Archives.

21 Price, *Anthropological Intelligence*, 239.

22 Muddassir Ali Shamsee, "Suggestions and Themes on Morale Operations Among Moslems in the Japanese-Occupied Areas," n.d., RG 226, Entry A1139, Box 135, Folder 1820, National Archives at College Park, College Park, MD.

23 Susan Grace Oppenheim, "Undermining Japanese Authority in Muslim Areas by Promoting Antagonism between Shinto and Islam," August 29, 1944, RG 226, Entry 139, Box 179, Folder 2415, National Archives at College Park, College Park, MD.

24 For an important study of the Japanese side of this policy, see Kelly A. Hammond, "Managing Muslims: Imperial Japan, Islamic Policy, and Axis Connections during the Second World War," *Journal of Global History* 12, no. 2 (July 2017): 251–73, https://doi.org/10.1017/S1740022817000079. See also Price, *Anthropological Intelligence*, 234–36.

25 M. A. Shamsee, "Windpipe Project," September 5, 1944, RG 226, Entry 139, Box 179, Folder 2415, National Archives at College Park, College Park, MD; Susan Grace Oppenheim, "Undermining Japanese Authority."

26 Susan Grace, "MO Directed Toward Moslems in the Month of Ramadhan," August 24, 1944, RG 226, Entry A1139, Box 135, Folder 1820, National Archives at College Park, College Park, MD.

27 Shamsee, "Windpipe Project," September 5, 1944; M.A. Shamsee, "Windpipe Project," September 4, 1944, RG 226, Entry 139, Box 179, Folder 2415, National Archives at College Park, College Park, MD; Susan Grace, "Further Examples of MO Directed Toward Moslems by Mr. Shamsee," n.d., RG 226, Entry A1139, Box 135, Folder 1820, National Archives at College Park, College Park, MD; Susan Grace Oppenheim to Lt. Col. H. B. Little, "Undermining Japanese Authority in Muslim Areas by Promoting Antagonism between Shinto and Islam," August 29, 1944, RG 226, Entry 139, Box 179, Folder 2415, National Archives at College Park, College Park, MD.

28 Mikiya Koyagi, "The Hajj by Japanese Muslims in the Interwar Period: Japan's Pan-Asianism and Economic Interests in the Islamic World," *Journal of World History* 24, no. 4 (2013): 849–76, 874.

29 Shamsee, "Suggestions and Themes on Morale Operations."

30 Grace, "Further Examples of MO Directed Toward Moslems."

31 Stanley Lovell, *Of Spies and Stratagems: Incredible Secrets of World War II Revealed by a Master Spy* (Englewood Cliffs, NJ: Prentice-Hall, 1963), 28.

32 Lovell, *Of Spies and Stratagems*, 27–29.

33 Grace, "Further Examples of MO Directed Toward Moslems."

34 Grace, "Further Examples of MO Directed Toward Moslems."

35 Shamsee, "Suggestions and Themes on Morale Operations."

36 For more on the larger conversation around religion in Japan, see Josephson, *The Invention of Religion in Japan*; Thomas, *Faking Liberties*. For a contemporary approach to the study of Shinto, see Helen Hardacre, *Shinto: A History* (New York: Oxford University Press, 2016).

37 For a prominent critique of this tendency in academic work, see Bruce Lincoln, "Theses on Method," *Method and Theory in the Study of Religion* 8 (1996): 225–28.

38 Shamsee, "Suggestions and Themes on Morale Operations."

39 Shamsee, "Suggestions and Themes on Morale Operations."

40 Shamsee, "Suggestions and Themes on Morale Operations."

41 The creation of a monolithic "Muslim World" and its influence on American intelligence is explored in the final chapter. Also see Matthew F. Jacobs, "The Perils

and Promise of Islam: The United States and the Muslim Middle East in the Early Cold War," *Diplomatic History* 30, no. 4 (2006): 705–39; Melani McAlister, *Epic Encounters: Culture, Media, and U.S. Interests in the Middle East since 1945*, rev. ed. (Berkeley: University of California Press, 2005); Zareena Grewal, *Islam Is a Foreign Country: American Muslims and the Global Crisis of Authority* (New York: NYU Press, 2013); Cemil Aydin, *The Idea of the Muslim World: A Global Intellectual History* (Cambridge, MA: Harvard University Press, 2017); Sophia Rose Arjana, *Muslims in the Western Imagination* (New York: Oxford University Press, 2015); Karine V. Walther, *Sacred Interests: The United States and the Islamic World, 1821–1921* (Chapel Hill: University of North Carolina Press, 2015).

42 Grewal, *Islam Is a Foreign Country*, 5.

43 For a study of how this term came to be used in both Muslim and non-Muslim communities, see Aydin, *The Idea of the Muslim World*.

44 For example, see Christine Leigh Heyrman, *American Apostles: When Evangelicals Entered the World of Islam* (New York: Hill and Wang, 2015); Ussama Makdisi, *Artillery of Heaven: American Missionaries and the Failed Conversion of the Middle East* (Ithaca, NY: Cornell University Press, 2009), 215. Drawing on—and enhancing—Edward Said's arguments, Makdisi's work is a notable example of the subtle back-and-forth that went on between American missionaries and their Middle Eastern counterparts in the nineteenth century. Makdisi demonstrates that a postcolonial transnational history (such as of American missionaries in the Middle East) need not frame the colonial newcomers as all-powerful or the Ottoman subjects as entirely powerless to illustrate the complexities of the situation.

45 Quoted in John Davis, *The Landscape of Belief*, 1st ed. (Princeton, NJ: Princeton University Press, 1996), 14.

46 For accounts of several OSS and CIA officers from missionary families, see David Hollinger, *Protestants Abroad: How Missionaries Tried to Change the World but Changed America* (Princeton, NJ: Princeton University Press, 2017).

47 The tradition of the early CIA Arabists (most notably William Eddy) is also linked to prewar American experiences in the region. See Hugh Wilford, *America's Great Game: The CIA's Secret Arabists and the Shaping of the Modern Middle East* (New York: Basic Books, 2013).

48 American Consul, Jerusalem, Palestine, to Secretary of State and William Donovan, January 14, 1943, RG 226, Entry 210, Box 453, Folder 3, National Archives at College Park, College Park, MD.

49 "Black Report #13, 'Conditions Among the Arabs in Algiers,'" September 28, 1944, RG 226, Entry 210, Box 311, Folder 2, National Archives at College Park, College Park, MD.

50 Wilford, *America's Great Game*, 36.

51 "Black Report #13."

52 OSS Research and Analysis Branch, "Principal Social Groups [in North Africa],"
August 28, 1942, Director's Office Records, NARA Microfilm Publication M1642,
Roll 64, National Archives at College Park, College Park, MD, 9.

53 OSS Research and Analysis Branch, "Principal Social Groups," 15.

54 OSS Research and Analysis Branch, "Principal Social Groups," 22.

55 Robin Winks, *Cloak and Gown: Scholars in the Secret War, 1939–1961*, 2nd ed.
(New Haven, CT: Yale University Press, 1996), 184.

56 Douglas C. Waller, *Wild Bill Donovan: The Spymaster Who Created the OSS and
Modern American Espionage* (New York: Free Press, 2012), 131.

57 William A. Eddy, "Spies and Lies in Tangier," n.d., William A. Eddy Papers,
Box 17, Folder 1, Princeton University Library, 1.

58 William A. Eddy, "FDR Meets Ibn Saud" (America-Mideast Educational &
Training Services, Inc., 1954).

59 See Waller, *Wild Bill Donovan*, 132–33.

60 William A. Eddy, "Communist Allies," n.d., William A. Eddy Papers, Box 17,
Folder 1, Princeton University Library, 1.

61 Cave Brown, *The Last Hero*, 252.

62 Carleton Coon, *A North Africa Story: The Anthropologist as OSS Agent 1941–1943*
(Ipswich, MA: Gambit Publications, 1980), 11.

63 Coon, *A North Africa Story*, 14.

64 Quoted in Cave Brown, *The Last Hero*, 252–53.

65 Waller, *Wild Bill Donovan*, 137.

66 Rhodri Jeffreys-Jones, *The CIA and American Democracy* (New Haven, CT: Yale
University Press, 2003), 18–20; Christopher M. Andrew, *For the President's Eyes
Only: Secret Intelligence and the American Presidency from Washington to Bush*
(New York: HarperPerennial, 1996), 134.

67 Eddy, "The Moors Draw Their Knives in Tangier," 3.

68 Eddy, "Communist Allies," 6.

69 William A. Eddy, "How Arabs See the West Today," December 19, 1950, William A. Eddy Papers, Box 15, Folder 16, Princeton University Library, 8.

70 Quoted in Wilford, *America's Great Game*, 27.

71 JAW ED, "Criticism of 'Suggested Directive to O.W.I. Covering Propaganda to the Near East—August 10, 1942,'" August 15, 1942, Director's Office Records, NARA Microfilm Publication M1642, Roll 64, National Archives at College Park, College Park, MD.

72 Ferdinand Mayer to William Donovan, July 17, 1945, RG 226, Entry 210, Box 338, Folder 1, National Archives at College Park, College Park, MD.

73 Mayer to Donovan.

74 William Donovan, "Intelligence: Key to Defense," *LIFE*, September 30, 1946, 118.

75 Donovan, "Intelligence," 117.

76 For more on the "Tri-Faith" movement, see Kevin M. Schultz, *Tri-Faith America: How Catholics and Jews Held Postwar America to Its Protestant Promise* (New York: Oxford University Press, 2011).

77 David Chidester wrote that "Ironically, therefore, the historical origin of the academic discipline of comparative religion can be traced back to European discoveries of the absence of religion." See Chidester, *Savage Systems*, 11.

Chapter Four

1 Dwight Eisenhower, "Farewell Address," January 17, 1961, Our Documents Project, https://www.ourdocuments.gov/doc.php?flash=false&doc=90.

2 W. G. Wyman to Allen Dulles, March 30, 1956, CIA-RDP80B01676R0012000 60037-5, National Archives (CREST Database).

3 Allen Dulles to W. G. Wyman, April 10, 1956, CIA-RDP80B01676R0012000 60036-6, National Archives (CREST Database).

4 Dianne Kirby's work is foundational in the study of religion and the Cold War. For work on the early years of the conflict, including Truman's role, from a transnational perspective, see Kirby, "Christian Anti-Communism," *Twentieth Century Communism*, no. 7 (Autumn 2014), 126–52; Kirby, "Britain and the Origins of the Religious Cold War, 1944–47," in *Britain in Global Politics Volume 2: From Churchill to Blair*, ed. J. W. Young, E. G. H. Pedaliu, and M. D. Kandiah (New York: Palgrave Macmillan, 2013); Kirby, "Religion and the Cold War in Europe," in *The Oxford Handbook of Religion and Europe*, ed. Lucian Leustean and Grace Davie (Oxford: Oxford University Press, 2021).

5 For additional work on religion and the Cold War, important contributions include Dianne Kirby, "The Religious Cold War," in *The Oxford Handbook of the Cold War*, ed. Richard H. Immerman and Petra Goedde (New York: Oxford University Press, 2013), 540–64; William Inboden, *Religion and American Foreign Policy, 1945–1960: The Soul of Containment* (Cambridge and New York: Cambridge University Press, 2008); Jonathan P. Herzog, *The Spiritual-Industrial Complex: America's Religious Battle against Communism in the Early Cold War* (New York: Oxford University Press, 2011); Lori L. Bogle, *The Pentagon's Battle for the American Mind: The Early Cold War* (College Station: Texas A&M University Press, 2004).

6   Wolfgang Saxon, "Edward L. R. Elson Dies at 86; Influential Cleric in Washington," *New York Times*, August 28, 1993, sec. Obituaries, https://www.nytimes .com/1993/08/28/obituaries/edward-l-r-elson-dies-at-86-influential-cleric-in -washington.html.

7   Quoted in Patrick Henry, "'And I Don't Care What It Is': The Tradition-History of a Civil Religion Proof-Text," *Journal of the American Academy of Religion* 49, no. 1 (March 1981): 35–49, 37.

8   Will Herberg, *Protestant—Catholic—Jew: An Essay in American Religious Sociology* (Chicago: University of Chicago Press, 1955), 84–85.

9   Robert Bellah, "Civil Religion in America," *Dædalus* 96, no. 1 (Winter 1967).

10   Henry, "'And I Don't Care What It Is,'" 42.

11   Inboden, *Religion and American Foreign Policy, 1945–1960*, 259–60, 277–78. Inboden's chapter on Eisenhower is an excellent analysis of the president's personal views in relation to the work of his office.

12   Henry, "'And I Don't Care What It Is,'"; Inboden, *Religion and American Foreign Policy, 1945–1960*, 259–60.

13   Quoted in Anthony Cave Brown, *The Last Hero: Wild Bill Donovan* (New York: Times Books, 1982), 2.

14   K. Healan Gaston's work is essential in understanding the genealogy of "Judeo-Christian." See Gaston, "The Judeo-Christian and Abrahamic Traditions in America," *Oxford Research Encyclopedia of Religion* (Oxford: Oxford University Press, January 24, 2018), https://doi.org/10.1093/acrefore/9780199340378.013.425. Also see K. H. Gaston, "The Cold War Romance of Religious Authenticity: Will Herberg, William F. Buckley Jr., and the Rise of the New Right," *Journal of American History* 99, no. 4 (March 1, 2013): 1133–58, https://doi.org/10.1093/jahist /jas588, 1136. For example, Herberg is what Gaston terms a "Judeo-Christian exceptionalist."

15   Bogle, *The Pentagon's Battle for the American Mind*, 119–23.

16   Eisenhower administration officials who dealt with psychological warfare were particularly concerned about this. For example, see Edward Lilly to C. D. Jackson, "The Religious Factor," July 21, 1953, White House Office, National Security

Council Staff Papers, OCB Secretariat Files, Moral Factor (4), Dwight D. Eisenhower Presidential Library; Edward Lilly to Elmer B. Staats, "The Religious Factor and OCB," March 3, 1954, White House Office, National Security Council Staff Papers, OCB Central Files 000.3 [Religion] (File #1) (1), Dwight D. Eisenhower Presidential Library; Byron K. Enyart to Elmer B. Staats, "The Religious Factor and OCB," March 8, 1954, White House Office, National Security Council Staff Papers, OCB Central Files 000.3 [Religion] (File #1) (1), Dwight D. Eisenhower Presidential Library; Horace S. Craig to George A. Morgan, "Subjects for Possible UN Exploitation," April 28, 1953, Document #CK2349007476, US Declassified Documents Online; Psychological Strategy Board, "PSB Planning Objectives," April 7, 1952, Document #CK2349007455, US Declassified Documents Online. Also see the explanation of Soviet intentions in *A Report to the National Security Council—NSC 68*, 1950, https://www.trumanlibrary.gov/library/research -files/report-national-security-council-nsc-68.

17 "C. D. Jackson Dies; Time, Inc., Official; Adviser to Eisenhower Had Been Publisher of Fortune," *New York Times*, September 20, 1964, https://www.nytimes .com/1964/09/20/archives/c-d-jackson-dies-time-inc-official-adviser-to-eisen hower-had-been.html.

18 Edward Lilly to C. D. Jackson, "The Basic Factor," June 3, 1953, Document #CK2349089986, US Declassified Documents Online.

19 For more on the religious factor, see Kenneth Osgood, *Total Cold War: Eisenhower's Secret Propaganda Battle at Home and Abroad* (Lawrence: University Press of Kansas, 2006), 310–12.

20 Lilly to Jackson, "The Religious Factor."

21 Lilly to Jackson, "The Religious Factor."

22 Lilly to Staats, "The Religious Factor and OCB."

23 The PSB was abolished and became part of the OCB by executive order in 1953. See Eisenhower, Dwight, "Executive Order 10483," September 5, 1953, https:// www.cia.gov/library/readingroom/docs/CIA-RDP80B01676R002700040039 -9.pdf.

24 Enyart to Staats, "The Religious Factor and OCB."

25 "Foundation for Religious Action in the Social and Civil Order Brochure," n.d., Collection 165, Box 68, Folder 11, Billy Graham Center Archives. Also see Inboden, *Religion and American Foreign Policy, 1945–1960*, 279.

26 "Dr. Charles Wesley Lowry," n.d., Collection 165, Box 68, Folder 11, Billy Graham Center Archives.

27 "Foundation for Religious Action in the Social and Civil Order Brochure."

28 Will Herberg, "The Biblical Basis of American Democracy," 1954, Collection 165, Box 68, Folder 11, Billy Graham Center Archives.

29 Theodore Hesburgh, "The Necessity of Faith in a Living Democracy," 1954, Collection 165, Box 68, Folder 11, Billy Graham Center Archives.

30 Charles W. Lowry, "Democracy's Answer to the Marxian Dialectic," 1954, Collection 165, Box 68, Folder 11, Billy Graham Center Archives.

31 For more on Trueblood and his office, see Inboden, *Religion and American Foreign Policy, 1945–1960*, 303–4.

32 "Foundation for Religious Action in the Social and Civil Order Brochure." Also see Inboden, *Religion and American Foreign Policy, 1945–1960*, 279–85.

33 Eisenhower, Dwight, "Remarks by the President of the United States at the First National Conference on the Spiritual Foundations of American Democracy," November 9, 1954, Collection 165, Box 68, Folder 11, Billy Graham Center Archives.

34 Gaston, "Cold War Romance," 1133. One achievement of FRASCO, as Inboden notes, is that it came close to producing a pan-religious statement of principles desired by Lilly and others in the administration. See Inboden, *Religion and American Foreign Policy, 1945–1960*, 285–86.

35 Richard Nixon to Walter Bedell Smith, September 10, 1954, White House Office, National Security Council Staff Papers, OCB Central Files 000.3 [Religion] (File #1) (1), Dwight D. Eisenhower Presidential Library.

36 "Proposal to OCB by Foundation for Religious Action," August 9, 1954, White House Office, National Security Council Staff Papers, OCB Central Files 000.3 [Religion] (File #1) (1), Dwight D. Eisenhower Presidential Library.

37 "Proposal to OCB by Foundation for Religious Action."

38 It is unclear whether the authors misspelled "God" as "Good," or were instead making a broader claim about the value of theistic religion. See "A Proposal: A Spiritual Counteroffensive in Southeast Asia," n.d., White House Office, National Security Council Staff Papers, OCB Central Files 000.3 [Religion] (File #1) (1), Dwight D. Eisenhower Presidential Library.

39 This operation is the subject of chapter 5.

40 "National Security Council Report (NSC 5612/1)," in *Foreign Relations of the United States, 1955–1957, East Asian Security; Cambodia; Laos, Volume XXI* (US Government Printing Office, 1956), Document 119.

41 "Operations Coordinating Board Memorandum of Meeting: Committee on Buddhism," June 29, 1956, Document #CK2349148155, U.S. Declassified Documents Online.

42 Kenneth Landon, interview by Albert Atwood, April 1982, Association for Diplomatic Studies and Training Foreign Affairs Oral History Project, Library of Congress, http://lcweb2.loc.gov/service/mss/mfdip/2004/2004lan02/2004lan02.pdf.

43 Kenneth Young to Kenneth Landon, "Comments on Memorandum for Committee on Buddhism," August 27, 1956, Document #CK2349474903, U.S. Declassified Documents Online; White House, "Proposals Regarding U.S. Relations with Therawada Buddhist Countries in Southeast Asia, Including Ceylon, Thailand, Burma, Cambodia and Laos," September 7, 1956, Document #CK2349143740, US Declassified Documents Online.

44 "Operations Coordinating Board Memorandum of Meeting: Committee on Buddhism." For the proposed plan, see "Outline Plan Regarding Buddhist Organizations in Ceylon, Burma, Thailand, Laos, Cambodia," January 16, 1957, Document #CK2349143796, US Declassified Documents Online.

45 White House, "Proposals Regarding U.S. Relations."

46 Young to Landon, "Comments on Memorandum for Committee on Buddhism."

47 Baghdad 933 to Department of State, "Anti-Communist Poster Material Prepared by USIS Baghdad," March 10, 1951, Electronic Briefing Book No. 78, Document #21, National Security Archive, https://nsarchive2.gwu.edu/NSAEBB/NSAEBB78/essay.htm; Inboden, *Religion and American Foreign Policy, 1945–1960*, 289–291; Osgood, *Total Cold War*, 312–14.

48 William A. Eddy to Dorothy Thompson, June 7, 1951, Documentation on Early Cold War U.S. Propaganda Activities in the Middle East, Document #26, National Security Archive, https://nsarchive2.gwu.edu/NSAEBB/NSAEBB78/docs.htm.

49 Dan Lacy to Datus C. Smith Jr., October 27, 1952, Documentation on Early Cold War U.S. Propaganda Activities in the Middle East, Document #78, National Security Archive, https://nsarchive2.gwu.edu/NSAEBB/NSAEBB78/docs.htm.

50 Helen Anderson to Richard H. Sanger, May 8, 1953, Documentation on Early Cold War U.S. Propaganda Activities in the Middle East, Document #94, National Security Archive, https://nsarchive2.gwu.edu/NSAEBB/NSAEBB78/docs.htm; Bayard Dodge to Richard H. Sanger, February 2, 1953, Documentation on Early Cold War U.S. Propaganda Activities in the Middle East, Document #90, National Security Archive, https://nsarchive2.gwu.edu/NSAEBB/NSAEBB78/docs.htm.

51 "NSC 155/1: United States Objectives and Policies with Respect to the Near East," July 14, 1953, Document #CK2349454798, US Declassified Documents Online.

52 "Memorandum: Ad Hoc Working Group on Islam," January 30, 1957; "Inventory of US Government and Private Organization Activity Regarding Islamic Organizations as an Aspect of Overseas Operations," May 3, 1957.

53 "Inventory of US Government and Private Organization Activity."

54 "A Psychological Strategy Program for the Middle East," January 8, 1953, Document #CK2349474052, US Declassified Documents Online.

55 "A Psychological Strategy Program for the Middle East."

56 "A Psychological Strategy Program for the Middle East." For concerns about Islam and modernity, see "Memorandum: Ad Hoc Working Group on Islam"; "Inventory of US Government and Private Organization Activity"; "Evaluation of Iran Program," August 15, 1957; James Gustin to Elmer B. Staats, "Briefing Memo on Islamic Inventory Paper," May 2, 1957, Document #CK2349505037, US Declassified Documents Online.

57 Edward L. R. Elson to Dwight Eisenhower, July 24, 1958, Dwight D. Eisenhower Records as President, White House Central Files, Official File, Middle East (6), Dwight D. Eisenhower Presidential Library.

58 Dwight Eisenhower to Edward L. R. Elson, July 31, 1958, "National Security Archive Electronic Briefing Book No. 78: U.S. Propaganda in the Middle East— The Early Cold War Version," Document #133, National Security Archive, https://nsarchive2.gwu.edu/NSAEBB/NSAEBB78/essay.htm.

59 Dwight Eisenhower, "Farewell Address."

60 Eisenhower to Elson.

61 Randall Balmer, "Broger, John C.," in *Encyclopedia of Evangelicalism* (Waco, TX: Baylor University Press, October 14, 2004); Bogle, *The Pentagon's Battle for the American Mind*, 127–31.

62 See the foreword in Gleason H. Ledyard, *Sky Waves: The Incredible Far East Broadcasting Company Story* (Chicago: Moody Bible Institute of Chicago, 1963).

63 Deputy Chief, Psychological and Paramilitary Staff to Director of Central Intelligence, "Militant Liberty," September 27, 1957, CIA-RDP80B01676R00120013 0013-3, National Archives (CREST Database).

64 Balmer, "Broger, John C."; Lori L. Bogle, "Militant Liberty," in *Encyclopedia of War and American Society*, ed. Peter Karsten (Thousand Oaks, CA: SAGE, 2005); William Harlan Hale, "'Militant Liberty' and the Pentagon," *The Reporter*, February 9, 1956, 30–34.

65 "A Report to the National Security Council—NSC 162/2," October 20, 1953, 14, https://fas.org/irp/offdocs/nsc-hst/nsc-162-2.pdf.

66 "Militant Liberty" (Department of Defense, November 5, 1954), 1–2, 6–7, Document #CK2349092981, US Declassified Documents Online.

67 See, for example, Lilly to Jackson, "The Basic Factor."

68 "Militant Liberty," 1–2, 6–7.

69 "Militant Liberty," 26.

70 "Militant Liberty," 21.

71 "Militant Liberty," 30–37, 37.

72 "Militant Liberty," 39.

73 "Militant Liberty," 44–45.

74 "Militant Liberty," 12.

75 "Militant Liberty," 14.

76 "Militant Liberty," 15.

77 "Militant Liberty," 18.

78 For more on American perceptions of "brainwashing," see Matthew Dunne, *A Cold War State of Mind: Brainwashing and Postwar American Society* (Amherst: University of Massachusetts Press, 2013).

79 Radford, Arthur W., to Allen Dulles, "Brainwashing," June 7, 1956, CIA-RDP80 R01731R000300200018–2, National Archives (CREST Database); Radford even spoke on the same themes when he gave a speech at FRASCO's 1955 conference on "The Mind and the Spirit in National Security." See Inboden, *Religion and American Foreign Policy, 1945–1960*, 285.

80 Quoted in Hale, "'Militant Liberty' and the Pentagon."

81 Deputy Chief, Psychological and Paramilitary Staff to Director of Central Intelligence, "Militant Liberty," September 27, 1957.

82 Deputy Chief, Psychological and Paramilitary Staff to Director of Central Intelligence, "Militant Liberty."

83 Interestingly, CIA staff prepared a more polite letter for Dulles to send, but the director revised it to be more direct before sending. See Deputy Chief, Psychological and Paramilitary Staff to Director of Central Intelligence.

84 Allen Dulles to Arthur W. Radford, October 9, 1957, CIA-RDP80B01676R001200 130012–4, National Archives (CREST Database).

85 This office would later be reorganized as the Armed Forces Information Service, which would itself be abolished in 2008 and renamed the Defense Media Activity.

86 While versions of Militant Liberty were developed by the Department of Defense for use in various countries under the "Project Action" moniker, the program seems to only have been deployed to mixed results in Ecuador, and the program was never fully operationalized in the way its authors hoped. See Osgood, *Total Cold War*, 318–19.

87 Tony Shaw, *Hollywood's Cold War* (Amherst: University of Massachusetts Press, 2007), 203–4.

88 For similar plans, see "Outline Plan of Operations for the U.S. Ideological Program (D-33)," January 14, 1955, Document #CK2349114669, US Declassified Documents Online. Also see Greg Barnhisel, *Cold War Modernists: Art, Literature, and American Cultural Diplomacy* (New York: Columbia University Press, 2015), 112; Audra J. Wolfe, *Freedom's Laboratory: The Cold War Struggle for the Soul of Science* (Baltimore: Johns Hopkins University Press, 2018), 91–95; Osgood, *Total Cold War*, 289–94.

89 For a helpful introduction to this understanding of secularism, see Ann Pellegrini and Janet Jakobsen, "Times Like These," in *Secularisms*, ed. Janet Jakobsen and Ann Pellegrini (Durham, NC: Duke University Press, 2008). In the specific context of American religion, two useful starting points are Tracy Fessenden, *Culture and Redemption: Religion, the Secular, and American Literature* (Princeton, NJ: Princeton University Press, 2007); John Lardas Modern, "Evangelical Secularism and the Measure of Leviathan," *Church History: Studies in Christianity and Culture* 77, no. 4 (2008): 801–76, https://doi.org/10.1017/S0009640708001613.

90 Theodore Hesburgh to Thomas A. Dooley, April 12, 1960, Thomas Dooley Collection, St. Mary's Notre Dame 1960 Binder, Saint Louis University Archives. For Hellmuth's ties to the CIA, see Hugh Wilford, *The Mighty Wurlitzer: How the CIA Played America* (Cambridge, MA: Harvard University Press, 2008), 180.

91 Joel Kramer, "NSA's 15's Year Lie Was Finally Too Much," *The Harvard Crimson*, February 25, 1967, http://www.thecrimson.com/article/1967/2/25/nsas-15-year -lie-was/.

92 While the CIA was involved, its influence has also been exaggerated by American and Italian actors for various reasons. See Kaeten Mistry, "Approaches to Understanding the Inaugural CIA Covert Operation in Italy: Exploding Useful Myths," *Intelligence and National Security* 26, no. 2–3 (April 2011): 246–68, https://doi.org /10.1080/02684527.2011.559318; Burton Hersh, *The Old Boys: The American Elite and the Origins of the CIA* (New York: Charles Scribner's Sons, 1992), 294.

93 Wilford, *The Mighty Wurlitzer*, 189.

94 Wilford, *The Mighty Wurlitzer*, 190.

Chapter Five

1 Thomas A. Dooley, "Mike Wallace Asks Tom Dooley: How Much Can One Man Do?," interview by Mike Wallace, March 18, 1958, Thomas Dooley Collection, Scrapbook MEDICO 1 (1958), Saint Louis University Archives.

2 Jim Winters, "Tom Dooley: The Forgotten Hero," *Notre Dame Magazine*, May 1979, 10.

3 For one excellent study of the American memory of the Vietnam War, see Edwin A. Martini, *Invisible Enemies: The American War on Vietnam, 1975–2000* (Amherst: University of Massachusetts Press, 2007).

4 On how the early CIA absorbed these capabilities, see Richard H. Immerman, *The Hidden Hand: A Brief History of the CIA* (Chichester, West Sussex: Wiley-Blackwell, 2014), 19–29.

5 James T. Fisher, *Dr. America: The Lives of Thomas A. Dooley, 1927–1961* (Amherst: University of Massachusetts Press, 1997), 25.

6 Under the terms of the Geneva Agreement, the land around Haiphong was turned over to the Viet Minh in phases. This acts as an important plot device, and a looming existential threat, in Dooley's writings.

7 Thomas A. Dooley, *Deliver Us from Evil* (Farrar, Straus & Giroux, 1956).

8 Seth Jacobs, *America's Miracle Man in Vietnam: Ngo Dinh Diem, Religion, Race, and U.S. Intervention in Southeast Asia, 1950–1957* (Durham, NC: Duke University Press, 2004), 138.

9 Dooley, *Deliver Us from Evil*, 114.

10 Dooley, *Deliver Us from Evil*, 26.

11 The best overall biography on Tom Dooley remains Fisher, *Dr. America*. Also see chapter 8 in Wilford, *The Mighty Wurlitzer*; chapter 4 in Jacobs, *America's Miracle Man in Vietnam*.

12 Of course, Operation Passage to Freedom—the movement of hundreds of thousands of North Vietnamese to the South in 1954–1955—certainly took place, even if it was less a one-man show than depicted in Dooley's book. As Peter Hansen and other scholars have noted, there were plenty of injustices visited upon Northern Catholics, and some of these injustices likely factored into the decision by many to move south. See Peter Hansen, "Bắc Đi Cú: Catholic Refugees from the North of Vietnam, and Their Role in the Southern Republic, 1954–1959," *Journal of Vietnamese Studies* 4, no. 3 (October 2009): 173–211, https://doi.org/10.1525/vs.2009.4.3.173.

13 Fisher, *Dr. America*, 74.

14 Among much else, see Jonathan P. Herzog, *The Spiritual-Industrial Complex: America's Religious Battle against Communism in the Early Cold War* (New York: Oxford University Press, 2011); Andrew Preston, *Sword of the Spirit, Shield of Faith: Religion in American War and Diplomacy* (New York: Anchor Books, 2012); William Inboden, *Religion and American Foreign Policy, 1945–1960: The Soul of Containment* (Cambridge and New York: Cambridge University Press, 2008); Wilford, *The Mighty Wurlitzer*; Russell T. McCutcheon and William Arnal, "'Just Follow the Money': The Cold War, the Humanistic Study of Religion, and the Fallacy of Insufficient Cynicism," in *The Sacred Is the Profane* (Oxford: Oxford University Press, 2012), 72–90; Dianne Kirby, ed., *Religion and the Cold War* (New York: Palgrave Macmillan, 2002).

15 Dooley, *Deliver Us from Evil*, 58.

16 Dooley, *Deliver Us from Evil*, 54–57.

17 Kenneth A. Osgood, "Hearts and Minds: The Unconventional Cold War," *Journal of Cold War Studies* 4, no. 2 (2002): 85–107, 102.

18 For a concise look at the relationship between American religion and support for Diem, see Seth Jacobs, "'Our System Demands the Supreme Being': The US Religious Revival and the 'Diem Experiment,' 1954–55," *Diplomatic History* 25, no. 4 (2001): 589–624.

19 Diana Shaw, "The Temptation of Tom Dooley," *Los Angeles Times Magazine*, December 15, 1991, 44.

20 Quoted in Christian G. Appy, *Patriots: The Vietnam War Remembered from All Sides* (New York: Penguin Books, 2004), 48.

21 Shaw, "The Temptation of Tom Dooley," 44.

22 William Lederer to DeWitt Wallace, February 20, 1957, William J. Lederer Papers (MS 158), Special Collections and University Archives, University of Massachusetts Amherst Libraries; William Lederer and Eugene Burdick, *The Ugly American* (New York: W. W. Norton, 1958).

23 Lansdale was technically a member of the US Air Force on loan to the CIA.

24 Quoted in Appy, *Patriots*, 50.

25 For example, see "The Man with the Innocent Air," *Time* 62, no. 5 (August 3, 1953): 12–15.

26 On the relationship between Diem and the US religious context, see Jacobs, *America's Miracle Man in Vietnam*; Seth Jacobs, *Cold War Mandarin: Ngo Dinh Diem and the Origins of America's War in Vietnam, 1950–1963* (Lanham, MD: Rowman & Littlefield Publishers, 2006). For a survey on how US officials understood the domestic religious context in South Vietnam, and how it related to the broader conflict, see James McAllister, "'Only Religions Count in Vietnam': Thich Tri Quang and the Vietnam War," *Modern Asian Studies* 42, no. 4 (July 2008), https://doi.org/10.1017/S0026749X07002855. For other coverage, see Edward Garvey Miller, *Misalliance: Ngo Dinh Diem, the United States, and the Fate of South Vietnam* (Cambridge, MA: Harvard University Press, 2013); Jessica M. Chapman, "The Sect Crisis of 1955 and the American Commitment to Ngô Đình Diệm," *Journal of Vietnamese Studies* 5, no. 1 (February 2010): 37–85, https://doi.org/10.1525/vs.2010.5.1.37.

27 Quoted in Jacobs, *Cold War Mandarin*, 53.

28 T. Jeremy Gunn, *Spiritual Weapons: The Cold War and the Forging of an American National Religion* (Santa Barbara, CA: ABC-CLIO, 2008), 171. US Information Agency, "Come South," August 5, 1954, RG 306: Records of the U.S. Information Agency, 1900–2003; U.S.I.A. Bureau of Programs, Press and Publications Service, Publications Division, 1953–1978, National Archives, https://catalog.archives.gov/id/6949142.

29 Gunn, *Spiritual Weapons*, 171.

30 Ralph McGehee, *Deadly Deceits: My 25 Years in the CIA* (New York: Sheridan Square Publications, 1983), 131.

31 Drawing in part on oral histories conducted with Vietnamese survivors, Peter Hansen argues that this traditional interpretation rests "on the rather patronizing assumption that the Bắc Đi Cú ['Northern Refugees from Fifty-four'] left because they were superstitious and therefore susceptible to such simplistic attempts at manipulation." See Hansen, "Bắc Đi Cú," 182–83. Also see Jacobs, *Cold War Mandarin*, 51–56.

32 "Memorandum of Discussion at the 183d Meeting of the National Security Council (Thursday, February 4, 1954)," in *Foreign Relations of the United States, 1952–1954, Indochina, Volume XIII, Part 1* (US Government Printing Office, 1982), 1013–17, https://history.state.gov/historicaldocuments/frus1952-54v13p1/d534, Document 534. See also Jacobs, *America's Miracle Man in Vietnam*, 46–49.

33 Allen Dulles to Felix Stump, May 11, 1955, William J. Lederer Papers (MS 158), Special Collections and University Archives, University of Massachusetts Amherst Libraries. Also see Fisher, *Dr. America*, 273.

34 Quoted in Fisher, *Dr. America*, 71.

35 Wilford, *The Mighty Wurlitzer*, 173.

36 On the relationship between FSG and the CIA, see Boris Kachka, *Hothouse: The Art of Survival and the Survival of Art at America's Most Celebrated Publishing House, Farrar, Straus, and Giroux*, repr. ed. (New York: Simon & Schuster, 2014).

37 Kachka, *Hothouse*, 50.

38 Kachka, *Hothouse*, 113.

39 "The Man with the Innocent Air (Condensed from Time)," *Reader's Digest*, October 1953.

40 DeWitt Wallace to Thomas A. Dooley, May 15, 1956, Thomas Dooley Collection, Box 1, Binder MEDICO, Saint Louis University Archives.

41 DeWitt Wallace to Thomas A. Dooley, August 24, 1956, Thomas Dooley Collection, Box 1, Binder MEDICO, Saint Louis University Archives.

42 Lynn Caine to C. L. Douglas, March 9, 1956, Thomas Dooley Collection, Teresa Gallagher Papers, Saint Louis University Archives.

43 DeWitt Wallace to William Lederer, December 16, 1955, William J. Lederer Papers (MS 158), Special Collections and University Archives, University of Massachusetts Amherst Libraries.

44 On these changes during World War II, see Kevin M. Schultz, *Tri-Faith America: How Catholics and Jews Held Postwar America to Its Protestant Promise* (New York: Oxford University Press, 2011).

45 Dooley, *Deliver Us from Evil*, 34.

46 Dooley, *Deliver Us from Evil*, 84.

47 Dooley, *Deliver Us from Evil*, 132.

48 Dooley, *Deliver Us from Evil*, 21.

49 Dooley, *Deliver Us from Evil*, 112.

50 This strategy, even if not consciously employed by Dooley, has a long tradition in American religious history. For the classic treatment of this pattern, see R. Laurence Moore, *Religious Outsiders and the Making of Americans*, new ed. (Oxford: Oxford University Press, 1987).

51 Quoted in Jacobs, *America's Miracle Man in Vietnam*, 141.

52 Dooley, *Deliver Us from Evil*, 39.

53 "Ideas of Indochina Communists as Bad as Their Cruelties," *Catholic View*, May 13, 1956, Thomas Dooley Collection, Lecture Binder 1, Saint Louis University Archives.

54 Pope Leo XIII issued *Testem Benevolentaie* in 1899 in response to perceived liberal trends in the Church, particularly those involving church-state separation in the

United States. The encyclical was addressed to the American Cardinal James Gibbons and came in the midst of church-state tension in Europe.

55 "Christian Influences in United States Democracy," January 1959, CIA-RDP78–02771R0005000160002–5, National Archives (CREST Database).

56 Elizabeth Fenton, *Religious Liberties: Anti-Catholicism and Liberal Democracy in Nineteenth-Century U.S. Literature and Culture*, 1st ed. (New York: Oxford University Press, 2011); Peter R. D'Agostino, *Rome in America: Transnational Catholic Ideology from the Risorgimento to Fascism* (Chapel Hill: University of North Carolina Press, 2004); Philip Hamburger, *Separation of Church and State* (Cambridge, MA: Harvard University Press, 2004); Mark S. Massa, "Anti-Catholicism in the United States," *Oxford Research Encyclopedia of American History*, June 9, 2016, https://doi.org/10.1093/acrefore/9780199329175.013.316. Also see the more extensive references on this topic in chapter 1 and the introduction.

57 For one excellent study exploring these themes, particularly in the case of colonial Maryland, see Maura Jane Farrelly, *Papist Patriots: The Making of an American Catholic Identity* (Oxford: Oxford University Press, 2012).

58 Dooley, "Mike Wallace Asks Tom Dooley: How Much Can One Man Do?"

59 John T. McGreevy, *Catholicism and American Freedom: A History* (New York: W. W. Norton, 2003), 164.

60 Dooley, *Deliver Us from Evil*, 62.

61 For examples of this work, see Tomoko Masuzawa, *The Invention of World Religions: Or, How European Universalism Was Preserved in the Language of Pluralism* (Chicago: University of Chicago Press, 2005); David Chidester, *Savage Systems: Colonialism and Comparative Religion in Southern Africa* (Charlottesville: University of Virginia Press, 1996); Brent Nongbri, *Before Religion: A History of a Modern Concept* (New Haven, CT: Yale University Press, 2013). Additional references on this topic are provided in the introduction.

62 William Lederer, "They'll Remember the Bayfield," *Reader's Digest*, March 1955.

63 This position is also shared by many of the historians who have written about Dooley. For one recent example, see Christian G. Appy, *American Reckoning: The Vietnam War and Our National Identity* (New York: Viking, 2015), 27.

64 Quoted in Appy, *Patriots*, 49.

65 Quoted in Appy, *Patriots*, 45.

66 Quoted in Shaw, "The Temptation of Tom Dooley," 46.

67 Quoted in Shaw, "The Temptation of Tom Dooley," 45.

68 Thomas A. Dooley to Bart, "Draft of the 'Dear Bart' Letter," n.d., Thomas Dooley Collection, Teresa Gallagher Papers, Box of Posthumous Material, Saint Louis University Archives.

69 Dooley, *Deliver Us from Evil*, 115.

70 Thomas A. Dooley, "Deliver Us from Evil," *Reader's Digest*, April 1956, 161.

71 Howard R. Simpson, *Tiger in the Barbed Wire: An American in Vietnam, 1952–1991* (Washington, DC: Brassey's (US), 1992), 129.

72 Simpson, *Tiger in the Barbed Wire*, 127.

73 The Saint Louis University Archives preserves a large collection of Dooley fan mail. See Clare DuBrock to Thomas A. Dooley, April 3, 1958, Thomas Dooley Collection, Clippings Binder 6, Saint Louis University Archives.

74 Ngo Dinh Diem to Thomas A. Dooley, June 25, 1956, Thomas Dooley Collection, Box 1, Binder MEDICO, Saint Louis University Archives.

75 Quoted in Appy, *Patriots*, 49.

76 On the broader role of the Peace Corps, see David Allen, "The Peace Corps in US Foreign Relations and Church-State Politics," *The Historical Journal* 58, no. 1 (March 2015): 245–73, https://doi.org/10.1017/S0018246X14000363.

77 John F. Kennedy, "Speech of Senator John F. Kennedy, Cow Palace, San Francisco, CA—(Advance Release Text)," November 2, 1960, American Presidency Project, University of California Santa Barbara, https://www.presidency.ucsb .edu/documents/speech-senator-john-f-kennedy-cow-palace-san-francisco-ca.

78 This is a darkly ironic statement, especially considering Nixon's later role as president in expanding American military operations into Laos.

79 Ruth Dean, "It Was Tom Dooley's Day at Capitol Hill Luncheon," *Washington Star*, June 15, 1960, Thomas Dooley Collection, Clippings Binder 1960, Saint Louis University Archives.

80 "Book by Doctor Tells Story of Red Cruelty in Vietnam," *Visitor Register*, April 6, 1956; Marchmont Kovas, "Dooley Tells of Red Torture," *South Bend Tribune*, April 14, 1956.

81 William McGaffin, "Exclusive: How Reds Tortured Indo Catholics," *Chicago Daily News*, February 11, 1956. Dooley's mother, Agnes, subscribed to a clipping service after her son became famous. She filled numerous binders with newspaper clippings from around the country. Conveniently, these binders are available for review at the Saint Louis University archives, making it an ideal location to get a sense of how Dooley was received around the country.

82 June Bove to Thomas A. Dooley, September 22, 1958, Thomas Dooley Collection, International Book Covers / Reprint Box, Saint Louis University Archives.

83 Jacobs, *America's Miracle Man in Vietnam*, 174.

84 McGehee, *Deadly Deceits*, 132. As noted earlier in this chapter, there are other, less generous assessments of the Agency's success.

85 Quoted in Fisher, *Dr. America*, 239.

86 Fisher, *Dr. America*, 237.

87 Quoted in Appy, *Patriots*, 49.

88 Fisher, *Dr. America*, 117.

89 Heinrich to J. Edgar Hoover, "SUBJECT: Thomas A. Dooley, M.D.," February 8, 1957, FBI Personality Files, Box 8, Thomas Dooley Folder, National Security Archive.

90 C. D. DeLoach, "Religious Heritage of America, Inc.," March 9, 1960, FBI Personality Files, Box 8, Thomas Dooley Folder, National Security Archive.

91 Fisher, *Dr. America*, 98–103.

92 Shaw, "The Temptation of Tom Dooley," 47.

93 John Cooney, *The American Pope: The Life and Times of Francis Cardinal Spellman* (New York: Times Books, 1984), 243. The cardinal's aides seem to have been concerned about the propriety of the visit, but Spellman went anyway. See Shaw, "The Temptation of Tom Dooley."

94 Winters, "Tom Dooley: The Forgotten Hero," 10.

95 Thomas A. Dooley, "Thomas Dooley's Final Letter to Father Hesburgh," *Chicago's American*, January 15, 1961, Thomas Dooley Collection, Box 1 Assorted Letters, Saint Louis University Archives.

96 Shaw, "The Temptation of Tom Dooley," 46.

97 Marguerite Shepard, "Dr. Dooley's Mother Getting Letters From Around World," *St. Louis Globe-Democrat*, n.d., Thomas Dooley Collection, Clippings Binder 1960 #2, Saint Louis University Archives.

98 Dalai Lama to the Director, MEDICO, January 30, 1961, Thomas Dooley Collection, Teresa Gallagher Papers, Saint Louis University Archives.

99 Angier Biddle Duke to Agnes Dooley, February 2, 1961, Thomas Dooley Collection, Box 1, Saint Louis University Archives.

100 "Sermon Delivered by the Rt. Rev. Msgr. George J. Gottwald at the Funeral of Dr. Thomas Dooley Held at the Saint Louis Cathedral," January 23, 1961, Thomas Dooley Collection, Scherck Papers, Saint Louis University Archives.

101 For a slightly earlier example, see Lederer, "They'll Remember the Bayfield."

102 An American Officer, "The Report the President Wanted Published," *Saturday Evening Post*, May 20, 1961.

103 Don A. Schanche to Edward Lansdale, May 8, 1961, Edward Geary Lansdale Papers, Box 49, Folder 1375, Hoover Institution Archives.

104 Edward Lansdale to Robert McNamara, "Film on Vietnam," March 26, 1962, Edward Geary Lansdale Papers, Box 49, Folder 1375, Hoover Institution Archives.

105 Stan Atkinson to Edward Lansdale, April 12, 1962, Edward Geary Lansdale Papers, Box 49, Folder 1375, Hoover Institution Archives.

106 The Lansdale Papers have numerous examples of these donations. See in particular Box 49, Folder 1375.

107 "DCAS Vietnam Conflict Extract File Record Counts by HOME OF RECORD STATE CODE," April 29, 2008, National Archives and Records Administration, http://www.archives.gov/research/military/vietnam-war/casualty-statistics .html#date.

108 John A. McCone to McGeorge Bundy, May 27, 1963, NSF/CF/Vatican, Box 191A, John F. Kennedy Presidential Library.

109 CIA Office of National Estimates, "Staff Memorandum No. 27–63, 'Change in the Catholic Church,'" May 13, 1963, NSF/CF/Vatican, Box 191A, John F. Kennedy Presidential Library, 15.

110 "Special Report #80: Vatican Relations with Russia and France," March 7, 1945, RG 226, Entry 210, Box 311, Folder 2, National Archives at College Park, College Park, MD.

111 "Preliminary Comments on the Encyclical 'Pacem in Terris,'" April 15, 1963, CIA-RDP79T00429A0013000300012–0, National Archives (CREST Database), 2.

112 CIA Office of National Estimates, "Staff Memorandum No. 27–63, 'Change in the Catholic Church.'"

113 Quoted in Jeffrey M. Burns, "No Longer Emerging: 'Ramparts' Magazine and the Catholic Laity, 1962–1968," *US Catholic Historian* 9, no. 3 (1990): 321–33, 323. Burns's article is a thorough, scholarly investigation of the relationship between *Ramparts* and the changing nature of American Catholicism in the 1960s.

114 Peter Richardson, *A Bomb in Every Issue: How the Short, Unruly Life of Ramparts Magazine Changed America* (New York: New Press, 2009), 21.

115 The magazine would be resurrected a few years later and published until 1975 under the same name, but it was functionally a separate publication from the Catholic *Ramparts* that had come before it.

116 Burns, "No Longer Emerging," 322. Burns argues that this is one of the magazine's most important legacies.

117 Quoted in Richardson, *A Bomb in Every Issue*, 32.

118 Quoted in Burns, "No Longer Emerging," 332.

119 Richardson, *A Bomb in Every Issue*, 19–33.

120 Quoted in Burns, "No Longer Emerging," 328.

121 It is important to note that Scheer overemphasized the role played by the CIA in the early days of American involvement. For more on this, see Hansen, "Bắc Đi Cú."

122 Robert Scheer, "Hang Down Your Head Tom Dooley," *Ramparts*, 1965, 28.

123 Burns, "No Longer Emerging," 332–33.

124 Robert Scheer and Warren Hinckle, "The Vietnam Lobby," *Ramparts*, 1965, 22.

125 Scheer and Hinckle's errors, and the consequences of those errors, have been explored by a number of scholars. See James T. Fisher, "The Second Catholic President: Ngo Dinh Diem, John F. Kennedy, and the Vietnam Lobby, 1954–1963," *US Catholic Historian* 15, no. 3 (1997): 119–37; James T. Fisher, "The Vietnam Lobby and the Politics of Pluralism," in *Cold War Constructions: The Political Culture of United States Imperialism, 1945–1966* (Amherst: University of Massachusetts Press, 2000); Joseph G. Morgan, *The Vietnam Lobby: The American Friends of Vietnam, 1955–1975* (Chapel Hill: University of North Carolina Press, 1997); Burns, "No Longer Emerging."

126 Fisher, "The Second Catholic President," 120.

127 See Fisher, "The Second Catholic President," 120.

128 Rhodri Jeffreys-Jones, *The CIA and American Democracy* (New Haven, CT: Yale University Press, 2003), 153.

129 For an account of the Ramparts situation from inside the CIA, see Cord Meyer, *Facing Reality: From World Federalism to the CIA* (Lanham, MD: University Press of America, 1982). Meyer contends that the *Ramparts* exposés harmed the liberal

internationalist wing within the CIA, which was funding the National Student Association (NSA) to do what the NSA wanted to do of its own accord. See Meyer, *Facing Reality*, 86–89.

130 John Ranelagh, *The Agency: The Rise and Decline of the CIA* (New York: Simon and Schuster, 1986). Similar to the argument advanced by Cord Meyer, Ranelagh's scholarly study shows how some of these funding programs resulted from a creative and flexible engagement with a variety of anti-Communist associations, the cancellation of which only strengthened conservative elements within the Agency. See Ranelagh, *The Agency*, 251–52.

131 Nicholas Dujmovic, ed., "Reflections of DCIs Colby and Helms on the CIA's 'Time of Troubles,'" *Studies in Intelligence* 51, no. 3 (1988): 39–56.

132 Perhaps coincidentally, Angleton was the intelligence officer who, during his time working for OSS in Rome during World War II, determined VESSEL to be fraudulent.

133 Michael Howard Holzman, *James Jesus Angleton, the CIA, and the Craft of Counterintelligence* (Amherst: University of Massachusetts Press, 2008), 231–36.

134 Quoted in Evan Thomas, *The Very Best Men: Four Who Dared: The Early Years of the CIA* (New York: Touchstone, 1995), 329–30.

135 "IRS Briefing on Ramparts," February 2, 1967, CNSS Documents Collection Box 9 File C-48, National Security Archive.

136 "Ramparts Tax Returns," February 15, 1967, CNSS Documents Collection Box 9 File C-48, National Security Archive.

137 Fisher, *Dr. America*, 79.

138 Rosemary Rawson, "18 Years After Dr. Tom Dooley's Death, a Priest Insists He Was a Saint, Not a CIA Spook," *People*, July 30, 1979.

139 Arthur W. Arthur, "A Damned American Patriot," *Washington Post*, July 14, 1979, sec. Letters to the Editor.

140 Fisher, *Dr. America*.

141 Lederer, "They'll Remember the Bayfield," 3.

142 Ferdinand Mayer to William Donovan, July 17, 1945, RG 226, Entry 210, Box 338, Folder 1, National Archives at College Park, College Park, MD.

Chapter Six

1   William Lederer to Fritz, April 7, 1959, William J. Lederer Papers (MS 158), Special Collections and University Archives, University of Massachusetts Amherst Libraries.

2   Chaplain Corps Planning Group, "The Religions of South Vietnam in Faith and Fact" (US Navy Bureau of Naval Personnel, 1967), Edward Geary Lansdale Papers, Box 62, Folder 1619, Hoover Institution Archives, 93.

3   Rev. John Ireland Gallery to Edward Lansdale, October 13, 1976, Edward Geary Lansdale Papers, Box 3, Folder 79, Hoover Institution Archives.

4   Quoted in Cecil B. Currey, *Edward Lansdale, the Unquiet American* (Boston: Houghton Mifflin, 1988), 293.

5   Quoted in Jonathan Nashel, *Edward Lansdale's Cold War* (Amherst: University of Massachusetts Press, 2005), 21.

6   Edward Lansdale, Interview I, interview by Ted Gittinger, June 5, 1981, Edward Geary Lansdale Papers, Box 78, Folder 285, Hoover Institution Archives, Part I, 11.

7   Nashel, *Edward Lansdale's Cold War*, 21.

8   Edward Lansdale, "The Upside-Down Wars" (unpublished manuscript, n.d.), Edward Geary Lansdale Papers, Box 76, Folder 265, Hoover Institution Archives, 3.

9   William Egan Colby, "The Ten Greatest Spies of All Time," n.d., Edward Geary Lansdale Papers, Box 70, Memoranda Folder, Hoover Institution Archives.

10   US Marine Corps, "Selections from 'Small Wars Manual, United States Marine Corps,'" 1940, Edward Geary Lansdale Papers, Box 9, Hoover Institution Archives.

11   Edward Lansdale, interview by William Gibbons and Patricia McAdams, November 19, 1982, Edward Geary Lansdale Papers, Box 79, Hoover Institution Archives, 9.

12   Edward Lansdale, "Warfare Systems School, CI Course," May 28, 1964, Edward Geary Lansdale Papers, Box 74, Folder 241, Hoover Institution Archives.

13   Max Boot, *The Road Not Taken: Edward Lansdale and the American Tragedy in Vietnam* (New York: Liveright, 2018), 33–34.

14   Edward Lansdale, "From the Serpent's Mouth," October 25, 1943, Edward Geary Lansdale Papers, Box 31, Folder 694, Hoover Institution Archives.

15   For more information on Lansdale's early life, see Nashel, *Edward Lansdale's Cold*

War, 26–29. "USAF Official Biography: Major General Edward G. Lansdale" (US Air Force, October 1962), http://www.af.mil/AboutUs/Biographies/Display/tabid /225/Article/106443/major-general-edward-g-lansdale.aspx.

16   Lansdale, "From the Serpent's Mouth."

17   Eric Pace, "Edward Lansdale Dies at 79; Adviser on Guerilla Warfare," *New York Times*, February 24, 1987, sec. Obituaries, http://www.nytimes.com/1987/02/24 /obituaries/edward-lansdale-dies-at-79-adviser-on-guerrilla-warfare.html.

18   Lansdale, Interview I, Part I, 2.

19   "USAF Official Biography: Major General Edward G. Lansdale."

20   Lansdale, Interview I, Part I, 7.

21   Nashel, *Edward Lansdale's Cold War*, 31.

22   Edward Lansdale, "Notes on Magsaysay," n.d., Edward Geary Lansdale Papers, Box 80, Assorted Writings Folder, Hoover Institution Archives.

23   Edward Geary Lansdale, *In the Midst of Wars: An American's Mission to Southeast Asia* (New York: Harper & Row, 1972), 71–75.

24   Jeffrey Wheatley, "US Colonial Governance of Superstition and Fanaticism in the Philippines," *Method & Theory in the Study of Religion* 30, no. 1 (January 2, 2018): 21–36, https://doi.org/10.1163/15700682–12341410, 33.

25   On leveraging others' credulity, see Emily Ogden, *Credulity: A Cultural History of US Mesmerism* (Chicago: University of Chicago Press, 2018).

26   Edward Lansdale, "Military Psychological Operations: Part One," January 7, 1960, Edward Geary Lansdale Papers, Box 45, Folder 1279, Hoover Institution Archives, 4–5.

27   Lansdale, "Military Psychological Operations: Part One," 4–5.

28   Edward Lansdale, "Military Psychological Operations: Part Two," March 29, 1960, Edward Geary Lansdale Papers, Box 45, Folder 1279, Hoover Institution Archives, 6–7.

29   Evan Thomas, *The Very Best Men: Four Who Dared: The Early Years of the CIA* (New York: Touchstone, 1995), 57.

30   Lansdale, "Military Psychological Operations: Part Two," 7.

31   Lansdale, "Military Psychological Operations: Part Two."

32 Matthew 7:12: "Therefore all things whatsoever ye would that men should do to you, do ye even so to them: for this is the law and the prophets" (KJV).

33 Edward Lansdale, "There Is My Country" (unpublished manuscript, 1969), Edward Geary Lansdale Papers, Box 75-76, Hoover Institution Archives, 215-17.

34 Lansdale, "There Is My Country," 215-16.

35 Lansdale, "Military Psychological Operations: Part Two."

36 Edward Lansdale, "Magsaysay Mambo," n.d., Edward Geary Lansdale Papers, Box 34, Folder 753, Hoover Institution Archives.

37 Nick Cullather, *Illusions of Influence: The Political Economy of United States-Philippines Relations, 1942-1960* (Stanford, CA: Stanford University Press, 1994), 108.

38 Lansdale, interview by William Gibbons and Patricia McAdams, 3.

39 Lansdale, Interview I, Part 1, 7.

40 Edward Lansdale, "Connection with CIA," December 15, 1985, Edward Geary Lansdale Papers, Box 70, Folder Memoranda, Hoover Institution Archives.

41 Currey, *Edward Lansdale*, 186-88.

42 Edward Lansdale to Allan Millett, June 15, 1977, Edward Geary Lansdale Papers, Box 81, Folder 318, Hoover Institution Archives.

43 Lansdale, "There Is My Country," Box 75, Folder 259, 64.

44 Richard Helms, "Interview II," interview by Ted Gittinger, September 16, 1981, Lyndon Baines Johnson Presidential Library, Austin, TX.

45 Lansdale, "There Is My Country," Box 76, Folder 264, 21.

46 Lansdale, interview by William Gibbons and Patricia McAdams, 17.

47 Edward Lansdale to Secretary of Defense Robert McNamara, "Vietnam," January 17, 1961, Edward Geary Lansdale Papers, Box 49, Folder 1376, Hoover Institution Archives, 2.

48 Lansdale to McNamara, 15.

49 The most famous example of this alternative approach to the study of religion is likely Mircea Eliade's work. See Eliade, *The Quest: History and Meaning in Religion* (Chicago: University of Chicago Press, 1969), 7.

50 Lansdale, Interview I, 6.

51 Lansdale, interview by William Gibbons and Patricia McAdams, 16–7.

52 Lansdale, interview by William Gibbons and Patricia McAdams, 17.

53 Lansdale, interview by William Gibbons and Patricia McAdams, 14.

54 US Senate, "Alleged Assassination Plots Involving Foreign Leaders" (US Government Printing Office, 1975), 142–43.

55 Edward Lansdale to Frank Church, January 1, 1976, Edward Geary Lansdale Papers, Box 10, Folder 360, Hoover Institution Archives.

56 Jonathan Nashel suggests Lansdale may have been more involved than he acknowledged. He points to a document, attributed to Lansdale, titled "Illumination by Submarine." See Nashel, *Edward Lansdale's Cold War*, 239n105.

57 For information on similar projects, see Lansdale, "There Is My Country," Box 76, Folder 263, 849–53.

58 Lansdale, "Connection with CIA."

59 Lansdale, Interview I, 57–58; Nashel, *Edward Lansdale's Cold War*, 78.

60 Lansdale, "There Is My Country," Box 76, Folder 263, 849–53.

61 Edward Lansdale to Ellsworth Bunker, "Vietnamese Soothsaying," June 1968, Edward Geary Lansdale Papers, Box 62, Folder 1619, Hoover Institution Archives.

62 Edward Lansdale to Ellsworth Bunker, "Soothsayers," May 18, 1967, Edward Geary Lansdale Papers, Box 62, Folder 1619, Hoover Institution Archives.

63 Lansdale to Bunker, "Vietnamese Soothsaying."

64 Edward Lansdale to Ellsworth Bunker, "Superstitious Dates," January 26, 1968, Edward Geary Lansdale Papers, Box 62, Folder 1619, Hoover Institution Archives.

65 Lansdale to Bunker, "Vietnamese Soothsaying."

66 Lansdale, "There Is My Country," Folder 76, Box 263, 854.

67 Edward Lansdale, "The 'True American,'" June 3, 1960, Edward Geary Lansdale Papers, Box 45, Folder 1286, Hoover Institution Archives.

68 Edward Lansdale, "The Older Vietnamese [Redacted]," n.d., Edward Geary Lansdale Papers, Box 62, Folder 1619, Hoover Institution Archives.

69 William G. Samways, "Indigenous Religious Beliefs and Practices of Vietnam"

(97th Civil Affairs Group, 1966), Edward Geary Lansdale Papers, Box 62, Folder 1619, Hoover Institution Archives.

70 Chaplain Corps Planning Group, "The Religions of South Vietnam in Faith and Fact," 91.

71 CIA programs in South Vietnam were particularly keen on using anthropologists. See David H. Price, *Cold War Anthropology: The CIA, the Pentagon, and the Growth of Dual Use Anthropology* (Durham, NC: Duke University Press Books, 2016), 301–2.

72 Chaplain Corps Planning Group, "The Religions of South Vietnam in Faith and Fact."

73 Edward Lansdale to Ellsworth Bunker, "Political Leaflet," August 31, 1967, Edward Geary Lansdale Papers, Box 62, Folder 1619, Hoover Institution Archives.

74 Lansdale to Bunker, "Vietnamese Soothsaying."

75 Edward Lansdale, "Soldiers and the People" (Lecture at the Special Warfare School, Fort Bragg, August 30, 1962), Edward Geary Lansdale Papers, Box 73, Folder 240, Hoover Institution Archives.

76 For important introductions to this idea, see Tomoko Masuzawa, *The Invention of World Religions: Or, How European Universalism Was Preserved in the Language of Pluralism* (Chicago: University of Chicago Press, 2005); Christopher R. Cotter and David G. Robertson, eds., *After World Religions: Reconstructing Religious Studies* (London and New York: Routledge, 2016). Also see the more extensive references on this topic in the introduction.

77 Lansdale's interest in the WRP echoes Jonathan Z. Smith's famous gloss on world religions as traditions that have "achieved sufficient power and numbers to enter our history to form it, interact with it, or thwart it. We recognize both the unity within and the diversity among the world religions because they correspond to important geopolitical entities with which we must deal." Smith, "Religion, Religions, Religious," in *Critical Terms for Religious Studies*, ed. Mark C. Taylor (Chicago: University of Chicago Press, 1998), 280.

78 Recently these critiques have even found commercial success when aimed at popular audiences. See Stephen Prothero, *God Is Not One: The Eight Rival Religions That Run the World*, repr. ed. (New York: HarperOne, 2011).

79 The Staff of *LIFE*, ed., *The World's Great Religions, Volume 1: Religions of the East* (New York: Time Incorporated, 1955).

80 One of the earliest responses is provided by Wilfred Cantwell Smith, *The Meaning and End of Religion* (Minneapolis: Fortress Press, 1962); Smith identifies many of the problems with how (largely American and European) academics understood

the category "religion," and he called for a more critically minded approach to studying religion. For a more recent and comprehensive study, see Masuzawa, *The Invention of World Religions*.

81 Tomoko Masuzawa's work demonstrated how the "research" like that conducted by Lansdale in the Philippines is part of a larger academic trajectory, one that presupposes "Europe as a harbinger of universal history, as a prototype of unity amid plurality." See Masuzawa, *The Invention of World Religions*, xi.

82 Edward Lansdale, "Meanings of Colors for Vietnamese People," n.d., Edward Geary Lansdale Papers, Box 62, Folder 1619, Hoover Institution Archives.

83 Stanley Karnow, "On Duty, 'Dirty Tricks,' and Democracy," *Washington Post*, December 10, 1972.

84 Edward Lansdale to Leo Kowatch, March 13, 1978, Edward Geary Lansdale Papers, Box 70, Memoranda Folder, Hoover Institution Archives.

85 Lansdale, "The 'True American.'"

86 Masuzawa, *The Invention of World Religions*.

87 Edward Lansdale, "Freedom and Democracy," October 3, 1961, Edward Geary Lansdale Papers, Box 74, Hoover Institution Archives.

88 Lansdale to Bunker, "Vietnamese Soothsaying."

89 Mary McAuliffe, interview with Ambassador Richard M. Helms, 1989, 9.

90 Directorate of Intelligence, "Near East and South Asia Review," October 11, 1985, CIA-RDP87T00289R000100230001-3, National Archives (CREST Database).

91 Price, *Cold War Anthropology*; Donald Wiebe, "Religious Studies in North America during the Cold War," in *The Academic Study of Religion during the Cold War: East and West*, ed. Iva Dolezalova, Luther Martin, and Dalibor Papousek, Toronto Studies in Religion 27 (New York: Peter Lang, 2001).

92 Russell T. McCutcheon and William Arnal, "'Just Follow the Money': The Cold War, the Humanistic Study of Religion, and the Fallacy of Insufficient Cynicism," in *The Sacred Is the Profane*, 2013, 72–90; Sarah Imhoff, "The Creation Story, or How We Learned to Stop Worrying and Love Schempp," *Journal of the American Academy of Religion* 84, no. 2 (June 2016): 466–97, https://doi.org/10.1093/jaarel /lfv060, 476.

93 Russell T. McCutcheon, *Manufacturing Religion: The Discourse on Sui Generis Religion and the Politics of Nostalgia*, 1st ed. (Oxford: Oxford University Press, 1997), 162–63. David H. Price, *Anthropological Intelligence: The Deployment and Neglect of American Anthropology in the Second World War* (Durham, NC: Duke Univer-

sity Press, 2008); Price, *Cold War Anthropology*; Peter Mandler, *Return from the Natives: How Margaret Mead Won the Second World War and Lost the Cold War* (New Haven, CT: Yale University Press, 2013).

94 Imhoff, "The Creation Story, or How We Learned to Stop Worrying and Love Schempp," 481.

95 Jacob Neusner and Noam M. M. Neusner, *The Price of Excellence: Universities in Conflict during the Cold War Era* (New York: Continuum, 1995), 33.

96 *School District of Abington Township, Pennsylvania v. Schempp*, 374 U.S. 203 (1963).

97 See Sarah Imhoff's important and persuasive essay on this reimagining of Schempp. See Imhoff, "The Creation Story, or How We Learned to Stop Worrying and Love Schempp."

98 Neusner and Neusner, *The Price of Excellence*, 37.

99 Huston Smith, *The Religions of Man* (New York: Harper & Row, 1958), 8–9.

100 This approach surely appealed to some in the national security community, and Smith himself was president of the World University Service of the United States when media reports linked the organization to a network of private organizations that had received, or were rumored to receive, CIA funds, though Smith himself was not implicated. Special to the *New York Times*, "Johnson Prodded on Oaths to CIA," *New York Times*, March 9, 1967; Special to the *New York Times*, "University Service Clarifies Resolution on CIA Funds," *New York Times*, March 10, 1967.

101 Smith, *The Religions of Man*, 8–9.

102 Quoted in Peter Braestrup, "Researchers Aid Thai Rebel Fight: U.S. Defense Unit Develops Antiguerrilla Devices," *New York Times*, March 20, 1967, https://nyti.ms /2vHUyc9.

103 Lansdale, "Freedom and Democracy," 21–22. Emphasis original.

104 Edward Lansdale, Interview II, interview by Ted Gittinger, September 15, 1981, Edward Geary Lansdale Papers, Box 78, Folder 285, Hoover Institution Archives, 80.

105 Boot, *The Road Not Taken*, 13. Boot provides good coverage of Lansdale's biographical information.

106 Hurd details a trinary of expert, governed, and lived religion in order to study how the category of religion has come to be used in academic studies of global religion and secularity. See Elizabeth Shakman Hurd, *Beyond Religious Freedom: The New Global Politics of Religion* (Princeton, NJ: Princeton University Press, 2015), 8.

Chapter Seven

1   William Egan Colby and Ted Gittinger, William E. Colby Oral History Interview I, June 2, 1981, Internet Copy, LBJ Presidential Library, 23.

2   Mary McAuliffe, interview with Ambassador Richard M. Helms, 1989.

3   Glenn E. Curtis and Eric Hooglund, eds., *Iran: A Country Study*, Area Handbook Series (Library of Congress Federal Research Division, 2008), 276.

4   On the idea of the "Muslim world," see Zareena Grewal, *Islam Is a Foreign Country: American Muslims and the Global Crisis of Authority* (New York: NYU Press, 2013); Cemil Aydin, *The Idea of the Muslim World: A Global Intellectual History* (Cambridge, MA: Harvard University Press, 2017).

5   "Memorandum from the President's Assistant for National Security Affairs (Brzezinski) to President Carter, December 28, 1978," in *Foreign Relations of the United States, 1977–1980, Volume I, Foundations of Foreign Policy* (US Government Printing Office, 2014), 511, Document 106.

6   Ruhollah Khomeini, *Islamic Government* (Institute for Compilation and Publication of Imam Khomeini's Works, 1970), http://www.iranchamber.com/history/rkhomeini/books/velayat_faqeeh.pdf.

7   Susan Grace, "MO Directed Toward Moslems in the Month of Ramadhan," August 24, 1944, RG 226, Entry A1139, Box 135, Folder 1820, National Archives at College Park, College Park, MD.

8   See, for example, "Anti-Communist Statements by Mullah Kashani," November 17, 1951, CIA-RDP82–00457R009400360010-2, National Archives (CREST Database); "SE-33: Prospects for Survival of Mossadeq Regime in Iran," October 7, 1952, CIA-RDP79S01011A000800020005-5, National Archives (CREST Database); Ian Johnson, *A Mosque in Munich* (New York: Houghton Mifflin Harcourt, 2010).

9   On this, see Charles Kurzman's sharp and creative account of the various interpretations of the Revolution (including especially from an Iranian perspective) as part of what he terms an "anti-explanation." See *The Unthinkable Revolution in Iran* (Cambridge, MA, and London: Harvard University Press, 2005), 5–7.

10 Jacques Waardenburg, "The Study of Religion during the Cold War: Views of Islam," in *The Academic Study of Religion during the Cold War: East and West*, ed. Iva Dolezalova, Luther Martin, and Dalibor Papousek, Toronto Studies in Religion 27 (New York: Peter Lang, 2001), 31–32.

11 Odd Arne Westad, *The Cold War: A World History* (Basic Books, 2017), 4.

12 James E. Miller, "Taking Off the Gloves: The United States and the Italian Elections of 1948," *Diplomatic History* 7, no. 1 (1983): 35–56. For a more recent

evaluation arguing that the CIA's role has been exaggerated, see Kaeten Mistry, "Approaches to Understanding the Inaugural CIA Covert Operation in Italy: Exploding Useful Myths," *Intelligence and National Security* 26, no. 2-3 (April 2011): 246-68, https://doi.org/10.1080/02684527.2011.559318.

13   Among the many good studies on this topic, see Kevin Kruse, *One Nation Under God: How Corporate America Invented Christian America* (New York: Basic Books, 2015); Kevin M. Schultz, *Tri-Faith America: How Catholics and Jews Held Postwar America to Its Protestant Promise* (New York: Oxford University Press, 2011); Dianne Kirby, "The Religious Cold War," in *The Oxford Handbook of the Cold War*, ed. Richard H. Immerman and Petra Goedde (New York: Oxford University Press, 2013), 540-64; Sylvester A. Johnson and Steven Weitzman, eds., *The FBI and Religion: Faith and National Security before and after 9/11* (Oakland: University of California Press, 2017); Matthew Avery Sutton, "Was FDR the Antichrist? The Birth of Fundamentalist Antiliberalism in a Global Age," *Journal of American History* 98, no. 4 (March 1, 2012): 1052-74, https://doi.org/10.1093/jahist/jar565; Andrew Preston, *Sword of the Spirit, Shield of Faith: Religion in American War and Diplomacy* (New York: Anchor Books, 2012).

14   For histories that trace this link, see Talal Asad, *Genealogies of Religion: Discipline and Reasons of Power in Christianity and Islam* (Baltimore: Johns Hopkins University Press, 1993); Tomoko Masuzawa, *The Invention of World Religions: Or, How European Universalism Was Preserved in the Language of Pluralism* (Chicago: University of Chicago Press, 2005); Peter Harrison, *"Religion" and the Religions in the English Enlightenment* (Cambridge and New York: Cambridge University Press, 2002); Wilfred Cantwell Smith, *The Meaning and End of Religion* (Minneapolis: Fortress Press, 1962); Jonathan Z. Smith, *Imagining Religion: From Babylon to Jonestown* (Chicago: University of Chicago Press, 1982); Russell T. McCutcheon, *Manufacturing Religion: The Discourse on Sui Generis Religion and the Politics of Nostalgia*, 1st ed. (Oxford: Oxford University Press, 1997).

15   This is best illustrated through tradition-specific studies that demonstrate how these expectations about specific religions were implemented in and through the colonial project. See Nicholas B. Dirks, *Castes of Mind: Colonialism and the Making of Modern India* (Princeton, NJ: Princeton University Press, 2001); Anna Sun, *Confucianism as a World Religion: Contested Histories and Contemporary Realities* (Princeton, NJ: Princeton University Press, 2013); Jason Ananda Josephson, *The Invention of Religion in Japan* (Chicago: University of Chicago Press, 2012); Jolyon Thomas, "Religions Policies During the Allied Occupation of Japan, 1945-1952: Occupation Policy and Religion in Postwar Japan," *Religion Compass* 8, no. 9 (September 2014): 275-86, https://doi.org/10.1111/rec3.12117; Donald S. Lopez, *Curators of the Buddha: The Study of Buddhism under Colonialism* (Chicago: University of Chicago Press, 1995).

16   The Staff of *LIFE*, ed., *The World's Great Religions, Volume 1: Religions of the East* (New York: Time Incorporated, 1955), 11.

17   For the most comprehensive account of how this came to be, see Hugh Wilford,

America's Great Game: The CIA's Secret Arabists and the Shaping of the Modern Middle East (New York: Basic Books, 2013), especially xix–xxi.

18   Office of Research Estimates, "Consequences of Partition of Palestine" (Central Intelligence Agency, November 28, 1947), FOIA Electronic Reading Room, http://www.foia.cia.gov/sites/default/files/document_conversions/89801/DOC_0000 256628.pdf. There is some evidence to suggest that this assessment was written by William Eddy. See Wilford, *America's Great Game*, 305n13.

19   The Staff of *LIFE, The World's Great Religions, Volume 1: Religions of the East,* 12, 51.

20   Huston Smith, *The Religions of Man* (New York: Harper & Row, 1958), 217.

21   This contradictory thinking is explored in Matthew F. Jacobs, "The Perils and Promise of Islam: The United States and the Muslim Middle East in the Early Cold War," *Diplomatic History* 30, no. 4 (2006): 705–39.

22   With the notable exception of Dina Rezk's pioneering work on Orientalism's influence on American intelligence, this is an avenue requiring further study. See Rezk, "Orientalism and Intelligence Analysis: Deconstructing Anglo-American Notions of the 'Arab,'" *Intelligence and National Security*, September 3, 2014, 1–22, https://doi.org/10.1080/02684527.2014.949077.

23   The Staff of *LIFE, The World's Great Religions, Volume 1: Religions of the East,* 12. For more on popular Iranian understandings of the relationship between science and religion, see Alireza Doostdar, *The Iranian Metaphysicals: Explorations in Science, Islam, and the Uncanny* (Princeton, NJ: Princeton University Press, 2018).

24   Smith, *The Religions of Man*, 251.

25   This relationship began shortly after the United States became independent in the eighteenth century. On this, see Christine Leigh Heyrman, *American Apostles: When Evangelicals Entered the World of Islam* (New York: Hill and Wang, 2015); John Davis, *The Landscape of Belief*, 1st ed. (Princeton, NJ: Princeton University Press, 1996); Ussama Makdisi, *Artillery of Heaven: American Missionaries and the Failed Conversion of the Middle East* (Ithaca, NY: Cornell University Press, 2009); Robert Allison, *The Crescent Obscured: The United States and the Muslim World, 1776–1815* (Chicago: University of Chicago Press, 2000), Karine V. Walther, *Sacred Interests: The United States and the Islamic World, 1821–1921* (Chapel Hill: University of North Carolina Press, 2015).

26   Kai Bird, *The Good Spy: The Life and Death of Robert Ames* (New York: Crown, 2014), 31–32.

27   Bernard Lewis, "Communism and Islam," *International Affairs (Royal Institute of International Affairs 1944–)* 30, no. 1 (January 1954): 1, https://doi.org/10.2307/2608416, 1.

28 Lewis, "Communism and Islam," 1, 6, 9.

29 Lewis, "Communism and Islam," 2–3.

30 Mattin Biglari, "'Captive to the Demonology of the Iranian Mobs': U.S. Foreign Policy and Perceptions of Shi'a Islam During the Iranian Revolution, 1978–79," *Diplomatic History* 40, no. 4 (September 2016): 579–605, https://doi.org/10.1093/dh/dhv034, 589. For a study of this change in understanding, see Jacobs, "The Perils and Promise of Islam."

31 Francis Hollyman, "Intelligence Gathering in an Unlettered Land," *Studies in Intelligence* 3, no. 3 (1959), https://www.cia.gov/library/center-for-the-study-of-intelligence/kent-csi/vol3no3/html/v03i3a02p_0001.htm, 1.

32 Hollyman, "Intelligence Gathering in an Unlettered Land," 1.

33 Hollyman, "Intelligence Gathering in an Unlettered Land," 3.

34 Hollyman, "Intelligence Gathering in an Unlettered Land," 3–4.

35 Peter A. Naffsinger, "'Face' Among the Arabs (1994 Declassified Version)," *Studies in Intelligence* 8, no. 3 (Summer 1964), https://www.cia.gov/library/center-for-the-study-of-intelligence/kent-csi/vol8no3/pdf/v08i3a05p.pdf, 1.

36 Naffsinger, "'Face' Among the Arabs," 4.

37 Donald Wilber, "Clandestine Service History: Overthrow of Premier Mossadeq of Iran, November 1952–August 1953," March 1954; Malcolm Byrne, ed., "National Security Archive Electronic Briefing Book No. 435: CIA Confirms Role in 1953 Iran Coup," accessed May 21, 2017, http://nsarchive.gwu.edu/NSAEBB/NSAEBB435/. One of the enduring curiosities of the 1953 coup is that, even over half a century later, no one is quite sure why it played out the way it did. While the CIA's Kermit Roosevelt was quick to claim a stake in its success (even if he had to do so secretly), it remains unclear to what extent American or British involvement is responsible for the coup. CIA internal documents acknowledge that the coup was carried out "under CIA direction," a claim challenged by recent histories. What is clear is that both British and American forces tried to effect regime change in Iran, and that fact remains a potent influence on US-Iranian relations. See Michael Axworthy, *Revolutionary Iran: A History of the Islamic Republic* (New York: Oxford University Press, 2013), 55–56; Hugh Wilford, "'Essentially a Work of Fiction': Kermit 'Kim' Roosevelt, Imperial Romance, and the Iran Coup of 1953," *Diplomatic History* 40, no. 5 (November 2016): 922–47, https://doi.org/10.1093/dh/dhv048. Quoted in Dan Merica and Jason Hanna, "In Declassified Document, CIA Acknowledges Role in 1953 Iran Coup," CNN, accessed May 29, 2017, http://www.cnn.com/2013/08/19/politics/cia-iran-1953-coup/index.html. For a comprehensive account of the coup itself, see Darioush Bayandor, *Iran and the CIA: The Fall of Mosaddeq Revisited* (New York: Palgrave Macmillan, 2010).

38 "Anti-Communist Statements by Mullah Kashani."

39 Henry Byroade to H. Freeman Matthews, "Proposal to Organize a Coup d'etat
    in Iran," November 26, 1952, National Security Archive, http://nsarchive2.gwu
    .edu//dc.html?doc=3914379-01-State-Department-Memorandum-of-Conver
    sation.

40 "Telegram from the Station in Iran to the Central Intelligence Agency (October 2,
    1952)," in *Foreign Relations of the United States, 1952–1954, Iran, 1951–1954* (US Gov-
    ernment Printing Office, 2017), 363, https://history.state.gov/historicaldocuments
    /frus1951-54Iran/d127, Document 127; "Telegram from the Station in Iran to
    the Central Intelligence Agency (September 5, 1952)," in *Foreign Relations of
    the United States, 1952–1954, Iran, 1951–1954* (US Government Printing Office,
    2017), 337, https://history.state.gov/historicaldocuments/frus1951-54Iran/d120,
    Document 120; "Telegram from the Embassy in Iran to the Department of State
    (September 28, 1952)," in *Foreign Relations of the United States, 1952–1954, Iran,
    1951–1954* (US Government Printing Office, 2017), 357–58, https://history.state
    .gov/historicaldocuments/frus1951-54Iran/d124, Document 124.

41 Department of State, "British Proposal to Organize a Coup d'etat in Iran,"
    December 3, 1952, National Security Archive, http://nsarchive2.gwu.edu//dc
    .html?doc=3914380-02-State-Department-Memorandum-of-Conversation.

42 "Telegram from the Embassy in Iran to the Department of State (November 11,
    1952)," in *Foreign Relations of the United States, 1952–1954, Iran, 1951–1954* (US Gov-
    ernment Printing Office, 2017), 405–6, https://history.state.gov/historicaldocu
    ments/frus1951-54Iran/d142, Document 142.

43 "Anti-Communist Statements by Mullah Kashani."

44 Kermit Roosevelt, "Zahedi-Kashani Meeting," October 20, 1953, http://nsarchive
    .gwu.edu/NSAEBB/NSAEBB435/docs/Doc%2019%20-%201953-10-20%20
    Zahedi-Kashani%20meeting.pdf, National Security Archive.

45 Bayandor, *Iran and the CIA*, 152–54; Axworthy, *Revolutionary Iran*, 55–56.

46 Bayandor, *Iran and the CIA*, 57.

47 Baqer Moin, "Khomeini's Search for Perfection: Theory and Reality," in *Pioneers
    of Islamic Revival*, ed. Ali Rahnema, updated ed. (New York, Kuala Lumpur, and
    Beirut: Zed Books, 2005), 64–97, 84.

48 See Bayandor, *Iran and the CIA*, 21–22, 57–58.

49 Moin, "Khomeini's Search for Perfection: Theory and Reality," 84–87.

50 For how this worked with respect to the Muslim Brotherhood specifically, see
    Johnson, *A Mosque in Munich*, 177.

51 Anthony Mark Lewis, "Re-Examining Our Perceptions on Vietnam," *Studies in*

Intelligence 17, no. 4 (1973), https://www.cia.gov/library/center-for-the-study
-of-intelligence/kent-csi/vol17no4/html/v17i4a01p_0001.htm, 44.

52 Smith, *The Meaning and End of Religion*, 16.

53 "Memorandum from the President's Assistant for National Security Affairs (Brze-
zinski) to President Carter, December 2, 1978," in *Foreign Relations of the United
States, 1977–1980, Volume I, Foundations of Foreign Policy* (US Government Printing
Office, 2014), Document 100.

54 Quoted in Jimmy Carter, *Keeping Faith: Memoirs of a President*, reprint edition
(Fayetteville: University of Arkansas Press, 1995), 332.

55 The 2,500-year celebration of the Persian Empire, a pet project of the shah's, is
one of the most famous examples. See Axworthy, *Revolutionary Iran*, 76–77.

56 Axworthy, *Revolutionary Iran*, 171.

57 Biglari, "'Captive to the Demonology of the Iranian Mobs,'" 583.

58 "Islam in Iran" (Central Intelligence Agency, National Foreign Assessment Center,
March 1980), CIA-RDP81B00401R000400110013–5, National Archives (CREST
Database), 23.

59 "Islam in Iran," 12.

60 To understand the fast-developing American understandings of Shiism during the
Revolution, see Biglari, "'Captive to the Demonology of the Iranian Mobs.'"

61 National Foreign Assessment Center, "Iran: The Meaning of Moharram," November 29, 1978, CIA-RDP80T00634A000500010011–9, National Archives (CREST
Database).

62 See discussion in Biglari, "'Captive to the Demonology of the Iranian Mobs,'" 592.
In general, this is a confusing way to approach Islam because it presumes a local
change in Christianity during the Reformation's aftermath (which itself is the subject of much debate) to be a universal historical trait across religious systems.

63 Quoted in David Farber, *Taken Hostage: The Iran Hostage Crisis and America's First
Encounter with Radical Islam*, new ed. (Princeton, NJ: Princeton University Press,
2006), 148.

64 "Islam in Iran," 7.

65 "Islam in Iran," 12–13.

66 For a study of how this thinking continued after 1979, see Grewal, *Islam Is a Foreign Country*.

67 "Islam in Iran," 8–9.

68 "Islam in Iran," 9.

69 National Foreign Assessment Center, "The Politics of Ayatollah Ruhollah Kho-
    meini," November 20, 1978, CIA-RDP80T00634A000500010002–9, National
    Archives (CREST Database), 13–14.

70 Retired US Army intelligence source, telephone interview with author, April 2017.

71 On the changing culture of Tehran in 1977–1979, see Axworthy, *Revolutionary
    Iran*, 81.

72 Robert Dreyfuss, *Devil's Game: How the United States Helped Unleash Fundamen-
    talist Islam* (New York: Metropolitan Books, 2005), 217.

73 National Foreign Assessment Center, "The Politics of Ayatollah Ruhollah Kho-
    meini," 2.

74 Axworthy, *Revolutionary Iran*, 96–97.

75 Khomeini, *Islamic Government*.

76 Ervand Abrahamian, *Khomeinism: Essays on the Islamic Republic* (Berkeley: Uni-
    versity of California Press, 1993), 2–3.

77 Dreyfuss, *Devil's Game*, 240.

78 Melani McAlister, *Epic Encounters: Culture, Media, and U.S. Interests in the Middle
    East since 1945*, rev. ed. (Berkeley: University of California Press, 2005), 211–12.

79 "Khomeinism: The Impact of Theology on Iranian Politics," November 1983, CIA-
    RDP84S00927R000100150003–5, National Archives (CREST Database), 21.

80 Khomeini, *Islamic Government*, 8.

81 Khomeini, *Islamic Government*, 8.

82 Khomeini, *Islamic Government*, 16–17.

83 Khomeini, *Islamic Government*, 16–17.

84 See Said's example of the British in Egypt (11) or his identification of the connec-
    tion between Oriental studies and Christian supernaturalism (122) in Edward W.
    Said, *Orientalism* (New York: Vintage, 1979). Among contemporary observers, it
    was not only Americans who would fail to reckon with Khomeini's revolutionary
    politics. As the philosopher Michel Foucault read the tea leaves, "One thing
    must be clear. By 'Islamic government,' nobody in Iran means a political regime
    in which the clerics would have a role of supervision or control." See Foucault,

"What Are the Iranians Dreaming About?," in *Foucault and the Iranian Revolution: Gender and the Seductions of Islamism*, ed. Janet Afary and Kevin B. Anderson (Chicago: University of Chicago Press, 2005), https://press.uchicago.edu/Misc/Chicago/007863.html.

85   See, for example, Masuzawa, *The Invention of World Religions*; Harrison, *"Religion" and the Religions in the English Enlightenment*; Smith, *Imagining Religion*.

86   Khomeini, *Islamic Government*, 9.

87   Among the most formative examples of this critique are Asad, *Genealogies of Religion*; Masuzawa, *The Invention of World Religions*.

88   Retired US Army intelligence source, telephone interview with author.

89   National Foreign Assessment Center, "The Politics of Ayatollah Ruhollah Khomeini," 8.

90   This area of study has received much attention in recent years. For a foundational text, see Talal Asad, *Formations of the Secular: Christianity, Islam, Modernity*, 1st ed. (Stanford, CA: Stanford University Press, 2003). Also see Janet Jakobsen and Ann Pellegrini, eds., *Secularisms* (Durham, NC: Duke University Press, 2008). For examples in an American context, see John Lardas Modern, *Secularism in Antebellum America* (Chicago: University of Chicago Press, 2011); Tracy Fessenden, *Culture and Redemption: Religion, the Secular, and American Literature* (Princeton, NJ: Princeton University Press, 2007); Finbarr Curtis, *The Production of American Religious Freedom* (New York: NYU Press, 2016).

91   "Islam in Iran," 2.

92   "Islam in Iran," 14.

Conclusion

1   Alan Scaife to Frederic Dolbeare, January 7, 1944, RG 226, Entry 210, Box 414, Folder 1, National Archives at College Park, College Park, MD.

2   Quoted in Ian Linden, *Global Catholicism: Diversity and Change Since Vatican II* (New York: Oxford University Press, 2009), 143.

3   Special to the *New York Times*, "Salvador Archbishop Assassinated by Sniper While Officiating at Mass," *New York Times*, March 25, 1980, sec. A1; Charles D. Brockett, *Political Movements and Violence in Central America* (Cambridge and New York: Cambridge University Press, 2005), 240.

4   Gustavo Gutierrez, *A Theology of Liberation: History, Politics, and Salvation*, rev. ed. (Maryknoll, NY: Orbis Books, 1988), xiii.

5   Craig L. Nessan, "Liberation Theologies in America," *Oxford Research Encyclopedia of Religion*, December 19, 2017, https://doi.org/10.1093/acrefore/97801993 40378.013.493. See chapters 5 and 6 in Linden, *Global Catholicism*; Joseph Cardinal Ratzinger, "Instruction on Certain Aspects of the 'Theology of Liberation,'" 1984, http://www.vatican.va/roman_curia/congregations/cfaith/documents /rc_con_cfaith_doc_19840806_theology-liberation_en.html; "Introduction," in Christopher Rowland, ed., *The Cambridge Companion to Liberation Theology* (Cambridge and New York: Cambridge University Press, 2007). These debates also spilled beyond Catholicism into other forms of social Christianity in Latin America. See David C. Kirkpatrick, *A Gospel for the Poor: Global Social Christianity and the Latin American Evangelical Left* (Philadelphia: University of Pennsylvania Press, 2019).

6   Ratzinger, "Instruction on Certain Aspects of the 'Theology of Liberation.'"

7   Linden, *Global Catholicism*, 142; Marie Gayte, "The Vatican and the Reagan Administration: A Cold War Alliance?," *Catholic Historical Review* 97, no. 4 (2011): 713–36, https://doi.org/10.1353/cat.2011.0170, 719.

8   Examples include Directorate of Intelligence, "Egypt: Islamic Cults, Crisis and Politics," August 1982, CIA-RDP06T00412R000200960001-3, National Archives (CREST Database), https://www.cia.gov/library/readingroom/docs/CIA-RDP 06T00412R000200960001-3.pdf; Directorate of Intelligence, "Morocco: Islam and Politics," February 1983, CIA-RDP84S00556R000100070002-7, National Archives (CREST Database), https://www.cia.gov/library/readingroom/docs /CIA-RDP84S00556R000100070002-7.pdf.

9   Directorate of Intelligence, "Islam and Politics: A Compendium," April 1984, CIA-RDP84S00927R000300110003-7, National Archives (CREST Database), https:// www.cia.gov/library/readingroom/docs/CIA-RDP84S00927R000300110003-7 .pdf.

10   Directorate of Intelligence, "Islam and Politics," 1.

11   CIA Office of National Estimates, "Staff Memorandum No. 27-63, 'Change in the Catholic Church,'" May 13, 1963, NSF/CF/Vatican, Box 191A, John F. Kennedy Presidential Library.

12   William J. Casey to Director of Global Issues, August 29, 1985, CIA-RDP87M0053 9R002003170045-7, National Archives (CREST Database), https://www.cia.gov/ library/readingroom/docs/CIA-RDP87M00539R002003170045-7.pdf; "DCI Speaking Engagements," n.d., CIA-RDP88G01117R001004030001-2, National Archives (CREST Database), https://www.cia.gov/library/readingroom/docs /CIA-RDP88G01117R001004030001-2.pdf.

13   Directorate of Intelligence, "Liberation Theology: Religion, Reform, and Revolution," April 1986, CIA-RDP97R00694R000600050001-9, National Archives (CREST Database), vi.

14 Robert M. Kimmitt, "Request for Clearance of White House Digest Draft: Persecution of Christian Groups in Nicaragua," December 14, 1983, CIA-RDP86M00886R001400140039-3, National Archives (CREST Database), https://www.cia.gov/library/readingroom/docs/CIA-RDP86M00886R001400140039-3.pdf; Directorate of Intelligence, "Liberation Theology: Religion, Reform, and Revolution."

15 Directorate of Intelligence, "Liberation Theology," 2.

16 Directorate of Intelligence, "Liberation Theology," 5.

17 Directorate of Intelligence, "Haiti: The Churches, Voodoo, and Politics," February 18, 1988, CIA-RDP04T00907R000100460001-2, National Archives (CREST Database), 5.

18 Directorate of Intelligence, "Haiti."

19 Kimmitt, "Request for Clearance of White House Digest Draft." Emphasis original.

20 In the study of religion, one famous statement of these challenges is Bruce Lincoln, "Theses on Method," *Method and Theory in the Study of Religion* 8 (1996): 225–28.

Index